PUZZLING IDENTITIES

INSTITUTE FOR HUMAN SCIENCES
Vienna Lecture Series

The Institute for Human Sciences
(Institut für die Wissenschaften vom Menschen, or IWM),
founded in 1982, is an independent international institute
for advanced study based in Vienna, Austria.
The IWM publishes books in cooperation
with Harvard University Press,
Suhrkamp Verlag (Frankfurt),
and Znak (Kraków).

PUZZLING IDENTITIES

VINCENT DESCOMBES

TRANSLATED BY

STEPHEN ADAM SCHWARTZ

HARVARD UNIVERSITY PRESS

Cambridge, Massachusetts, and London, England | 2016

Originally published as *Les embarras de l'identité* © Éditions Gallimard, 2013

First printing

Epigraph: Ludwig Wittgenstein, *Wittgenstein's Lectures on Philosophical Psychology 1946–47,*
ed. P. T. Geach (Chicago: University of Chicago Press, 1988), 243. © 1998 P. T. Geach,
K. J. Shah, A. C. Jackson. Reprinted by permission.

Library of Congress Cataloging-in-Publication Data

Descombes, Vincent.
[Embarras de l'identité English]
Puzzling identities / Vincent Descombes ; translated by Stephen Adam Schwartz.
pages cm
Includes bibliographical references and index.
ISBN 978-0-674-73214-8
1. Identity (Philosophical concept) I. Title.
BD236.D5213 2015
126—dc23   2015015936

A difficulty in philosophy
is that it's hard to be both intelligent
and non-intelligent enough
at the right time.

—WITTGENSTEIN

CONTENTS

PUZZLING IDENTITIES

PART I

"IDENTITY CAN BE A COMPLICATED MATTER"

1

LEARNING THE LANGUAGE OF IDENTITY

Identity Questions: A Lexical Puzzle

"Who am I?" "Who are we?" It might be said that these are the kinds of questions that we ask ourselves when reflecting upon our own identities. To ask, "Who am I?" is to ask what is sometimes called a "question of identity." We know what it involves because we have a model for it: to know someone's identity is to know what he is called. Yet can it be said, when I ask the first-person question of my own identity, that my intention is to be informed about my *surname, forenames*, and *occupation*, in much the same way as I might be expected to provide this information upon entering a public building and being subject to what is aptly called an "identity check"? Certainly not. My aim in this book will thus be to ask what the word "identity" means when it is used with the possessive (e.g., "my identity," "our identity") and where it does not simply refer to the statement of my surname, forenames, and occupation—i.e., my civil status.[1]

This use of the word "identity" (e.g., "my identity") is of relatively recent coinage. In the past, a question of identity would have had the

---

1. [Translator's note: The French term *état civil* originates in the eighteenth century to refer to the principal facts about a person that are relevant to the state: citizenship, circumstances of birth, marital status, etc. Owing perhaps to the centrality and importance of the French state within French life, the notion is much more commonly used and referred to in French than any corresponding term is in English. I will usually translate it as "civil status."]

trivial sense expressed by the question "Who is he?"—i.e., an inquiry bearing on a person we can neither name nor place within our surroundings. Thus, when the nineteenth-century French *Littré* dictionary discusses "questions of identity" in the article on "identity," it explains that the word, as used in this expression, is a "jurisprudential term" employed during investigations seeking to establish "whether an individual is who he claims to be" or whether a corpse is that of a particular person, "the presumed victim of a crime," identified by the elements of his civil status. Understood in this way, questions of identity arise only in the third person. If someone were to raise such a question about herself, it could only be because she had become a stranger to herself, having been struck by amnesia or delirium and thus unable to state her name or identify her parents, etc.

When "identity" came to be understood as a matter of civil status, it entered into common parlance. But it retains the earlier meaning it had for philosophers who used it to formulate identity judgments. How does one move from this classical, philosophical sense to the new sense relating to civil status?

In its earliest editions, which date from the late seventeenth century, the *Dictionnaire de l'Académie française* makes clear that the word "*identité*" is a scholarly term that is rarely used: "It is only used in Didactics." The definition offered in editions after 1794, by contrast, is philosophically perplexing: "That which makes it the case that two or more things are but a single thing."

What is this quality or force called "identity" that is defined by its prodigious ability to make *two things* into *a single thing*? Perhaps we are to understand the definition as an elliptical one to be interpreted as follows: "That which makes it the case that what one (erroneously) took to be two or more things is (in reality) but a single, selfsame thing." This definition would avoid falling into a dialectic of identity resulting from positing *two* things only so as to be able to claim that there is but *one*. The concept of identity thus defined is what one finds in statements of identity: to say that thing A is identical to thing B is to say that there is in reality but a single, selfsame thing that we sometimes call A and sometimes call B.

§§ I came to understand that the word "identity" had ceased to be an exclusively scholarly or "didactic" word and had become part of the most ordinary sort of language when I came upon a passage in a tourist guide to Rome that stated of the San Lorenzo district that it was "one of the working-class neighborhoods whose identity has been best preserved."[2] Identity is now a quality that can be preserved, which means that it is also a quality that one can lose or that one can seek to defend against whatever threatens to destroy it.

Can we explain what is meant by the "identity" of a working-class neighborhood? An older guidebook might have referred to the *character* of the neighborhood, suggesting a charm or quaintness attaching to its originality and distinctiveness, all the more so if this character has been maintained when other neighborhoods have become uniform or gentrified. This might even have been referred to as a "personality" or a "soul" of the neighborhood thanks to an analogy between the feelings we have for people and those we have for places imbued with human presence.

Nevertheless, the word "identity" today says something more than this. In the example of a neighborhood that has retained its identity, it is clear that what is at issue is both a territory that could have been absorbed by the rest of the city that surrounds it and also the population that inhabits it. This allows the word "identity" to designate not just a quality of this part of the city, but also the inhabitants' attachment to their way of life within it, their local customs, their surroundings. What would become of the neighborhood if, as is said, it "lost its identity"? It would never be the same, would be the response. But does this mean that it would have disappeared altogether or that it would still exist but in an indistinct way, blended as it would be with the city around it?

How can the word "identity" bear all of these meanings? How have we moved from the meaning given to the word in the *Dictionnaire de l'Académie française* to that given to it in the tourist guide? My aim in what follows is now set: departing from the idea that in times past the word "identity" exclusively meant (and still can mean) *that there is only a single selfsame thing* where one might have thought there to be two, I will seek to explain how in the past few decades it has come to sometimes mean something completely different—*that there is a thing that has the virtue of being itself* even though it might well have no longer been or not yet become itself.

§§§ One way of measuring the distance between these two meanings of the word "identity" is to consider its associated adjectives. We may say,

---

2. *Rome: Le guide du routard* (Paris: Hachette, 2008), 215.

for example, of two people that their behavior is *identical*. This means that they are doing the same thing—for example, they are both drinking coffee. By contrast, if we say that they are both engaged in "identity behavior" [*un comportement identitaire*], we mean that a certain way of acting provides them with a means for affirming their membership in a community or for claiming a social bond from which they derive their feeling of dignity or of their proper place in the world.[3] In the latter case, the important point is that this characterization of their behavior is not simply something observed by us from outside—as it is for the tourists who admire the charm of San Lorenzo—but comes from the people involved themselves. In order for their conduct to be identitarian, they must be aware of it and be able to say, "It is not possible for me to give up acting as I do; it is a 'question of identity' for me in which the very conception that I have of myself is at stake." Or, if they are speaking in the first-person plural, "The very conception that we have of ourselves is at stake." It will be claimed, for example, that the linguistic conflict dividing a country—Belgium, for instance—is an *identitarian* conflict. To say this is to indicate that the conflict involves much more than opposing interests and that, in a sense, no compromise is possible. Indeed, the conflict will be said to be such that both sides would feel diminished and lose self-esteem if they were to give in on the matter in dispute.

For anyone not in thrall to a narrow utilitarian conception of human existence, there is nothing particularly enigmatic about the fact that people may come into conflict over questions that do not involve their material interests properly understood. Yet there remains a *lexical* enigma: why is it my "identity" that carries the burden of signifying the stakes and the object of such conflicts? My discussion in what follows will bear on this precise point: what do the word and the concept of "identity" have to do with all of this?

---

3. [Translator's note: French has two adjectives associated with the noun *identité*. One of them, *identique*, is unproblematic and is the equivalent of the English "identical." The other, *identitaire*, is of recent coinage, arising in the mid-1970s precisely to translate Erikson's notion of an "identity crisis" (*une crise identitaire* in French). It has no direct translation into English other than "identity" used as an adjective, as it is in "identity crisis" or "identity politics." Unfortunately, the English adjective "identity" cannot always be used without leading to confusion. For example, sometimes this new adjective in French is itself nominalized as *l'identitaire*, which can only be rendered by a neologism: "the identitarian." Where it is felicitous, I will translate *identitaire* by the adjective "identity." Where it is not, I will use the neologism "identitarian."]

Declaring One's Identity

Between identity in the sense of the identical and identity in the identitarian sense, there is an intermediary in the form of the juridical and administrative usage, which assigns to individuals an identity that makes them identifiable (and thus able to be recognized as *identical* to the person named by a given name) but at the same time also provides them with an identity proper to their person in the form of their names, forenames, and occupations (thereby also providing them with a potential source of *identitarian* feelings).

In his book *Identity and Violence*, Amartya Sen criticizes intellectuals who promote an "identity politics."[4] He reproaches these theorists for enclosing human beings within identities that are exclusive. In particular, he vigorously attacks a British proposal that sought to reconceive the country as a "federation of cultures."[5] With regard to diversity, he observes, what is proposed is more like a juxtaposition of what he calls "monoculturalisms."[6] Indeed, such a proposal would inevitably wind up confining everyone within his or her community of origin. In the name of celebrating diversity and respecting the customs of everyone, one would in reality end up giving official structure to the segmentation of the country into "communities" that could then remain oblivious to one another.

Sen raises a principled objection to this proposal, reminding us of the meaning we bestow on citizenship within a regime of popular sovereignty (i.e., a democratic regime). This objection is key: democratic citizenship assumes that the citizen is a member of his country directly, without the mediation of a community.

> [The problem] concerns whether citizens of immigrant backgrounds should see themselves as members of particular communities and specific religious ethnicities first, and only *through* that membership see themselves as British, in a supposed federation of communities.[7]

---

4. Amartya Sen, *Identity and Violence: The Illusion of Destiny* (New York: Norton, 2006).
5. Ibid., 158.
6. Ibid., 156.
7. Ibid., 164.

Sen happens to begin his book with a personal anecdote meant to introduce his subject while stressing the way our use of the word "identity" can lead to difficulties—difficulties of communication that themselves lead to conceptual difficulties of a philosophical sort.

Here is the anecdote. The scene is Heathrow Airport. At the time, Amartya Sen was teaching at Cambridge, where he was *Master of Trinity College*. Passing through immigration after a trip abroad, he presents his immigration form to the immigration officer, who sees that his English address is *Master's Lodge, Trinity College, Cambridge*. Taken aback, the officer seeks to find out how it is that the Indian traveler before him has come to live with the Master of the College. He asks whether Sen is a close friend of the Master. Clearly, it has never dawned on him that Trinity College might have appointed a professor of Indian nationality as its *Master*.

Mischievously, Sen points out that such a question when asked of him could be taken in a deeply philosophical sense. Since antiquity, philosophers have asked if an individual could be his own friend or have with himself a relation of friendship. If the officer's question were asked in this sense, Sen would have to see whether the feelings he had for himself were friendly ones.

From this little incident at Heathrow, Sen draws the lesson that "identity can be a complicated matter," as philosophers have taught us.[8] Sen then proceeds to cite one of the best-known philosophers of his college, Ludwig Wittgenstein, who wrote the following warning to which Sen refers:

"A thing is identical with itself."—There is no finer example of a useless sentence, which nevertheless is connected with a certain play of the imagination. It is as if in our imagination we put a thing into its own shape and saw that it fitted.[9]

One does of course find in philosophy books the idea that our thought rests on a great principle according to which every thing is identical to

---

8. Ibid., xi.
9. Ludwig Wittgenstein, *Philosophical Investigations*, rev. 4th ed., ed. P. M. S. Hacker and Joachim Schulte, trans. G. E. M. Anscombe, P. M. S. Hacker, and Joachim Schulte (1953; Oxford: Wiley-Blackwell, 2009), § 216 (91).

itself. Wittgenstein's complaint is that this principle is in fact completely vacuous. It seems to be saying something only because it suggests a certain game of representation. It is as if we said that every material body is exactly the same size as itself and then sought to illustrate this relation by applying a measure to the thing that would in fact be the thing itself or a tracing of it.

Wittgenstein's remark becomes clearer if read in the context of the preceding remark (§ 215), where he writes:

> For identity we seem to have an infallible paradigm: namely, in the identity of a thing with itself. I feel like saying: "Here at any rate there can't be different interpretations. If someone sees a thing, he sees identity too."
>
> Then are two things the same when they are what *one* thing is? And how am I to apply what the one thing shows me to the case of two things?

In short, Wittgenstein derides the idea that the property of self-identity might be put forward as a *paradigm* of what we call *identity*. Since the property of self-identity is universal, one would only have to inspect an object present before one—for example, the philosopher's table—to be able to extract from it an understanding of the meaning of the predicate "to be self-identical." Wittgenstein playfully asks how he might go about applying to *two objects* the predicate that he abstracted from his perception of a *single object*, a predicate that signifies the property by which the object is not two but one. It is clear that Wittgenstein would not accept the explanation proposed by the *Académie française* according to which identity is what makes it the case that two or more things are but a single thing.

Of course, Wittgenstein is not suggesting that the concept of identity is empty, but rather that it must be explained by means of authentic "paradigms"—i.e., instructive models that allow us to understand how we are doing something meaningful when we apply the concept of identity to a situation. In fact, we have just been considering an example of such a meaningful application of the concept. The immigration officer at Heathrow learned something: this man named Mr. Amartya Sen is the same person as the one answerable to the title *Master of Trinity College*. The principle that "every thing is identical to itself" says nothing as yet, which means that a meaningful example of its application has not yet been found. By contrast, the statement "Amartya Sen is the Master of Trinity College" is a good example of what it is to have an identity, since it makes clear that we understand by such identity what makes an individual *identifiable* and even *re-identifiable*.

§§ Be that as it may, Amartya Sen himself draws our attention to these obscurities only as a way of preparing the ground for the presentation of different difficulties inherent, in his view, in another kind of identity. It is common today to speak about "sharing an identity" with others—for example, sharing a national identity with one's compatriots, a religious identity with others of the same faith, a professional identity with one's colleagues, etc. Sen provides several examples of this sort of identity, all constructed from the same basic framework. The identity of a person is presented as a list of various attributes such as her nationality or, perhaps, her origins, her profession, her religious affiliation, her family status, her sex, her opinions, her commitments, her aesthetic preferences. These are so many "categories" and "groups" to which an individual may be attached in one way or another—so many "identities." "I am," writes Sen,

> at the same time, an Asian, an Indian citizen, a Bengali with Bangladeshi ancestry, an American or British resident, an economist, a dabbler in philosophy, an author, a Sanskritist, a strong believer in secularism and democracy, a man, a feminist, a heterosexual, a defender of gay and lesbian rights, with a nonreligious lifestyle, from a Hindu background, a non-Brahmin, and a nonbeliever in an afterlife (and also, in case the question is asked, a nonbeliever in a "before-life" as well).[10]

Why such a miscellaneous inventory of the various positions and statuses the author recognizes himself as having? The intention is clear. If it is true that each of us can similarly list as part of his or her identity all manner of commitments and interests, then it goes without saying that identity politics rests on a sophism, acting as if an individual can only ever attach herself or himself to a single group. If this were the case, one

---

10. Sen, *Identity and Violence*, 19.

might well believe that everyone's conduct is dictated by this unique social identity. But, in fact, social identities are "robustly plural":[11] "We do belong to many different groups, in one way or another, and each of these collectivities can give a person a potentially important identity."[12]

According to Amartya Sen, to emphasize this point is all that is required to demolish the idea of deriving my politics from a reference to my identity. Because each of us has several identities, we must each time *choose*, from among the various groups that can lay claim to our allegiance, the group that will prevail on a given occasion.

There is of course a great deal of truth in Sen's reflections on the matter: the social life of each of us is multifaceted, none of us belong to only one group, and therefore there is a measure of personal responsibility implicit in the act of casting one's lot with one group rather than another. All of this is correct but perhaps also insufficient. We want to ask: in what way are social identities *social*? And in what sense are they *identities*? Of course, these questions are not aimed specifically at Sen— and perhaps less at him than at others—for he himself points out that he took up the term "identity" as it is currently used in the social sciences and politics, while at the same time warning us that dealing with questions of identity is more complex than it seems at first glance, so much so that it calls for a detour through philosophy.

§§ For starters, what is Sen's list a list *of*? Is it a list of *identities* in the sense in which a proper name (e.g., "Amartya Sen") or an exclusive title ("the Master of Trinity College") can be held to be identities belonging to a single person? To speak of identity in such cases would mean that, each time, a *single person* is intended. There could be no question of sharing anything at all. In reality, the paradigm of the identity check (at a border crossing, for example) is that of an identity that is always "robustly singular."

It might be claimed that the list sets out Sen's "social identities." The list of my social or shared identities is the list of the groups I belong to. A sociological objection then arises. The list, we are told, is that of the groups to which an individual acknowledges belonging. Yet in order to count elements and draw up a list of them, these elements have to be of

---

11. Ibid.
12. Ibid., 24.

the same type (I cannot count apples among the pears but must count them all as fruits). We will therefore have to recognize multiple groups. Indeed, Sen's list includes two different kinds of membership:

1. membership in a class in the *logical* sense of the set of individuals that possess an attribute (for example, having such and such an opinion or preference);
2. membership in a community in the sociological sense—i.e., in a sense in which the fact of my being in the same group as another person creates a *social bond* between us (for example, being in the same family or from the same country).

Some believe that such a bond can be created through an awareness of shared interests or circumstances, along the lines of the classical theory of class consciousness (i.e., people who recognize that they are being exploited come to realize that they have class interests and perhaps even a class "identity"). Some of Sen's examples fall under this theory of group formation through the simultaneous awareness in multiple individuals of the fact that they have a shared attribute that determines their circumstances and thus perhaps gives them a reason to get together to defend their shared interests. So it is, writes Sen, that the simple fact that individuals "share" a particular *individual* attribute—for example, wearing size 8 shoes or having been born between nine and ten o'clock in the morning—is not sufficient to give them a reason to think of themselves as a group.[13] But if we suppose that these individuals are treated unjustly *and* that this is so precisely because they have that shoe size or were born at that time, then we can imagine them moving from the "objectively" shared circumstance to a consciousness of that circumstance. One might imagine, for example, that size 8 shoes are no longer available (due to some bureaucratic foul-up); at that point, those who wear that size may have the impression of having been overlooked and may well propose the formation of a coalition to defend themselves. The common struggle might give rise to the emergence of a collective feeling that we will call the "sense of a common identity."

However, another, more important distinction will have to be drawn. One does not share an attribute with others in the same way when one is *from the same country* as other people as when one is *of the same opinion* as others. By definition, to have a given nationality is to be from the

---

13. Ibid., 26–27.

same country as the other citizens of that country. Or, to be from the same family assumes that said family exists, and this is therefore not an attribute that a single individual could possess. By contrast, there are attributes that are contingently shared. This is clearly the case with opinions and tastes. It is of course rare to be so original that one is alone in liking a particular work or in having a particular opinion. Nevertheless, it cannot be ruled out in principle. Only in the case of the latter sort of attributes can we speak of a resemblance (such as the fact of being the same color). By contrast, someone who speaks her own language is not someone who just happens to have a linguistic resemblance with other individuals, as if her ability to speak her own language were an individual attribute that she could possess on her own. Her language is (usually) her native language, which she learned in childhood. She speaks the same language that her mother does not because she bears a resemblance to her mother (such as the resemblance that leads others to say that she has the same eyes or nose as her mother) but because she learned the language from her mother.

Thus Amartya Sen's list of identities mixes up two sorts of groups: groupings that are purely notional or *nominal*—which are, in reality, mere taxonomical classes—and the *real* groups that are historical communities. There is therefore an ambiguity here: in the cases of nationality, language, or genealogical relation, we can speak of a group that confers an identity on the individual, and this is because we can identify the group and recount its history *separately* from the individual. In the case of an opinion such as "the concert was wonderful," there is no identity proper to the group of people who have it, since the only identity the group has is that of a *complete list* of the individuals whose opinion it is.

The recent use of the word "identity" can therefore not be explained by beginning from the ordinary meaning according to which things are "identical"—and thus have an "identity"—because they *resemble* each other.

What is therefore required is an inquiry into the word "identity," taken in the identitarian sense. And it is entirely appropriate to begin that inquiry with a historical investigation into identitarian language.

An American Concept

We are lucky to have available to us a very well-documented historical study of the word "identity" in the identitarian sense. The study is the work of the American historian Philip Gleason, a specialist in American history.[14] The author tells of how he had been tasked with writing an article about American identity for an encyclopedia of American ethnic groups.[15] It was then that he noticed that the term "identity" was frequently used by those working in the social sciences but that they never took the trouble to explain it. It was as if it were an everyday notion with which readers would necessarily be familiar. And in a sense this was the case, since at the time the word was increasingly coming to be used in ordinary language. Nevertheless, he goes on to say, when it came time to provide a meaning for the expression "American identity," nothing came to mind. The minimal explanation might be: the identity of a thing is what a thing is. But this is an explanation that explains nothing more than that a thing that stops being what it is also stops being itself. Gleason was therefore led to wonder about the term itself: what does "identity" mean in phrases such as "American identity," "Jewish identity," etc.? Good historian that he is, he estimated that the lexical inquiry into the term would have to take the form of a "historical semantics." The results of that investigation are those published in his article.

When and where did the notion of identity appear as it is used in the social sciences? The first conclusion of Gleason's inquiry is clear: the idea of identity in this sense first arose in the United States. In the 1950s, the word starts to be used in this new way in the social sciences. Gleason cites a work by Will Herberg from 1955 that defends the following thesis: Americans before the Second World War would answer the question "Who are you?" by referring to their national origins (Italian, Irish, etc.), whereas they later find such identity in their religious affiliation.[16] One might say, then, that American identity had ceased to be defined in "ethnic" terms (in the American sense), for it no longer involved reference to the country of one's ancestors but rather to

---

14. Philip Gleason, "Identifying Identity: A Semantic History," *Journal of American History* 69 (1983): 910–931. Reprinted in Philip Gleason, *Speaking of Diversity: Language and Ethnicity in Twentieth-Century America* (Baltimore: Johns Hopkins University Press, 1992), 123–149.

15. Gleason recounts this in *Speaking of Diversity*, 123. The article on "American Identity and Americanization" eventually appeared in Stephan Thernstrom, Ann Orlov, and Oscar Handlin, eds., *Harvard Encyclopedia of American Ethnic Groups* (Cambridge, MA: Harvard University Press, 1980), 31–58.

16. The work in question is Will Herberg, *Protestant-Catholic-Jew: An Essay in Religious Sociology* (1955; Chicago: University of Chicago Press, 1983).

one's own religious affiliation. That at least is the thesis of Herberg's book, which Gleason mentions only as a way of illustrating the sense of the word "identity" that has since become widespread.

A meaning has begun to take shape: the individual locates himself within society (here, in the overarching society that provides him with his nationality) through the assertion of a distinctive trait that separates the group he belongs to from other groups. In doing so, Gleason takes on board Tocqueville's characterization of American society:

> The relationship of the individual to society has always been problematic for Americans because of the surpassing importance in the national ideology of the values of freedom, equality, and the autonomy of the individual.[17]

From then on, the success of the term can be explained by the fact that this word allows people who are profoundly individualistic nevertheless to express the force of their social ties:

> What then *was* the decisive cause? The most important consideration, I would say, was that the word *identity* was ideally adapted to talking about the relationship of the individual to society as that perennial problem presented itself to Americans at midcentury. More specifically, *identity* promised to elucidate a new kind of conceptual linkage between the two elements of the problem, since it was used in reference to, and dealt with the relationship of, the individual personality and the ensemble of social and cultural features that gave different groups their distinctive character.[18]

The Idea of an Identity Crisis

So it was that the term "identity" in the identitarian sense became established within American social science. But where did it come from? Even if the current usage first appeared in America, in some ways it was *imported* there, since it is widely recognized as having been initially

---

17. Gleason, "Identifying Identity," 926–927.
18. Ibid., 926.

derived from the psychoanalyst Erik Erikson's notion of an "identity crisis." Unfortunately, as Gleason points out, the father of our psycho-social concept of identity never really defined what he meant by it. Erikson himself admitted as much. For example, he wrote:

So far I have tried out the term identity almost deliberately—I like to think—in many different connotations. At one time it seemed to refer to a conscious sense of individual uniqueness, at another to an unconscious striving for a continuity of experience, and at a third, as a solidarity with a group's ideals.[19]

Because we lack a definition, we will have to begin by seeking out the intellectual sources of this notion in Erikson's own biography. Here are the points most relevant to our present inquiry.

First is the most striking fact: Erikson was actually not called Erikson when he arrived in the United States and began to publish his first articles. He took this name when he became an American citizen in 1939. "Erikson" is a name he invented (one that makes him his own son!). This detail gives a certain piquancy to the fact that he spent his life con-structing a theory of *identity crises*. He himself admitted that, in so doing, he gave a universal scope to his own symptom.[20]

What was his name before he took on the name by which he is now known? His father is unknown; his mother (Karla Abrahamsen, who was both Danish and Jewish), married Erik's pediatrician when Erik was three years old. From that time, Erik was known as Erik Homberger, taking the name of his stepfather, Dr. Theodor Homberger. The family moved to Karlsruhe, in Germany. After a turbulent adolescence, the future Erik Erikson did his training analysis with Anna Freud, after which he was admitted to the Vienna Psychoanalytic Society, despite not having studied medicine. Until the end of his life, he would continue to claim to have been an orthodox Freudian, yet this claim may well be a half-truth: though there is nothing in Freudian doctrine that he dis-putes, he nevertheless contextualizes it within a global vision that no doubt comes from sources other than Freud. In 1933, he left Vienna with his family and emigrated to Copenhagen and then to Boston, taking the name Erikson at the moment he became an American citizen. It was

19. Erik Erikson, *Identity: Youth and Crisis* (New York: Norton, 1968), 208.
20. Ibid., 18.

during this period that he encountered great cultural anthropologists such as Ruth Benedict, Margaret Mead, and Gregory Bateson. These encounters had a major impact on his conception of personality.

One might thus say that our notion of identity in the identitarian sense is the result of the confluence, in the person of Erik Erikson himself, of two schools of thought. These are, on the one hand, the school of Freud and of Viennese psychoanalysts; on the other, the school of American cultural anthropology and, more specifically, the strain of thought that was known before the Second World War under the name "culture and personality." In fact, "identity" is a word that often takes the place that would previously have been occupied by terms such as "character," "personality," or "self."

It was in the United States, toward the end of the Second World War, that Erikson came up with the diagnosis of an "identity crisis." Such a crisis consists in a weakening, or even a loss, of what he calls "a sense of identity." One might imagine such a condition to be a variant of what nineteenth-century psychology called a "personality disorder": someone no longer knows "who he is" or exhibits symptoms of a double (or multiple) personality. This is not at all the case.

Erikson explains as much in recounting how he first diagnosed an "identity crisis." At the time, he was treating young soldiers returning from the Pacific and exhibiting the symptoms of a profound disturbance. Today, such soldiers might be said to be suffering from "combat fatigue." Erikson's diagnosis was that they were suffering from an "identity crisis." In what sense? Not in the sense that they had lost all concept of their "personal identity":

> They knew who they were; they had a personal identity. But it was as if, subjectively, their lives no longer hung together—and never would again. There was a central disturbance of what I then started to call ego identity. At this point it is enough to say that this sense of identity provides the ability to experience one's self as something that has continuity and sameness, and to act accordingly.[21]

Contrary to what the name "identity crisis" suggests, these young soldiers had not lost their sense of personal identity, if by that it is meant that they did not know their names, were struck with amnesia, or were

---

21. Erik H. Erikson, *Childhood and Society*, 3rd ed. (1950; New York: Norton, 1986), 42.

mentally confused. Something else was at work, though Erikson has difficulty explaining it. In the text cited above, he puts the emphasis on a *lived* sense of oneself as having "continuity" and "sameness." He then seeks an explanation in an application of the classical philosophical theory of the *self* as an entity that is distinct from the human being and on which a proper identity (*ego identity*) can be conferred, both in the sense of a continuity and a self-resemblance.

However, immediately after this passage, Erikson introduces an entirely different element: his patients' feelings of having failed, of not measuring up to what he describes as the ideals of a young American. Above all, the young soldiers that Erikson was charged with treating were disoriented; they were unable to make decisions or take action and were paralyzed in the face of their every future prospect. It was as if there were some sort of break between their lives before the traumatic episode and what they had become since their breakdown. Erikson interprets this breakdown in a normative or idealized way. In combat, these young soldiers discovered that they were unable to live up to the idea that they had hitherto had of themselves.

§§§ Is all of this Freudian? Erikson himself recounts the mixed reactions his theory elicited among orthodox psychoanalysts, beginning with Anna Freud herself, who had been his own analyst in Vienna. According to her, Erikson had strayed into a social or sociological approach to psychic conflicts, one that Freudians necessarily see as superficial.

Erikson sought to justify himself in the way that a historian might. He suggested that the disorders discussed by Freud were dependent on their fin de siècle Viennese context.

> [T]he patient of today suffers most under the problem of what he should believe in and who he should—or, indeed, might—be or become; while the patient of early psychoanalysis suffered most under inhibitions which prevented him from being what and who he thought he knew he was.[22]

Freud only failed to put forward the problem of ego identity, claims Erikson, because his patients were in no way disoriented: they knew

---

22. Ibid., 279.

what they were, or, more to the point, they knew *who they were*. They had no "identity problems." In their lives, however, they did experience being unable to measure up to ideals that were too strict. The context is thus that of a stable (or even conservative) society, and the goal of an analytic cure is then to liberate the individual from ideals that are too demanding or from social conventions that are too restrictive. By contrast, Erikson's patients suffered from being unable to find the mooring they needed within the ideals and models of the group.

Erikson goes so far as to say that the human predicament has changed between Freud's era and our own (i.e., after the Second World War):

> And so it comes about that we begin to conceptualize matters of identity at the very time in history when they become a problem. . . . The study of identity, then, becomes as strategic in our time as the study of sexuality was in Freud's time.[23]

More generally, Erikson claims to have *completed* Freud's theory by adding a fourth stage to the three infantile stages distinguished by Freud—an adolescent stage. According to him, Freudian theory lacks both a sense of the life cycle (i.e., of the individual) and a sense of the social milieu (i.e., of the context). Freud thought that his theory of infantile identifications accounted for the interactions of the child with his close relations. Yet, for Erikson, this theory is insufficient when it comes to treating adolescents. He goes so far as to write that "*Identity formation*, finally, begins where the usefulness of identification ends."[24]

More precisely, Erikson believes that Freud's disciples, following their master's lead, failed to provide sufficient place within the theory of personality formation for all that an individual derives from his environment (*Umwelt*).[25] In one of the rare passages in which Erikson points out a theoretical weakness of psychoanalysis, he calls into question its conception of the relation between the individual and his environment.

---

23. Ibid., 282.
24. Erikson, *Identity*, 159.
25. On the notion of what, in French, is called the *milieu ambiant* (and its translation into English by "environment" and into German as *Umwelt*), see the important investigation by Leo Spitzer, "Milieu and Ambiance: An Essay in Historical Semantics," *Philosophy and Phenomenological Research* 3:1 (Sept. 1942), 1–42, and 3:2 (Dec. 1942), 169–218.

Psychoanalysts speak of the "external world" and of "objective reality." They have not, however, taken up the notion of the *environment*.

> Certain habits of psychoanalytic theorizing, habits of designating the environment as "outer world" or "object world," cannot take account of the environment as a pervasive actuality. The German ethologists introduced the word *"Umwelt"* to denote not merely an environment which surrounds you, but which is also in you. And indeed, from the point of view of development, "former" environments are forever in us; and since we live in a continuous process of making the present "former" we never—not even as a new-born—meet any environment as a person who never had an environment.[26]

The environment is not the "objective" world (the world outside of one's representations of it), nor is it a mere ("subjective") *representation* of the real world. It is the subject's life environment, one that the subject makes her own by adapting to it, to such an extent that she ends up carrying it within her. From there, Erikson goes on to adopt an idea put forward by Gregory Bateson, among others: to have an identity is to have within one the environments of one's past history and thereby to be already oriented in the present and the future. The space in which the individual moves is never empty or indifferent. This space derives its meaning from the prior environments through which the individual has moved and within which she has developed a system of expectations and skills.

Erikson points out in this regard that, by following Freud's lead and always taking pains in the recounting of case histories to protect the private life of their patients by changing names, addresses, and professions, Freudian psychoanalysts have effectively rendered those case histories unintelligible.[27]

Identity according to Erikson: An Anthropological Notion

Among the sources of the psychosocial conception of identity is American cultural anthropology. Erikson himself twice engaged in

---

26. Erikson, *Identity*, 24.
27. Ibid., 44.

fieldwork, going first to the Indian reservations of South Dakota and subsequently to those on the Pacific coast. That is how he came to diagnose an "identity crisis" among adolescents in the Sioux tribe.

What is the difficulty for Sioux adolescents? It is not at all the result of a conflict between drives or urges on the one hand and superego-style repression on the other. Erikson describes the adolescents that have fallen prey to such a crisis as apathetic and unable to marshal their energies in the service of any particular project. He explains this by reference to the education of Sioux adolescents, which is shaped by two distinct moralities. According to the traditional morality of the Sioux, a man worthy of the name must prove himself to be generous such that whenever he comes into the possession of wealth, he must share it. By contrast, according to the morality of non-Sioux American teachers and authorities, a man worthy of the name proves himself to be moral by behaving in a sober and rational manner. He must calculate his expenditures, put money aside, etc. What the first system of customs advocates is what the second condemns.

The Sioux adolescent is thus paralyzed by the fact of having been educated—i.e., acculturated—within two heterogeneous systems. On the one hand, he has been inculcated with his people's morality (a morality of honor and expenditure), while, on the other, he has adopted the morality of Americans of European extraction (a morality of dignity and autonomy). These two systems are mutually exclusive. The morality of personal guilt (which speaks in the voice of one's moral consciousness) and the morality of shame (which speaks in the voice of the collective consciousness) pull the Sioux youth in opposite directions.

The contribution of American cultural anthropology to Erikson's theory was essential. I would claim that this contribution was perhaps made possible by the fact that Erikson had a "German" youth.[28] He himself experienced the difficulty of passing from childhood (a particular system of expectations and norms of recognition) to maturity (a different system). How does one go from the one to the other? The move cannot be a gradual one, because the subject will have to completely reconfigure his entire representation of what he can expect of others and what, in return, others can expect of him.

---

28. Other than his various personal revelations, see his notes on the German version of generational conflict in his study on the case of Hitler: "The Legend of Hitler's Childhood," in *Childhood and Society*, 326–358.

The idea is thus that adolescent crises are in fact a normal stage in the life cycle of human beings, one to which societies respond in different ways. Traditional societies give a structure and a public form to such transformations by imposing *rites of passage* on their young people, ones that are meant to change their status from that of a young person to that of an adult. Modern societies leave to the adolescent himself the task of reconfiguring his system of orientation. This is why, ultimately, we are not surprised when adolescents enter into conflict with their familial milieu. For us, the identity crisis is not taken up by the entire group but is, rather, a difficulty that the individual has to overcome on his own.

Among the elements in Erikson's biography that might have served to increase his sensitivity to the fact that a personality develops within an *Umwelt*, one might also mention—as he himself does—his experience as an immigrant to the United States. More generally, Erikson sees the twentieth century as distinguished by migration—not only waves of emigration and immigration but also the cases of political refugees, deportees, and displaced people. All in all, social change requires each of us to confront ceaselessly changing environments. Erikson diagnoses this as follows: "problems of identity become urgent wherever Americanization spreads. . . ."[29]

Identity after Erikson

So it is that, when we talk today about our "identities," we are using a term that Erikson put into circulation. Does this make us Eriksonians without knowing it? Is today's psychosocial identity Eriksonian? In his article, Gleason shows how, over time, new meanings were added to or substituted for those initially and approximately set out by Erikson.

Gleason distinguishes three different phases in the use of the term "identity" within American social science. The first phase is that of the "critical" American sociology of the 1950s. At that time, several works were published that dealt with "mass society" and the threat it represented for the American man. Could the American ideal of self-reliance

---

29. Erik H. Erikson, *Life History and the Historical Moment* (New York: W. W. Norton and Co., 1975), 44.

and autonomy survive the changes that produced "the organization man," "the lonely crowd," man as consumer, etc.?[30] The term "identity" is important because it allows sociologists to direct their attention to the individual and his concerns while simultaneously relating the questions that this individual confronts to changes in his social environment. Such an individual derives his idea of himself from the American ideal of self-reliance, but he is nevertheless aware of living within the context provided by a mass society that gives rise to conformism.

The next phase is that of the "rebels without a cause," including the revolts of college students on American campuses at the end of the 1960s. These revolts gave Erikson's ideas new currency, since they lent themselves to being interpreted by means of a schema that reworked the concept of the identity crisis into a "generational crisis," or a conflict between sons and their fathers, daughters and their mothers.

Finally, in the third phase set out by Gleason, the word "identity" enters into the vocabulary of political activists demanding civil rights for minorities. At this time, movements begin to appear that will be given partial theoretical expression in the ideas of multiculturalism and the struggle for recognition (which is to be understood as the recognition of a *minority* identity by the society *as a whole*).

§§ Nevertheless, Gleason explains, the salient fact is that, beginning in the 1960s, American social science began to use the word "identity" in a new way, one that was the opposite of Erikson's usage. The word "identity" began to replace the word "self." Gleason underscores the role played in this process by the so-called "symbolic interactionist" school. In 1963, in his book *Stigma*, Erving Goffman began to refer to identity where in the past he had spoken of "the self."[31] From then on, the word "identity" serves as a label that others apply to an individual according to her role or social position—a label that this individual can take on

---

30. Gleason mentions several classics of what he calls the "pop sociology" of the 1950s: David Riesman, *The Lonely Crowd: A Study of the Changing American Character* (New Haven: Yale University Press, 1950); William H. Whyte, *The Organization Man* (New York: Simon and Schuster, 1956); Vance Packard, *The Status Seekers: An Explanation of Class Behavior in America and the Hidden Barriers That Affect You, Your Community, Your Future* (New York: David McKay, 1959). Gleason, "Identifying Identity," 923.
31. Gleason, "Identifying Identity," 917–918. The reference is to Erving Goffman, *Stigma: Notes on the Management of Spoiled Identity* (Englewood Cliffs, NJ: Prentice Hall, 1963).

board as her own "identity" but whose content will have to be negotiated through her interactions with others.

Interactionist sociology is in reality a social psychology that promotes a dramaturgical conception of life in society. In life, we all play roles with regard to others. From the perspective of our interactions, two aspects of this game should retain our attention: (1) the definition of the role (in other words, what others expect of us) and (2) the level of conviction we bring to fulfilling it (in other words, the extent of the actor's identification with the role). Social psychology here takes up a theme from existentialist philosophy: though every role played by the individual constrains him while giving others a means for controlling his actions, the individual can regain a measure of freedom by showing his detachment while carrying out his tasks, as in Sartre's famous example of the "café waiter."[32] The waiter overdoes things and is in a sense playing his own social role, thereby showing that he is not taken in by it. His identity is *ironic*.

Yet something has been lost in this new use of the term "identity"—precisely what Erikson called *group identity*, the group's ethos or ideals out of which, during adolescence, an individual derives a definition of self. In fact, Gleason concludes, the social sciences have ever since used the term with two incompatible meanings.

If we take the term in Erikson's sense, identity is a configuration (*Gestalt*) of the personality that a human individual must construct throughout her life, but mainly at the moment of her *entry into life*, i.e., into responsible adult life. The work of identity construction is an effort of self-unification out of which should arise an appropriate relationship between the individual and her milieu. For Erikson, the adolescent's problem is one of developing *one* and *only one* identity, which is a condition for her integration within the group, a group that thereby gains further support for its ethos and collective ideals. The fragmentation of the adolescent's "identity" could only be pathological, in many ways the equivalent of the sorts of double personalities described by nineteenth-century psychiatry.

---

32. The "café waiter" as an example of bad faith is from Jean-Paul Sartre, *Being and Nothingness: An Essay on Phenomenological Ontology*, 2nd ed., trans. Hazel E. Barnes (1956; New York: Routledge, 2003), 59–60.

By contrast, if we take the term in the sense given to it by the interactionists, an "identity" is more like a role or a character that the individual must be able to play on the social stage yet still be able to abandon so as to move on to a different role. To remain fixated on a given role or *persona* would then be to exhibit an excessive inflexibility that is poorly adapted to social life, which requires a perpetual sliding from one interlocutor to another, from one role to another. As a result, it would be awkward and even pathological to have but a single identity for all of life's situations.

Thus if we stick to the first meaning, a multiplicity of identities would be pathological, a source of "confusion" and disorientation, whereas, if we embrace the second meaning, such a multiplicity is a trivial fact of human existence, while an attachment to a single self-definition would betoken the individual's inaptitude for a life with others.

§§ What does Gleason conclude from his investigation into the "historical semantics" of the term? He observes that the social sciences use it in (at least) two contrary ways and that a choice will have to be made, but he neglects to tell us which one to choose. Indeed, his conclusion is extraordinarily tentative:

> [A]s *identity* became more and more a cliché, its meaning grew progressively more diffuse, thereby encouraging increasingly loose and irresponsible usage. The depressing result is that a good deal of what passes for discussion of identity is little more than portentous incoherence.[33]

Should we or should we not refer to an "American identity"? And if we do, will it be in Erikson's sense or in Goffman's? Our goal was to explain the psychosocial use of the word, yet the difficulty of doing so remains before us. Nevertheless, our goal is now more precise: we must come to understand why "identity" was the word that came to be used to express the sorts of identitarian difficulties that we have been discussing, sometimes suggesting an analogy between adolescent crises and other sorts of disorientation, while at others calling to mind a disorder in the interactions and mutual recognition among people.

---

33. Gleason, "Identifying Identity," 931.

A Question of Language

According to Gleason's analysis, the word "identity" initially held out the promise of elucidating the "conceptual link" between the two elements of the problem raised for Americans by their individualist ideology. These two elements are, on the one hand, the upholding of the individual and his ability to get by on his own (self-reliance) and, on the other, the fact of social life. The problem for each individual is one of reconciling his idea of himself as an individual responsible for himself with his human experience of social dependency, a dependency that is less material than it is moral and psychological and one that the term *recognition* seeks to account for. That there is a demand for recognition means that the individual's own self-esteem is contingent upon esteem by those around him.

Nevertheless, a puzzle remains: what does the notion of identity have to do with a moral psychology of the conditions for personal pride or character formation? Why would one speak today of "identity" rather than, in each case, of "character," "personality," "social position," "associations and common cultures," "founding ideals," etc.? Here we must overcome a difficulty in the language itself. The history of the term "identity" in its social-scientific usages reveals a great confusion: at first, the word arose without having really been defined; then, as Gleason shows, the word was pulled in opposite directions, thereby introducing a certain measure of incoherence into social-scientific debates.

§§§ How do we move from identity in the sense in which things are *identical* to identity in the *identitarian* sense? The first thing to be aware of is that these are two different uses of the word, which can be called the *elementary* use and the *moral* use, respectively.

I will refer to the elementary use of the word "identity" whenever it is used as a "primitive word" in Pascal's sense. Pascal claims that the verb "to be" is a *primitive* word, one that cannot be defined through other words, since every conceivable definition would have to use it to relate the *definiens* to the *definiendum*, the verbal explanation to the word to be explained. The same is true of the word "identity." This word is also one that must be assumed in advance to have been understood by one's interlocutor if one is to be able to define anything at all for him. I will refer to an *elementary* usage of the word when the identity in question is the *primitive* one that allows us, in speaking for example of someone who has just entered the room, to make an identity statement such as "That's So-and-So." In other words, the person who just came in is none other than the bearer of that proper name.

As we have seen, a new usage has arisen since the 1950s. In fact, we are not dumbfounded to hear someone say that her language, her job, or her religious affiliation is part of her identity. Whatever we may think of such a claim, we understand it even though it uses the substantive "identity" not so as to make identity statements but in order to explain how it is that these diverse attributes (speaking a particular language or having a particular career, etc.) enter into her self-conception and how she would feel herself diminished—perhaps even reduced to nothing—if she had to give them up. The new usage concerns moral psychology: identity in this new sense is about pride, self-esteem, and self-affirmation by means of an idea of oneself that one expects others to respect. We may therefore call this a *moral identity* so as to distinguish it from identity in the elementary sense.

These two usages are distinct. Yet we are meant to understand the second by means of a paradigm based on the first: the model of self-presentation in which someone sets forth his identity by listing out his name and occupation. This sort of self-presentation involves making known and perhaps even confirming, for example, that the passenger who is present at the border crossing is Mr. Amartya Sen and then that Mr. Sen is the same person as the *Master of Trinity College*. This is, then, identity in the sense of what makes an individual identifiable. Identity is here understood in the elementary sense of the primitive word.

Things are clearly different when we encounter someone who intends to defend his identity. And when we speak about the success of the San Lorenzo district in preserving its identity (for the greater satisfaction of its inhabitants), the gap between the two conceptions of identity becomes an abyss. On the one hand, we are merely providing the name of the district we wish to discuss; it bears a name—the San Lorenzo district of Rome—and we can therefore identify it. On the other hand, we are delighted to learn that this district has *preserved* its identity. It might therefore have lost it, as so many others have.

Our problem arises because we have to understand the language of moral identity as deriving from identity in the elementary sense, even though the two senses are *logically* distinct.

§§§ The paradigm that should serve as our guide here is that of simple self-presentation in which someone identifies herself by saying, "I am so-and-so." The paradigm here is that of a question that is meant to be *incisive*: who is it that must be before us in order for it to be she who has provided us with her name rather than somebody else? Such an incisive question requires an equally clear-cut answer. Imagine a meeting at which someone who I do not know makes a speech that impresses me. I ask my neighbor "Who is that?" If my neighbor knows the speaker's *identity*, he tells me her name and perhaps also adds some details about her biography or position in the organization. Once I know her identity, I may wonder whether I have heard of her before. I ask myself "Is this the same woman, or is it someone else?" There are only two possible responses: either it is she or it is not. The only possible answers are yes or no. Even if the person before us *closely resembles* the one we are looking for, that will not be enough to make her *almost* or *half* the person in question. And if a person that we encounter after a long separation *only slightly resembles* the person we saw last, that does not mean that it is not she.

The new question of identity, by contrast, requires that we provide a *nuanced* response, one that does not require that the subject define himself exclusively by one of his attributes. To have an identity, we are told, is *to be oneself only under this or that condition*. If the conditions are not met, the individual will fail to have a sense of identity, which would seem to mean that he would be a stranger to himself—dispossessed or deprived of a self, alienated.

But of course the requisite conditions may impose themselves with greater or lesser urgency, and they may be more or less fulfilled, at which point *to be oneself* becomes a matter of degree. An adverb of intensity—like those that give nuance to the expression of one's feelings—will be required: e.g., "a little," "a lot," "intensely," "madly," "not at all." At a given moment, an individual is himself to a greater or lesser extent—a little, a lot, intensely, etc.—making it easy to imagine a clinical use of the notion of identity to characterize certain pathological states of the individual through either a loss of identity or an excessive will to be oneself.

One is reminded here of Rousseau expressing his delight in making solitary excursions on foot: "Never did I think so much, exist so vividly, and experience so much, never have I been so much myself—if I may use that expression—as in the journeys I have taken alone and on foot."[34] *Never have I been so much myself*: this observation presupposes that an individual can be and feel *more* or *less* himself. There are thus gradations in the feeling of being oneself.

The consequence of this is that the language of moral identity appears to be incoherent. If moral identity consists in various conditions that an individual must satisfy in order to have the feeling of being himself, then this sort of self-definition will necessarily be *composite*. It will require one do as Amartya Sen did and mention all of the kinds of things one cares about (to different degrees, which is what gives moral identity its intensive character). Identity will have to be *compound*. So we will have to describe moral identity as *plural*. As Sen puts it, "identities are robustly plural."

Yes, they are, but here we come up against a linguistic obstacle. The paradigm that was used to introduce the moral sense of the word "identity" was that of the question "Who am I?"—i.e., the paradigm of self-presentation. This paradigm does not allow any meaning to be given to the expression "plural identity." In its terms, the very idea of a plural identity appears incoherent.

How could identity be plural? In two ways: (1) through a succession of identities declared by the individual when she presents herself to others (in much the same way as an actor takes on a series of roles) or (2) through the distinction of multiple simultaneously occurring aspects of her person. I will take these two cases in turn.

Plural Identity

We are constantly invited to conceive of our "identities" as a diversity within our selves. My identity in the moral sense is necessarily *plural*. Each of the identities that comprise my description corresponds only to a part of what I am. One might even claim that my identity is plural two times over. It is plural at each instant, for I am never reducible to a single quality. And it is also plural over time, since (fortunately) I do not remain stuck within a single role.

Nevertheless, to speak about a "plural identity" may lead some to think that we have already discovered the solution to the problem

---

34. Jean-Jacques Rousseau, *Confessions*, trans. J. M. Cohen (New York: Penguin, 1953), 157.

posed. In reality, this is not the case. The words "plural identity" do no more than give expression to the problem—that of a single individual who is expected to exist in a "plural mode." But how can a single person carry off the amazing feat of existing in such a way that he is not only himself but also other people?

Our language today allows us to call upon what we call "his identity" in order to explain why carrying out an action (or even considering it) is ruled out. It is said, for example, that "I cannot do what you are asking me to do because it would be in conflict with my identity." Here, my "identity as X" explains why I do what I do: I act *qua X* and thus *as an X*. The phrases "qua X" and "as an X" are "labels" that convey the meaning of our actions.

Of course, there is more than one "label" that I might mention in order to explain myself. As a result, it must be the case that I can refer to several "identities." Just as one can have several passports if one has multiple citizenship, one can have several business cards—one for each of one's usual occupations. A moral identity would then be like a card that discloses the qualities that matter to me in a given context.

Yet such multiple business cards can easily give rise to conflicts. We will have to reconcile such a multiplicity with the fact that all of them present the services of *a single individual.* We are reminded of the scene in Molière's *The Miser* in which Harpagon is giving orders to Maître Jacques, who is serving as both coachman and cook.

MAÎTRE JACQUES: Is it your coachman or your cook you want to have a word with sir? I'm both.
HARPAGON: Both.
MAÎTRE JACQUES: But which do you want first?
HARPAGON: The cook.
MAÎTRE JACQUES: Just a minute, if you don't mind. (He removes his coachman's greatcoat and under it he is dressed as a cook.)[35]

Because he has two functions, Maître Jacques really does have, as we might say today, two "professional identities"—one for each function—since they entirely consume him when he takes them up, which is

---

35. Molière, *The Miser* in *The Miser and Other Plays: A New Selection*, trans. John Woods, rev. David Coward (New York: Penguin, 2000), act 3, scene 1 (181).

precisely what he wants Harpagon to understand. By donning his cook's uniform, Maître Jacques *enters into his role*, taking on the burdens, duties, and concerns associated with it. This stage business shows that the two functions—coachman and cook—exclude each other and cannot be carried out simultaneously. Maître Jacques's ploy of changing uniforms signifies that he cannot do it all at the same time; orders given to the coachman are of no concern to the cook.

One might say that Harpagon was hoping to have a *plural employee* at his service but that Maître Jacques has made clear to him that this plurality must respect the fact of human individuation. Of course, nothing prevents Maître Jacques from having a plural professional identity. But this means only that Maître Jacques has a surfeit of work and that the coachman's time infringes on that of the cook. It cannot mean that the man can *simultaneously* carry out both functions, since to do that he would have to have two bodies. If such a thing were possible, Harpagon would be able to address *simultaneously* both the coachman and the cook—i.e., to address an employee wearing both uniforms at the same time. In the play, plural identity is reduced to the mere accretion of the two functions, with no principle of composition other than the person of Maître Jacques.

§§ Can we conceive of a "plural identity" made of distinct elements X and Y, one whose plurality would allow its possessor to present himself simultaneously as an X and a Y? The condition under which this would seem to be possible is that he be able to distinguish what he does *qua X* from what he does *qua Y*. The plurality of identity would then be what logicians refer to as "reduplicative."

Ernst Kantorowicz, in his book on the king's two bodies, cites a marvelous example of this type of reasoning.[36] The illustration is that of a French bishop in the Middle Ages who admitted to being married but nevertheless insisted that, *as a bishop*, he was in perfect compliance with his vows of celibacy, for it was only *as a baron* that he was married. Kantorowicz explains that this person was making improper use of the medieval theory that ascribed to certain people a *persona mixta*, i.e., a double capacity, one temporal and the other spiritual. This theory of

---

36. Ernst Kantorowicz, *The King's Two Bodies: A Study in Mediaeval Political Theology* (1957; Princeton: Princeton University Press, 1981), 43.

the "plural person," as we might translate it, was a precursor to the theory of the *persona duplex*, the idea according to which the monarch has two bodies, one that is natural and mortal and another that is political and immortal.

Here then is the reasoning with which our baron-bishop seeks to defend himself. As a baron—a secular prince—he has a duty to ensure that he has legitimate heirs. As a bishop, he has a duty to remain celibate. How can an individual man fulfill both of these obligations? Our baron-bishop seems to think he can exonerate himself by appealing to a logical technique—that of the reduplicative proposition—so as to *compartmentalize* his activities. The theory of the *persona mixta* does indeed allow one to distinguish two capacities: what one can do *as a bishop* must be distinguished from what one can do *as a baron* and vice versa. The situation, he might argue, is like that of someone who is both a law professor and a psychoanalyst: in the first capacity, he can confer university degrees, while in the second capacity, he can receive patients on his couch.

Imagine that our man who is celibate *qua bishop* while married *qua baron* were able to avail himself of our identitarian language in order to mount his defense. He might then have said: "Like all of you, I am a plural being and have several identities. Sometimes I am entirely a bishop in complete control of my diocese. At others I am entirely a baron, giving myself totally to the flourishing of my barony. It would be reductive to seek to confine me to a single identity."

Such a defense would of course be a sophistical one. No theory of *plural identity* can result in the bishop not being married to the baron's wife. The reason for this is that a bishop is *a man* who has taken on the rank of bishop, while a baron is *a man* who owns a barony. Therefore, if the *same man* is involved, it is impossible for the woman to become a baroness by marrying the baron without, by this very fact, marrying the bishop that this baron also happens to be. In order for reduplication to compartmentalize these roles, keeping them separate from each other like distinct entities, the identity that the man who wears these roles retains in virtue of his individuation will have to be annihilated. Thus, behind so-called plural identity we find the identity (properly so called) of a human individual who has deluded himself into thinking he can occupy all of these social roles by somehow fragmenting the responsibility that he has for his own acts.

The discourse of plural identity seeks to bring peace and tolerance among people. In a word, it tells us this: we will more readily accept that others are different from us if we are aware that, at root, each of us is already different from himself or herself on various occasions. Yet this way of thinking risks producing an effect that is the opposite of the one desired. In fact, the word "identity," which is used here to shed light on the diversity of human beings, cannot fail to put each of us in mind of his or her individuation—i.e., what it is that gives each of us one and only one life.

This discourse seeks to reassure us that it is possible to live tranquilly in a complex world, since we find it normal to be the complex creatures that we ourselves are, busying ourselves in various ways, turned in multiple directions, and pursuing multiple goals. We need not see changes in our life environment as a threat, but rather as a sign of life. These changes are ones that we can meet with a new diversification of our interests and commitments.

Yes, but "identity" is the word used, and this immediately results in the advent of another message. It is as if the *manifest* discourse were erased in favor of a *hidden* one. The manifest discourse urges us not to worry. Yet each of us, upon hearing the discourse of plural identity, is given to understand that our own disappearance has been announced. All of us know what it is for an individual to preserve her identity as an individual. It means to remain the individual that she is and therefore to remain alive. If I am told that my identity is going to change tomorrow, how can I not understand this as meaning that the individual that I am will have to *give way* to another individual that I must allow to replace me?

When it pluralizes our collective identity, the discourse of plural identity thinks it is reassuring us: e.g., "You live in a society whose identity is 'plural,' therefore you live in a country that is *already* several countries. At every moment, this identity is alive, so that the country is constantly becoming a *different* country." But what does such a discourse really imply? "A different country" means a foreign country. The discourse ends up in fact saying this: at every moment, your country is already no longer your country, notwithstanding whatever efforts you might make to adjust to the changes around you. And the concerns of the public will only be exacerbated if the discourse of plural identity goes on to denounce the illusion of a constant identity. For the public will then come to understand this: the very idea of a country remaining constant is an illusion, which means that, in reality, you have never had a country that was *your* country for more than an instant.

§§§ So it is that by speaking of an incessantly plural identity, one presents as a *solution* to our problem something that is in fact precisely a statement of this problem itself.

Identitarian plurality is supposed to provide the solution to fanatical forms of identification. If someone stops imagining that she has only one identity—by which is meant the sense of satisfaction and self-confidence that she derives from the idea of belonging to the group to which she does belong—it will be more difficult for her to be intolerant. Whence the various invitations to interiorize the world's diversity: to have a single identity is tantamount to a kind of fanaticism or fundamentalism, whereas multiple identities represent the beginnings of liberalism.

Yet the word "identity" in such cases was explained through the question "Who am I?"—in other words, "Who am I as an individual?" Identity cannot then be severed from the sense that each of us has of his existence as an *individuated* being. That means that the plurality of identities is precisely the problem to be solved. If the word "identity" when taken in the moral sense continues to mean *identity*, then to invite me to embrace a plural identity is like asking a circle to be a square. And if "identity" taken in the moral sense does not mean *identity*, then why insist on using the word?

§§§ In the end, all of the justifications given for *pluralizing* the notion of identity and only attributing it to each of us *in the plural* would appear to be only so many reasons to avoid using the word "identity" in its psychosocial application.

Avoiding the word is precisely what some authors have proposed, while criticizing the notion of plural identity as a false solution and an impossible trade-off between two theoretical demands. In a hard-hitting article, Rogers Brubaker and Frederick Cooper—a sociologist and a historian, respectively—have called into question what they drolly refer to as "identity talk."[37]

---

37. Rogers Brubaker and Frederick Cooper, "Beyond 'Identity,'" *Theory and Society* 29 (2000): 1–47.

The authors describe the uneasy position of the contemporary identity theorist, which is like that of any cleric led to adopt a doctrine of
double truth. Indeed, the word "identity" is today found in two different types of discourse, since it appears in the vocabulary not only of
political activists (who use it as means for social and political critique)
but also in that of researchers (for whom it is a tool of analysis). A conflict between these two uses is inevitable if one is subject to a single
norm of truth.

In the activist's discourse, the word "identity" has what Brubaker and
Cooper call "reifying connotations."[38] This is to be understood in the
following way: to have an identity is to really exist. Every morning I
place my foot on *the same floor* in my bedroom, and it is the same floor
because it persists in its existence (until the day of its destruction, at
which time it will cease to be the same floor because it will cease to be a
floor altogether). The same goes for the group on behalf of which the
activist hopes to mobilize people. In order to be concerned about a
group having been mistreated, exploited, oppressed, humiliated, etc.,
one must be able to think of it as possessing a historical reality. To conceive of it in its identity is to conceive of it as really existing. As a result,
the activist's discourse must necessarily take the term "identity" in its
reifying sense, which is in the end entirely consonant with the meaning
of the word taken in its basic sense (i.e., that used in philosophy to discuss the conditions of identification of things). How could you mobilize
people (through an appeal to their feelings of solidarity and belonging)
on behalf of groups that are presented as being unreal?

On the other hand, in the sort of scholarly analysis undertaken
within critical sociology, what dominates is a certain *constructivism*, to
the point that it almost seems as if every social scientist worthy of the
name must be a "constructivist" to be taken seriously. From the critical
sociological point of view, there are no such real groups endowed with
an identity, for it would be "reifying" to make such a claim. What there
is, really, are people who have the *idea* that they belong to real groups
whose identity they share.

There is an obvious incompatibility between these two attitudes (one
of which is naively "realist," as the authors put it, while the other is
sophisticated and "critical," i.e., able to reduce the realities invoked by

---

38. Ibid., 1.

the activists to mere "social constructions"). How can the two be reconciled? Brubaker and Cooper condemn the false solution represented by a "soft constructivism." Like every doctrine of double truth, this theory is incoherent. The authors demonstrate with great verve how, in the very style of the texts in which the doctrine is put forward, this incoherence reveals itself through the frequent use of stereotypes: e.g., "yes" to identity but only on condition that it be fluid, multiple, ever-changing, and always in dispute. In other words, that it be completely watered down.

> Weak or soft conceptions of identity are routinely packaged with standard qualifiers indicating that identity is multiple, unstable, in flux, contingent, fragmented, constructed, negotiated, and so on. These qualifiers have become so familiar—indeed obligatory— in recent years that one reads (and writes) them virtually automatically.[39]

Brubaker and Cooper deride this way of speaking. They rightly criticize it for being so much verbiage, proposing that we give up such "identity talk."

But what are we meant to be giving up? Is it an identity that does not identify (or, if it does, only identifies a little bit)? Or is it *all* identity? In fact, Brubaker and Cooper's critique is not targeted only at moral identity—the kind that is often described as fluid, fragmented, constructed, negotiated, and so on. Following them to their conclusion, we will also have to condemn identity in the elementary sense as a concept with no place within the social sciences. One could refer to identity only within domains that deal with homogeneous, invariable realities that are neither context dependent nor riven with internal tensions nor even composite in their makeup. If this is the case, there would be no place within any human science for the concept of identity, since to seek out identities within human affairs would be to negate all historicity and anthropological diversity.

In the face of this suggestion that we abandon not only *identitarian* language but also all reference to the *identical* when describing historical phenomena or cultural transformations, we can only join Amartya Sen in reiterating that "identity can be a complicated matter."

---

39. Ibid., 11.

§§ Our task is now entirely clear. Our linguistic problem is a *philosophical* one. Indeed, it would appear that the ordinary language that we have no choice but to use makes us say things *that we do not mean* or prevents us from saying things *that we do mean*. A situation of this kind requires a philosophical treatment.

First and foremost, such treatment is needed for identity as it is used in moral psychology. But it is also needed for identity in the elementary sense of the identical. For we would like to be able to speak about *the same person* so as, for example, to tell his story and to do so without any implication that this person did not really have a story, that he was transformed by none of the things that he did or that happened to him. Similarly, we would like to be able to talk about *the same group*. But if we accept Brubaker and Cooper's view, the concept of identity is necessarily "reifying" and cannot be applied to a reality without immobilizing or homogenizing it. And this is certainly something that we do not wish to do with our language.

§§ If language *makes me say* what I do not want to say or *prevents me from saying* what I do want to say, then we have a properly philosophical difficulty. Aristotle studied this phenomenon, calling it a "sophistical refutation," by which he meant a trap we snare ourselves in by the manner in which we express our thought, a manner that allows the sophist to catch us in self-contradiction or entangle us in verbiage. This is precisely what has happened to us in the case of identity: by speaking of "plural identity," we lay ourselves open to saying only tenuous things, and a sophist would have no difficulty trapping us in self-contradiction, since we would have succeeded in providing individuals with neither *an* identity nor *several* identities.

We will therefore have to give ourselves the tools to avoid the "sophistical refutations" to which our way of speaking about identity risks finding itself subject. But how should we do this?

We will have to relearn the language of identity by acting as if we had never used it before (or at least had never really understood it). And we will have to relearn it starting from the correct understanding of the paradigm we were given: self-presentation in response to the question "Who am I?" or, in the plural, "Who are we?"

Yet it is not just the concept of moral identity that has proven problematic. The paradigm of self-presentation appeals to the elementary concept of identity, which allows us to judge what is or is not identical. But as we have just seen, such elementary usage is hardly beyond question. As a result, we will have to begin by rediscovering our use of the word "identity" taken in its primitive sense. We will have to relearn to speak of identity in all senses of the word, beginning, of course, with the elementary usage.

2

OF WHAT USE IS THE CONCEPT OF IDENTITY?

Is There Such a Thing as Identity in This World?

The question that we need to ask now is simply this: "Is the concept of identity applicable in this world?" There are two daunting arguments seeking to show that it is not. The first is *physical*, in the Greek sense of the word: i.e., this argument arises out of considerations bearing on the fact that the things of this world are always changing. The second argument derives from logical considerations concerning the form of identity statements of the type "a = b." This *logical* argument seeks to establish that we do not understand what we are saying when we speak of an "identity relation," i.e., the relation that we think we are positing by means of a sign of identity written thus: "=".

§§ Let us begin with the objections of a physical sort to the possibility of applying a concept of identity to the realities of this world.

In our world, according to the physical argument, all things are perpetually in a state of flux. We never have an opportunity to encounter anything that remains the same for more than an instant (or that *is itself* for more than an instant). At every moment, the thing is changing into something else. We must therefore conclude that not only is the concept of identity inapplicable to all things in this world, but the simple fact that we are able to say of a thing that it is possessed of identity is sufficient to establish that it belongs to *a different world* than this one. To be able to apply our concept of identity to an entity X is sufficient to show that this entity X does not exist in this world but only in some other (immaterial or ideal) world. This *other* world is one that some philosophers present as the only real world (as in Platonism, with its immutable Forms), while others will locate it solely within our mental representations (in which case, identity is a product of our understanding, which assimilates things to one another).

If we proceed along these lines, we will end up joining the chorus of thinkers in France who have presented themselves—if it even makes sense to talk about "presenting oneself" when it comes to thinkers who contest the very possibility of presence—as *philosophers of difference*. Philosophers of difference are those who have rejected what they call "our" Platonism, which is, according to them, a vain attempt to find *identity* in our world—i.e., to find stability, invariance, and uniformity.

Philosophies of difference take seriously the concept of identity, as it is usually explained, in order to conclude that this concept *is applicable to nothing real* but only to "idealities." How is it that we nevertheless continue to make use of this concept? The answer is that we are under the influence of an *illusion* that will have to be dispelled before we set about explaining its persistence as rooted in the way our minds function or the way we allow language to determine our thought. In a world where every (physical) thing is fluid, the concept of identity has no application. We only imagine ourselves able to apply it because we are insensitive to this instability. Perhaps we do not have the penetrating acuity to have noticed it. Or perhaps we do not want to notice it. Or maybe, despite being entirely aware of this fluidity, we nevertheless have decided to act *as if* things were stable and unchanging or at least possessed of a stable and unchanging core.

Whatever the case may be, there is a critical lesson to be drawn from these considerations. According to the "physical" argument, we do of course have the concept of identity within our intellectual vocabulary. However, this is not really the concept that we apply to things when we issue identity statements. In fact, we have so weakened the concept's conditions of application that we have no problem claiming that two merely similar things are *identical* so long as they follow each other under conditions in which their individual differences do not affect us or are undetectable by us—an identity "on the whole," as William James put it in regard to personal identity.[1] As a general rule it is in order to facilitate representation and action that we seek to represent things as similar to one another and as stable and self-identical. In reality, they are not.

§§§ Yet when we say that identity is not of this world, that it is not made for us, we nonetheless know—or believe we know—what the things of this world *would have to be* for us to be able to apply our concept of identity to them. In order to be able to apply this concept to them, they would have to be stable rather than changing, invariable rather than fluid; nothing could change in their composition from one moment to the next. We therefore also know what it is that prevents us from applying this concept to them: everything is changing all the time, and nothing remains in the state it was in. It nevertheless would appear to be possible to conceive of *another* world in which the concept would apply.

It is at this point that the *logical* argument comes in, bearing an apparently more radical critique that calls into question our very understanding of the concept of identity. This critique challenges us to explain the sign "=" in an intelligible way. Logic textbooks tell us that the concept of identity is that of a relation of comparison, which we express by saying that between two things *a* and *b* there may be either a difference or an identity. But this explanation does nothing to clear things up. As Wittgenstein remarked in a famous proposition from the *Tractatus Logico-Philosophicus*:

---

1. James writes:

> The identity which the *I* discovers, as it surveys this long procession [of thoughts], can only be a relative identity, that of a slow shifting in which there is always some common ingredient retained. The commonest element of all, the most uniform, is the possession of the same memories. However different the man may be from the youth, both look back on the same childhood, and call it their own.
>
> Thus the identity found by the *I* in its *me* is only a loosely construed thing, an identity "on the whole," just like that which any outside observer might find in the same assemblage of facts. We often say of a man "he is so changed one would not know him"; and so does a man, less often, speak of himself. These changes in the *me*, recognized by the I, or by outside observers, may be grave or slight.

William James, *The Principles of Psychology* (1890; Cambridge, MA: Harvard University Press, 1983), 351–352.

Roughly speaking, to say of *two* things that they are identical is nonsense, and to say of *one* thing it is identical with itself is to say nothing at all.[2]

What purpose can an identity statement serve? What do we learn from one? Certainly not that there is *one thing* that happens to be identical to *another thing*, if this sequence of words is supposed to mean that *two distinct things are a single thing*, for that would be nonsense. Nor can it mean that the thing that is the object of the identity statement is identical *to itself*, because that would amount to saying that the thing I am talking to you about is indeed the thing I am talking to you about. In saying it, I may hope to confirm the reference of my speech. But in reality, I have not yet said anything at all about the thing in question and certainly not that it possesses some important putative quality called "self-identity."

We do not know what to do with a property that consists in *being identical*. Of what could this property of identity be predicated? Of two objects? Such a thing is excluded in advance by these objects' very duality. Of a single object? But applying the concept of identity to a single object says nothing about it, even where we have the impression, in attributing this property to it, that we are saying something crucial— for example, providing it with the ability to be itself, to avoid being confused with some other object, as if "to be identical" could be understood as a kind of stability or steadiness that would guarantee the object's continuity in the face of the vicissitudes of existence.

§§ At this point, our question has become all the more urgent: of what use is the concept of identity? Are we to say that it serves no purpose? That is not Wittgenstein's view. In fact, in the *Tractatus*, Wittgenstein is not challenging the very *concept* of identity, the one that we make use of every day. What he is challenging is the explanation of identity offered by philosophers who turn it into a relation to be represented by "=", the logical sign of identity. In his view, such an explanation explains nothing. Wittgenstein therefore asks us to look instead at the way we in fact use the concept of identity.

---

2. Ludwig Wittgenstein, *Tractatus Logico-Philosophicus*, rev. ed., trans. D. F. Pears and B. F. McGuinness (1922; New York: Routledge, 1981), § 5.5303 (63).

Simply by doing this (if we manage it), we will have answered the *logical* objection to the very idea of applying this concept and will then be ready to respond to the *physical* objections, since we will be able to account for our usage of the primitive word "identical" in this world and not in some other, ideal one.

The Comedy of Identity

How do we ordinarily use the concept of identity? To answer this question, I suggest we return to the ancient origins of all of our speculation about identity—namely, the "Growing Argument" as it was formulated in Pre-Socratic Greek philosophy.

We know of this argument from Diogenes Laertius. In his chapter devoted to Plato's life and ideas, he reports the view according to which Plato was inspired by the poet Epicharmus (who lived at the beginning of the fifth century BC).[3] It is said that Epicharmus is the originator of an argument that bears on the identity conditions of things that are naturally in a state of flux. In the course of a subsequent debate between Academics and Stoics in which the former challenged the latter to account—within their materialist system—for the phenomenon of the growth of living things, it came to be called the "argument from growth" (*auxēsis*) or, literally, the "Growing Argument" (*auxanomenos logos*). Today, this argument is less well known than is the one concerning the paradox of the "Ship of Theseus." Yet, according to Plutarch, the paradox of the Ship of Theseus is no more than a version of the Growing Argument.[4] This argument was said to have been used by the poet Epicharmus in comic scenes that have unfortunately been lost but that have been mentioned by various authors, allowing us to at least have a sense of their spirit. It is my view that these scenes are of great interest for the philosophy of identity.

3. I will not be entering into the debate concerning the authenticity of the passages cited by Diogenes Laertius.

4. In the *Life of Theseus* (XXIII, 1), Plutarch presents the paradox of the Ship of Theseus as a variant of the Growing Argument. This is what he writes: "They [the Athenians] took away the old timbers from time to time, and put new and sound ones in their places, so that the vessel became a standing illustration for the philosophers in the mooted question of growth [*auxanomenos logos*], some declaring that it remained the same, others that it was not the same vessel. Plutarch, *Plutarch's Lives*, vol. 1, trans. Bernadotte Perrin (Cambridge, MA: Harvard University Press, 1914), 49.

§§§ Here is one possible version of the argument as reported by Diogenes Laertius:

> A. But suppose some one chooses to add a single pebble to a heap containing either an odd or an even number, whichever you please, or to take away one of those already there; do you think the number of pebbles would remain the same?
>
> B. Not I.
>
> A. Nor yet, if one chooses to add to a cubit-measure another length, or cut off some of what was there already, would the original measure still exist?
>
> B. Of course not.
>
> A. Now consider mankind in this same way. One man grows, and another again shrinks; and they are all undergoing change the whole time. But a thing which naturally changes and never remains in the same state must ever be different from that which has thus changed. And even so you and I were one pair of men yesterday, are another to-day, and again will be another to-morrow, and will never remain ourselves, by this same argument.[5]

Epicharmus is held to have put this highly philosophical argument into the mouths of his characters in scenes cited by Plutarch and others. In order to grasp both the logical force of the argument and the comic force of these scenes, it will be worth our while to reconstruct a scenario based on the information Plutarch provides. This has been done by David Sedley, a historian of classical philosophy, in an important article on the Stoic concept of identity.[6]

Imagine two people who meet, as often happens, in a public square. In order to keep things straight, we should give them names. The first person will be called Callias. Now, this Callias turns out to have previously borrowed money from a certain Coriscus, money that he never paid back. And so, upon meeting Callias the debtor in the agora, Coriscus the creditor asks him to repay his debt.

---

5. Diogenes Laertius, *Lives of the Eminent Philosophers*, vol. 1, trans. Robert Drew Hicks (Cambridge, MA: Harvard University Press, 1925), Book 3, Chapter 11 (287).
6. See David Sedley, "The Stoic Criterion of Identity," *Phronesis* 27 (1982): 255–275.

Callias responds with the Growing Argument above, with which Coriscus can find no fault. And since Coriscus is thus obliged to admit that nine pebbles plus one make a different number of pebbles (namely ten) and that men continually change, he must also admit that he does not have before him the same man who borrowed money from him but, rather, a different man. His debtor no longer exists.

The scene ends with a reversal of the situation. Coriscus the creditor, in a fit of rage, strikes Callias, who protests. But to these protestations Coriscus responds by saying that the man who struck him no longer exists because everything is always in a state of flux and therefore individuals are only ephemerally present in this world.

In this comical rewriting, the Growing Argument shows that the creditor can never manage to be repaid, because he will never be able to find the man to whom he lent the money. That man disappeared from the surface of the earth long ago. In fact, he was transformed into someone else shortly after contracting the debt (by, for example, taking in a deep breath of air or eating a Kalamata olive).

§§ It should be clear that the philosophy of identity is to be found not only in the argument that the poet deploys but also in the comical effects that arise out of his characters' tendentious use of it.

Consider the argument in itself, as it might be used in disputes among philosophers. The argument bears on every living body and, indeed, on any body whose size can be changed by a modification of its component parts. The Academics challenged the Stoics to reconcile their materialism with the common sense according to which living things are liable to grow: plants shoot up, animals get bigger until they reach their full adult size, etc.

However, if this argument is to be turned into a comedic scene, its scope will have to be limited to human affairs. Thus, it is the concept of a *human being* (*anthrōpos*) that enlivens these scenes. What is comical is that a character is entirely willing to redefine the concept of a human being if it will help him get out of trouble. Indeed, the entire exchange between the two characters bears upon what it means to be *the same man*, and therefore upon what it is that we will decide to refer to as a human being.

There is, however, a prior speculative question here: do we give the name Callias to an individual human so as to name him for his entire life and therefore at every age and regardless of his material composition? This is, of course, the ordinary conception of human beings and their proper names, such that if we were told that Callias was no longer of this world, we might ask, "What was done with his cadaver? Where is he buried?"

Here, the character Callias pretends to believe that this ordinary practice is lacking in rigor. He reckons that the name "Callias" was given to the *material man*, by which I mean the man in the material configuration that happens to be his at the moment the name is used for the first time. From that point on, any change in the material composition of the individual, any growth or deterioration, will have the effect of replacing this individual with a new one.

"I am not the Callias to whom you lent money": such an assertion amounts to asking us to rework our concept of *anthrōpos* (or of the human person) so as to tally with the Heraclitean idea that everything is in a state of flux. Yet, behind the metaphysical scruples expressed, the real motive, which is to get out of paying a debt, is plain to see. This debtor has discovered a new *technique for getting out of debt*: one need only avail oneself of a more "rigorous" and stringent concept of personal identity. While this may be true, it would seem to follow from it that nobody will be able to lend or borrow money, since the temporality of people is no longer on the same scale as the temporality of credit. In fact, one would only be able to lend money to someone on condition of being paid back at the very same instant, without any lapse of time between the two acts. Otherwise, the debtor will vanish into thin air.

What is comical here arises out of the discrepancy between the overt claims—to reform our way of thinking and speaking so as to make it more rigorous—and behavior that takes no account of these new ideas and pays no heed to the proposed reform as soon as there is an advantage to be had in returning to the old notions of what it is to be "the same person" or "the same man." It arises out of the gap between the fact of demanding that the other party embrace the conceptual reform (thereby abandoning the claim to be repaid) and the fact of exempting oneself from it, whether at the moment when one borrows the money or when one complains about being struck.

The practice of lending and incurring debt rests on a conception of personal identity in which identity is not ephemeral. It does not matter whether the debtor has gained weight or grown or lost weight or gone bald, etc. In other words, our practice presupposes that we are agreed on the application of the concept of identity to the concept of the human being. We are agreed about who must pay back and who must be paid back; neither is the material man in the sense of a being defined by the identity of his material parts.

In the end, what is comical is the fact that the character makes use of one conceptual system and then the other. In so doing, he reveals his indifference to Heraclitean philosophy and that he is only interested in finding a way not to honor his debts. Let us imagine that all of the other characters agree to reform their concepts so as to be in accord with Heraclitus's idea. If they wanted to retain the possibility of making loans, they would have to adjust the entire vocabulary used to talk about debt in order to be able to continue to make determinations about *who owes what to whom*; it will no longer be the ephemeral material man present at the moment of the loan but, rather, the "successor" whose (equally ephemeral) material identity was established in the site of his predecessor's individuation. But in that case, nothing will have changed in practice: they would simply have adopted another way of expressing the same facts.

Thus Epicharmus's comic scenes are, as is often the case, conservative in spirit. They show that it is not as easy as one might imagine to modify a conceptual system, for the entire system has to be changed. Yet if one does this without also modifying practices, what one has changed is nothing but a notation.

The Principle of Individuation

What do these comic scenes attributed to Epicharmus teach us? They teach us this: contrary to what was believed by those philosophers who proposed that we revise the concept of identity or distinguish different sorts of identity—some strict and some approximative—the concept of identity is not really what is at issue. These thinkers believed that certain uses, or perhaps all uses, of the concept had to be weakened if we were to account for a reality that was not amenable to being divided up into a set of immutable entities. The further one strayed from the ideal case where nothing changes in the composition of a physical entity, the more elastic one would have to make the conditions under which one could speak of identity. Here in this world, we would have to make do with identity of a second-rate kind.

Yet Epicharmus's scenes show that what is at issue is not the concept of identity itself. The issue in the Growing Argument is the concept of a living being and, in the comic scenes, the concept of a human being. What is it to be *the same human being*? Quine recalls the lesson of our Pre-Socratic comedy when he, rightly, writes:

> Some philosophers propound puzzles as to what to say about personal identity in cases of split personality or in fantasies about metempsychosis or brain transplants. These are not questions about the nature of identity. They are questions about how we might best construe the term "person." Again there is the stock example of the ship of Theseus, rebuilt bit by bit until no original bit remained. Whether we choose to reckon it still as the same ship is a question not of "same" but of "ship"; a question of how we choose to individuate that term over time.[7]

In another scene from a (lost) comedy by Epicharmus mentioned by Plutarch, a character invites someone he knows to dinner.[8] We can imagine the scene: when the invitee shows up for dinner on the appointed day, the man who invited him refuses to allow him to enter, claiming that he is not the man who had been invited because that man had a slimmer physique. Clearly the same reasoning could be used to maintain that the guests leaving a sumptuous dinner are not the same individuals who were earlier seated around the table, since they will certainly have put on weight in the interim. The dialectical argument makes it impossible to invite guests to a meal.

Our concept of the human being is that of a living being. It must therefore be possible for us to say that he has put on weight, grown, lost weight, become stronger, aged, etc. The interactions of our daily lives—lending money, dinner invitations, and so on—are carried out with just these sorts of individuals, who can put on or lose weight, etc. If we bear this in mind, the philosopher's question ("What is a human being?")

7. W. V. Quine, *Theories and Things* (Cambridge, MA: Harvard University Press, 1981), 12.
8. Plutarch, *Moralia*, vol. 7 (523c–612b), trans. Phillip H. de Lacy and Benedict Einarson (Cambridge, MA: Harvard University Press, 1959), 559b (244–247).

will have been honed so as to become this one: "How is it that the man Callias who arrives at my door at the appointed hour for dinner is the same human individual that I invited yesterday?" To answer this question is to provide what the Scholastics called a *principle of individuation* for human beings. Such a principle is what I appeal to each time I judge that what is before me is not *a* human being (as was the case yesterday when I encountered Callias and invited him) but *the same* human being as the one I encountered then.

The Growing Argument plays on a careless application of the principle of human individuation. What distinguishes two men—for example, Callias and Coriscus—and makes it the case that there are two men present and not just one is the fact that there are two materially distinct bodies present. The principle of individuation is thus matter. If I have invited not just Callias but also Coriscus to dinner, I will have to arrange to have an extra chair at the table, extra cutlery, etc., since there will be one more mouth to be fed. Matter is what distinguishes two *contemporaneous* individuals.

What, then, should we say if we contemplate one of those individuals over time? If we again appeal to the principle of material individuation for the individual Callias, we will have to say that *the identity of the matter* comprising the individual is what constitutes the identity of that individual. At this point, the paradox becomes inescapable: this individual will be destroyed if we change anything in his composition. Epicharmus's paradox therefore depends on a decision regarding the principle of individuation for human beings such that a change in the material composition of an individual results in the destruction of his identity and the production of a new individual. In other words, matter is not just the principle of individuation that we apply to contemporaneous human individuals; it is also what we use to identify an individual as himself throughout his personal history.

This must be the case, according to those philosophers who believe diachronic identity is material identity. To give up the material principle of individuation would entail *dematerializing* the individual identity of living things. But if the identity of an individual organism is dematerialized, then that individual itself, considered in what makes it the individual that it is, will have also been dematerialized. Having thus transformed living things into immaterial individuals, we will have adopted a spiritualist theory. At this point, according to these philosophers, if we want to resist such spiritualism we will have to accept the resultant paradox that there will be no place in our conceptual system for the phenomenon of growth. More generally, it will be impossible to take a *material* individual for a *historical* individual, for the subject of a story that will be *her* story, the story of *her* transformations over time. It will no longer be possible to recount, say, the history of the Lebanese cedar in the Jardin des Plantes in Paris.

§§§ At this juncture it should be clear that the roots of this paradox lie in the idea that there is an inherent contradiction in the very notion of diachronic identity once one moves away from the realm of immutable things (if indeed there are any such things). The presupposition governing the entire paradox is thus: *identity in time is the absence of change.* The physical argument against identity seeks to ensnare us in a dilemma: *how can something stay the same—remain itself—while nevertheless changing?* The argument seems unanswerable, for if the thing has changed, it can no longer be the same, and if it is the same, it cannot have changed.

Yet this argument is a sophism, one that is all the more disconcerting because it appeals to an idea that is incontrovertible—that there is an undeniable opposition between *remaining oneself* (i.e., preserving one's identity) and *changing* (i.e., *becoming other*). But, in reality, this opposition is an illusion. What is the meaning of "remaining oneself"? The archetype of a fluid entity is the Heraclitean river. Does the river cease to be itself, does it lose its identity, when its waters flow? On the contrary, only in such case is it itself! On the other hand, if its waters ceased to flow, it would at that point cease to be a river—and the same river—for having turned into a *lake* or an *inland sea.* It follows that we need not concede that "to change in its composition" is the equivalent of "to change into something else."

Does the river nevertheless stop being a material entity once it has a diachronic identity? But what would an immaterial river consist of? In fact, at each instant, the river consists of its flowing waters. What makes it the same river is that the waters flow in the same bed and in the same direction. In other words, the *diachronic* principle of the river's individuation is provided by the answer to the question of what makes these flowing waters into a river. And what makes these waters, that flow as they do, into a river—and, indeed, the same river as the one yesterday, which was made up of other waters that flowed in the same way—is the bed of the river and its geographical layout. Or, to put it in Aristotelian terms, the river's diachronic principle of individuation is derived from its "form." Moreover, it is precisely this analogy of the river that Aristotle uses in response to the Growing Argument.[9]

The error of the materialist who wants to determine the identity of an individual over time through his material identity at a given instant is to use the principle of synchronic individuation for diachronic ends. Such a materialism makes it impossible to conceive of historical individuals.

The Logic of Proper Names

What lesson should we draw from Epicharmus's comic scenes? That there is an ambiguity to the words "the same."

1. In one sense, a thing is the same if nothing in it has changed, if it remains exactly as it was. This is the sense applied by those who define the identity of a material thing through the identity of its material components, as in the case of a collection of ten pebbles that is distinguished from a collection that only contains nine. When we are talking about entities such as collections of pebbles, this sense of "the same" is the right one.

2. In another sense, a thing is the same if it continues to exist, regardless of the changes that may have affected it from time to time (provided that *it* is what was affected by these changes). It is in this sense that one can say, Look at how my flowers have shot up, how the tree I planted has grown, or how big my little dog has become.

If we do not distinguish between these two applications of the concept, we will find ourselves in a philosophical trap. In order to maintain that Coriscus has gotten fat or that Theaetetus has grown taller, we would appear to have to deny that these human beings are material individuals. But, if they are not material, how can they get fat or slim down? This is a philosophical trap, because the two positions imposed

---

9. On this response, see Elizabeth Anscombe, "The Principle of Individuation," in *The Collected Papers of G. E. M. Anscombe*, vol. 1, *From Parmenides to Wittgenstein* (Oxford: Blackwell, 1981), 64–65, as well as Richard Sorabji, *Self: Ancient and Modern Insights About Individuality, Life, and Death* (Chicago: University of Chicago Press, 2006), 57–59.

on us are indefensible. We want to adopt neither of them. We do not want to have to say that each of us possesses *multiple bodies* in succession over the course of our lives (through some strange application of the idea of metempsychosis to a single individual existence). But we also do not want to have to say that a human being has no biography because he exists for no more than a brief instant.

Is it possible to escape this trap? I believe that it can be done with support from the *logical critique* mounted by Wittgenstein of the relational conception of identity.

As early as the *Tractatus*, Wittgenstein asks: why do we need a concept of identity? Of what use is it to us? His intention is not to put its usefulness into question, but rather to criticize textbook explanations that do not account for it. Not for an instant does he doubt that the concept of identity is necessary for us. But he asks: must we necessarily express our concept of identity using the identity sign ("=")? And he answers: not at all. One could, he claims, do without the sign "=" entirely. To do so one need only decree that objects cannot have more than one proper name. If that were the case, if every difference in the noun used necessarily indicated (thanks to this convention) a difference in the object designated, we could give others to understand that we were speaking again of the same object as before, and we could do so without having to make an identity statement of the type "a = b." As he writes:

> Identity of object I express by identity of sign, and not by using a sign for identity. Difference of objects I express by difference of signs.[10]

Logicians require a sign for identity only because they accept that a thing can be referred to in several different ways or because some objects have several proper names (as in the textbook cases where Cicero = Tully or "the evening star = the morning star") or, finally, because we choose to treat certain expressions that are not really proper names as logical proper names, for example definite descriptions (as in Russell's example "the present king of France is bald").

If every object had only one proper name, one would only have to use the name a second time to make clear that one is speaking about the same object mentioned the first time. There is therefore an application of the concept of identity every time a proper name is used.

---

10. Wittgenstein, *Tractatus*, § 5.53 (62).

The lesson to be drawn from this critique is that we may derive the meaning that we give to the primitive word "identity" from our practice of using proper names. How is a proper name used? It can only be used after having been ascribed to an object so as to designate it. This leads us to wonder how it is that we ascribe a name to an object. To do this, a sign of our language has to be set aside that will henceforth serve to name the object that we identify in front of us through expressions such as "this baby," "this mountain," "this river," "this cat," etc. How is the sign assigned to each of these things as its name? The condition is that, at the moment we give the proper name to the object, we also put in place a rule for any possible future use of this same name. This rule for the use of the name consists in an *identity criterion* for the object, one that will allow us to individuate it among others of its kind. This is why such a criterion must include, to use Quine's terminology, an "individuative term."[11] We know that logicians and linguists distinguish between two sorts of general substantive terms: mass terms (such as "water," "gold," "paper," "cattle," etc.) and individuative terms (such as "steer," "tree," "river," "man," etc.). A mass term such as "cattle" does of course designate individual animals but only indistinctly. If we want to consider a mass of things as individuated—in order to count them, for example—we will have to refer to *a head* of cattle, *a glass* of water, *a bar* of gold, *a sheet* of paper, and so on. Individuative terms are those that allow one to move directly to the identification and enumeration of the objects designated, by saying, for example, "I have *two steer* in my stable."

In the comedic scene we have been considering, the proper name "Callias" was given to a human being, not to a collection of cells. In other words, every time someone uses the name "Callias," he conceives of the object named as being *the same man* that was once given this name.

Peter Geach has put forward a distinction that allows for an elegant reformulation of Wittgenstein's idea that the sign "=" is not the only way of expressing identity. He explains that identity can be applied in two ways: on the *predicate side* or on the *subject side*.[12] Logicians, Geach explains, tend to seek expressions of identity only in propositions that

---

11. W. V. Quine, *Ontological Relativity and Other Essays* (New York: Columbia University Press, 1969), 36–37.
12. Peter Geach, *Reference and Generality: An Examination of Some Medieval and Modern Theories*, 3rd ed. (Ithaca: Cornell University Press, 1980), 212–213.

contain a predicate such as " . . . is the same as . . ." or " . . . is identical to . . ." Geach speaks in this case of a *predicative use* of the expression "the same A." For example: "The evening star is the same planet as the morning star." This predicate is dyadic, meaning that it must be filled in with two proper names if it is to say something that will be either true or false. It seems entirely natural in such a case to speak about identity as a *relation*, in which case one runs up against Wittgenstein's paradox: to what is the thing related when it is claimed to be identical? To persist in the search for a real relation is to expose oneself to a dialectical refutation: if the thing must have a relation of identity with some *other* thing, that other thing must nevertheless necessarily once again be the subject of this relation; and if the thing must have a relation of identity with itself, then in one way or another it must be separated from itself—otherwise, what would be the point of placing it in a relation of identity with itself? If it is a relation, identity can only be a "dialectical" relation, an identity "in difference" or "as a result of difference" (the sort of "identity in difference" ridiculed by Russell).

Geach points out, however, that there are other ways for us to conceive of the identity of things than judgments of identity. We also apply the concept of identity on the *subject side*. We do this whenever we use a proper name a second time (or replace it by an anaphoric pronoun such as "he" or "she"). Geach characterizes such cases as "subject-uses" of "the same A." He illustrates the distinction with an example that he derives from thinking about the logic of narrative propositions and their connections within a single biographical narrative.[13] Here is a rudimentary biographical summary of the life of a man named Smith: "Smith committed seven burglaries, then Smith committed a murder, then Smith was hanged." Let us assume that we know nothing of the Smith in question. All that we learn from this narrative is the following, which gives the purely intelligible content, outside of any context of the narrative: "There is a man named Smith, and this same man committed seven burglaries, and this same man committed a murder, and this same man was hanged." It follows that to repeat an individual's proper name is to make use of the concept of identity: to name "Smith" is to posit that any subsequent use of the proper name "Smith" in the rest of

---

13. Peter Geach, *Mental Acts: Their Content and Their Objects* (London: Routledge and Kegan Paul, 1957), § 16 (71).

the narrative will have the function of referring to the *same man* as the one with whose name our story began.

Not only are there two possible kinds of use of the concept of identity, but use on the *subject side* clearly takes precedence over use on the *predicate side*. Indeed, in order to form an identity proposition of the kind "Cicero is the same man as Tully," we must already have the two proper names at our disposal, and therefore they must have been bestowed, along with their identity criteria, on the persons they name.

Identity Criteria

What do we mean by "identity criteria"? This notion, which was brought into use by Frege, is fundamental to the analytic philosophy of language. Its importance was captured by Quine's famous slogan according to which there is "no entity without identity," which would of course have to be complemented by its converse, put forward by Geach or Davidson: "no identity without entity."[14]

In § 62 of *The Foundations of Arithmetic*, Frege asks the question of how ideal (nonphysical) objects such as numbers are given to us. He replies that they are given to us in language. We then have to consider how numerical words (*Zahlwörter*) function within propositions. They function in the same way as proper names. Frege then formulates the condition under which one can use a word as a proper name:

> If we are to use the symbol *a* to signify an object, we must have a criterion for deciding in all cases whether *b* is the same as *a*, even if it is not always in our power to apply this criterion.[15]

What does Frege mean by "deciding" when speaking of an object *b* within a proposition, whether we are once again speaking of an object *a* (assuming it has already been mentioned) or of a different object? In the

14. Quine, *Ontological Relativity*, 23; Peter Geach, "Ontological Relativity and Relative Identity," in *Logic and Ontology*, ed. Milton K. Munitz (New York: New York University Press, 1973), 288; Donald Davidson, "The Individuation of Events," in his *Essays on Actions and Events* (New York: Oxford University Press, 1980), 164.

15. Gottlob Frege, *The Foundations of Arithmetic: A Logico-Mathematic Enquiry Into the Concept of Number*, 2nd rev. ed., trans. J. L. Austin (1950; New York: Harper Torchbooks, 1960), § 62 (73).

ordinary usage of the term, a "criterion of identity" is a means of judging or establishing whether there is identity or not. Strictly speaking, this is not what is at issue here, since Frege adds that we must have such a criterion even though, in practice, we cannot make use of it.

An identity criterion in Frege's sense is thus not some *mark* or *way of recognizing* or *proof* of the identity of the object named. It does not involve invoking resemblances, characteristic signs, or unique details. Rather, we might say that Frege's conception of the identity criterion is not epistemological but, as Wittgenstein would put it, grammatical. The criterion we need in order to determine the meaning of a proper name consists in determining what we mean when we speak of the "same man" (in the case of the name of a human) or of the "same river" (in the case of the name of a river).

§§ In order to illustrate this distinction between a *grammatical* criterion, on the one hand, and various kinds of *epistemological* criteria, on the other, imagine the following scenario. The police inform you that they have just recovered the Vermeer that had been stolen from you. Unfortunately, they simultaneously also inform you that the painting is a forgery, indeed a very well-made forgery, one that is so well made that only an expert's eye would be able to determine it as such. You protest: the painting that has been recovered cannot be yours; it must be a copy of the original that you owned, an original that therefore remains as yet unrecovered.

This is well and truly a question of identity. The problem is one of determining whether the recovered painting is the same as the one stolen from you or whether, alternatively, it is only a copy of that painting. But it is clear that a solution to this problem will appeal to two different kinds of criteria. For there are two separate questions raised: (1) How might you prove that your painting was not in fact this copy recovered from the thieves? (2) What is the difference between owning a painting made by the artist himself—what we call "the original"—and having in one's possession another painting that is almost entirely indistinguishable from it? One might imagine different ways of establishing that the recovered painting (the fake Vermeer) is the same one that the thieves took from your house: for example, if they were seen, or the movements of the painting were monitored, or, alternatively, if the forger admitted to having sold you the painting, etc. But for these various methods that we might come up with to seem conclusive to us, we must already know what we mean by "the same painting." And that is what we can call, following Frege, the criterion of identity for one kind of object: the meaning that we set down for the application of the concept of identity to an individuative term, in such a way as to form an expression of the type "the same X."

§§ David Wiggins has used some Aristotelian concepts in an instructive account of the Fregean idea of a criterion of identity. He shows how Frege's criterion corresponds to the Aristotelian notion of essence or *quiddity* taken in a *nominal* sense (as opposed to the *real* essence of the object, which derives not from any decision by us but from empirical research). In a nominal sense, the question of essence arises in the following conditions: before undertaking (empirical) investigation into whether something exists (*an est*), one must determine what one is talking about (*quid est*). If we are exploring a territory in order to know whether any X can be found there, we will have to have determined in advance, through a lexical decision, what counts as *an individual of type X* and thus also what will count as *the same X*.

Wiggins emphasizes that it is impossible to attribute mere diachronic identity to a thing and nothing more; one must specify "what it is for X to persist"—in other words, for it to have its own history.[16] The criterion we require to be able to use the concept "the same" is one that we derive from the question "What is it?"

> An answer to the *what is it* question does both less and more than provide that which counts as evidence for or against an identity.[17]

This response does *less*: to know that "Callias" is the (Greek) name of a man is not yet to be armed with a battery of tests or proofs to determine whether *this man*, present before us, is or is not Callias. It is therefore not a criterion of judgment in the way that a fingerprint, traces of DNA, or a signature might be. But, at the same time, the response does *more*: to note that "this is the name of a human being" makes clear what *existing*

---

16. David Wiggins, *Sameness and Substance Renewed* (Cambridge: Cambridge University Press, 2001), 57.
17. Ibid., 60.

consists in for the individual named Callias. To exist, for him, is to live a human life, to exist as a man, and, more precisely, to exist continually as the same man. The response here does more than simply provide a test, since it allows us to give a meaning to the operation by which the object named is reidentified. It thereby allows us to understand why it is that having the same animated body as Callias, or being born to the same mother at the same instant as Callias, means that one is the *same man* as Callias. The *quid est* allows us to understand why some clues are more probative than others.

Is Identity Relative?

I have already mentioned the classical example that has been discussed since ancient times: the Ship of Theseus that the Athenians continually repair by replacing old boards with new ones. The case is one of those difficult ones in which the spatio-temporal continuity of a material object is insufficient to assure its identity through time. Because the boat's boards are constantly being replaced, a moment arrives when none of the original material components remain. It might then be said, "At every moment there is a wooden object that we call the Ship of Theseus; yet, if we consider the material composition of this vessel, can we still say that we have the same boat before us?"

One solution that philosophers have often embraced is to maintain that there are in reality two sorts or two concepts of identity, one that is strict and philosophical and another that is lax and common. In applying the concept of identity, we sometimes attach rigorous conditions to its application. At other times, we agree to *act as if* there were not a succession of similar objects occupying the same space (i.e., the different bodies that we refer to as the same ship), but rather the durable and continuous existence of a single selfsame object. This theory has repeatedly been espoused from the eighteenth century to the present day.[18]

---

18. For examples of this view in the eighteenth century, see Joseph Butler, "Of Personal Identity" (excerpted from *The Analogy of Religion*, 1736) and Thomas Reid, "Of Identity" (from his *Essays on the Intellectual Powers of Man*, 1785), both in John Perry, ed., *Personal Identity*, 2nd ed. (1975; Berkeley: University of California Press, 2008), 99–105 and 107–112. For a modern expression of the theory, see Roderick M. Chisholm, "The Loose and Popular and the Strict and Philosophical Senses of Identity," in Norman S. Care and

We have already seen the impasse to which this dualistic solution (in which bodies have no real identity—only souls and mathematical concepts do) leads. In fact, the problem of the "same ship" is not a problem with the concept of identity but with our definition of a ship. If there is a difficulty here, it arises because the application of the term "ship" is indeterminate. It is incumbent upon us to say what we mean by it. No natural "essence" of the ship dictates what we mean by the word; our own conventions do. Once the identity criterion has been established, the question has a determinate (Fregean) sense: it can then be said whether the boat before us is the one we call the Ship of Theseus.

§§ I propose a rule governing the use of proper names in the identification of objects, one that we might call "Geach's Rule," a rule derived from a page in his *Mental Acts*, in which he offers a striking explanation. In his discussion of proper names, Geach is seeking to rule out the two most popular philosophical doctrines of the time: on the one hand, the empiricist doctrine according to which proper names are pure signifiers endowed with a referential value but devoid of meaning (this was John Stuart Mill's thesis) and, on the other hand, the doctrine according to which a proper name does have a meaning because it is an abbreviated form of a definite description (along such lines as these: "Napoleon" = "the victor in the battle of Austerlitz" = "the defeated party in the battle of Waterloo").[19]

On the one hand, a proper name is not an abbreviated form of a definite description, since the latter is necessarily derived from an episode or a feature in the life of the individual. Yet a proper name serves to designate an individual for her entire life, from infancy until death. Since it names the individual from birth, it cannot tell us anything about the life of that individual.

Robert H. Grimm, eds., *Perception and Personal Identity* (Cleveland: Press of Case Western Reserve University, 1969), 82-106, as well as Chisholm's *Person and Object: A Metaphysical Study* (London: George Allen & Unwin, 1976), 108-109.

19. Today the theory according to which proper names are associated with definite descriptions—and can thus be eliminated—has fallen into disfavor. By contrast, the opposing theory according to which they are meaningless has reappeared in new garb with Kripke's notion of the "rigid designator." See Saul Kripke, *Naming and Necessity* (Cambridge, MA: Harvard University Press, 1980).

On the other hand, the proper name must have a meaning, because such signs serve to designate *the same object* on multiple occasions, an object that must be specified (since the general term "object" is not an individuative term). As Geach puts it, "Proper names express identifications—e.g. 'the Thames' expresses the identification of something as one and the same *river*."[20] But if this is so, the concept of identity is already applied every time a word is used as a proper name. It is at this point that what I propose to call "Geach's Rule" comes into play: namely, that whenever we are faced with a question of identity regarding whether object *a* is *the same* as object *b*, we are always within our rights to ask, "the same *what*?" (so long as the answer is not made obvious by the context). Geach writes:

> "The same" is a fragmentary expression, and has no significance unless we say or mean "the same X," where "X" represents a general term (what Frege calls a *Begriffswort* or *Begriffsausdruck*).[21]

There is only one small part of this formulation that will need to be changed: a "general term" is not always sufficient to provide a criterion of identity (e.g., "the same X"), for some general terms are not *individuative*. Yet his examples ("man," "river") show that what Geach has in mind is an individuative term. Without such an individuative term, I cannot know what I have named with a proper name. And if I cannot know what I have named, I have not really named anything at all.

What is this rule's scope? Is it congruent with doctrines that tend to *relativize* identity? Geach apparently thought so and developed several different theories of so-called relative identity. Yet we need not follow him in this; David Wiggins has shown that we ought to distinguish two questions that were conflated during the debate between Quine and Geach on relative identity.[22]

1. First question: is simple spatio-temporal continuity in existence enough to ensure the diachronic identity of an individual? Can an individual continue to exist just by remaining "the same," or, rather, can it only remain the same individual of its type—i.e., the

---

20. Geach, *Mental Acts*, vii.
21. Ibid., 69.
22. See Wiggins, *Sameness and Substance Renewed*.

same *river* (if we are talking about the Thames), the same *man* (if we are discussing a man), and so on? Like Geach, Wiggins maintains that mere continuity is insufficient. The question "Does object *x* remain the same, or has it given way to an object *y*?" is incomplete in that it fails to specify what "remaining the same" consists in. Wiggins thus upholds "Geach's Rule," calling it the thesis of the "Sortal Dependency of Individuation."[23]

2. Second question: given two individuals, *a* and *b*, is it conceivable that they be nothing but a single individual under a description X but remain distinct under a description Y? Partisans of relative identity claim that such a thing is possible. Wiggins rejects this thesis of relative identity and, in my view, is right to do so. For, if we accepted that individuals *a* and *b* could be both distinct and identical, we would lose the advantages conferred by "Geach's Rule" or the "Sortal Dependency of Individuation." The doctrine of relative identity asks us to accept the possibility that individuals *a* and *b* might be a *single, selfsame X* while also being *two distinct Ys*. For example: Callias my debtor from yesterday and Callias encountered today are *a single selfsame man* but are *two different collections of cells*. To embrace such a thesis would entail that we could name objects *a* and *b* without identifying them using a criterion of identity. For example, we would not have to choose between giving the name "Callias" to a human being and giving it to a collection of cells.

In short, Geach's decisive contribution to the philosophy of identity does not lie in his parlous theory of relative identity, but rather in his Fregean and Wittgensteinian contention that the use of certain signs— proper names—rests on a grammatical criterion of identity. This leads to the revitalization of the notion of a nominal essence (quiddity) in the face of the empiricist school's attack on this kind of "Aristotelian essentialism."

§§ We have now taken a first step in (re)learning the identitarian idiom. We have uncovered the meaning of our elementary use of the word "identity" understood as a primitive word. We did this by returning to

---

23. Ibid., 22.

our linguistic use of the proper names that we give to the things we recognize as individuals. The key that allows us to understand the elementary concept of identity is the principle of what Wiggins calls the "sortal dependency" of questions of identity. More simply, it is "Geach's Rule" concerning the use of the words "the same." Taken alone, this rule in no way introduces relativity into identity, if by "relativity" we mean a deterioration (in relation to what an "absolute identity" would be: complete or perfect) in the concept's conditions of application or even in the sense of a contradiction internal to the concept itself, as would be the case if one wanted to claim that identity is never absolute—i.e., simple—because it is always an "identity in difference."

All of this, however, only concerns identity in the sense of what makes things *identical*. We will still have to see whether we can find a path that leads from the identical to the *identitarian*. As we have seen, the paradigm for the identitarian question is provided by two questions: "Who am I?" and "Who are we?" To this point, we have only discussed the question "Who is it?" asked about someone else, a question formulated in the third person.

The next step we will have to take is to learn to *appropriate* identity, to learn to speak of an identity experienced or conceived as belonging to a subject, at first in the first-person singular and subsequently in the first-person plural.

PART II

"WHO AM I?"

3

IDENTITY IN THE SUBJECTIVE SENSE

"Who Am I?"

We know how to ask, "Who is it?" but do we know how to ask, "Who am I?" Do we know how to ask the question of identity in the first person?

Today we are so accustomed to using the identitarian idiom that we are not surprised to learn that so-and-so is undergoing an identity crisis, by which we mean that *he no longer knows who he is.* Can we explain what it is that he no longer knows? The task may well be more difficult than it first appears.

Outside of exceptional situations, the question "Who am I?" is not strictly speaking a question that is ever asked other than as the echo-like reiteration of a question asked by an interlocutor. I can certainly take up, in the first person, the question you have asked me: e.g., "You have asked me who I am; I will therefore introduce myself to you." In this case, my "Who am I?" does nothing but reproduce your request for information. In such a case, although I do ask the question "Who am I?" I do not address it to myself and do not ask it with the aim of clearing up the matter for myself.

In exceptional circumstances, someone may be led to ask this question of himself. One might imagine a situation in which I do not know (or have forgotten) the role I am playing in a game or in a conspiracy. In such cases, the question would bear upon my identity within the game or my pseudonym within the clandestine activity. Or, one can imagine a case in which someone has lost his sense of self after an experience of amnesia or extreme distraction. This is Molière's way of staging a crisis undergone by the main character of *The Miser*. When Harpagon discovers that his moneybox has gone missing, he apostrophizes himself, even going so far as to grab himself by the arm as if he had laid his hands on the thief:

> Villain, give me back my money! Oh, it's me! I'm losing my mind, I don't know where I am, who I am or what I'm doing.[1]

Moreover, even if an occasion were to arise in which I were led to ask the question of *my own identity*, would this question really be in the first person? If it were merely about knowing my name and occupation, the question would only be half in the first person, since, on this hypothesis, I would be the one seeking to know *who I am*, but I could not be asking the question *of myself*. Indeed, assuming that, as a result of a case of amnesia, I no longer have this information, I would not get far asking myself for it; I would have to ask those around me, those who know the answer.

How does it happen that we want to ask a question that, on the face of it, would appear to be the very example of a question that does not arise? To understand the use of the term "identity" in its identitarian sense will entail finding a use, in everyday situations, for the question "Who am I?"

In order to explain this, one might appeal to the Scholastic theory according to which there are different kinds of identity, so that, alongside "numerical" identity (identity properly so called) there is also what is called "qualitative" identity, consisting in an individual having *the same quality* as other individuals. Identity crises would then be crises of qualitative identity.

During the 2007 French presidential election campaign, newspapers published articles claiming that "The candidate has been emphasizing her feminine identity." Is not *sexual identity* an excellent example of

---

1. Molière, *The Miser*, in *The Miser and Other Plays*, trans. John Wood (New York: Penguin, 2000), act 4, scene 7 (202).

qualitative identity? Yet if "sexual identity" is "qualitative," it can consist in only one thing: each of us is *of the same sex* as one of our two parents. What is identified, then, is which of the two sexes the person in question is; the person himself or herself is not identified. Now it happens that a great many individuals share this "quality." Imagine that you receive a telephone call and the person on the other end of the line is content to present herself to you only by "emphasizing her feminine identity" as a "qualitative identity." Having heard her say, "I am a woman," would you know who was on the line? If she had nothing else to tell you, you might at that point conclude that she was undergoing a serious "identity crisis"—in a literal sense this time; she would be incapable of telling you who she was.

Yet Harpagon's feverish monologue cited earlier suggests a path different from one leading to knowledge of facts about himself. It is not because he is short of information about himself that Harpagon admits, "I don't know where I am, who I am or what I'm doing." And it is not by asking others that he will be able to recover himself. The temporary alienation to which he has fallen prey is one that only he can overcome. Only he can come back to himself by recovering his wits. Clearly the key to the question "Who am I?" asked in the first person is to be sought in the fact that the answer must come from the subject himself.

§§§ Why is it necessary for the subject to ask himself *in person* the question of his own identity? Why is it impossible for such questioning to be delegated or subcontracted to someone else? What difference is there between someone else's response to the question and the subject's own? There are two conceivable ways of marking such a difference.

1. First explanation: it is possible that in response to the very *same question* about his personal identity, the subject concerned will have to offer a response *other than* a set of particular facts about himself. That such a thing is conceivable is implicit in the thesis according to which there are *multiple modes of personal individuation* as a result of the polysemy of the term "person."

2. A second explanation can also be imagined: it might be claimed that the question has to be asked and answered in the first person, because a subject who asks the question of himself in the first person is really asking a *different question* than the question of

identity as such—a different question than the *literal* question of identity. The question of identity, in the literal sense, takes this form: "Am I who you claim I am or am I someone else?" According to this explanation, the answer to the (nonliteral) question must come from the subject himself, because it consists not in any information to be communicated—which would be the literal sense—but in a *decision* the subject must make.

I will take up these two possibilities in turn. The first will prove to lead to an impasse. And we will only come to understand the second if we are able to move from our understanding of identity in the literal sense to an understanding of identity in a figural one.

An Identity at Once Objective and Subjective

We know that Erikson was not only the first—with his diagnosis of an "identity crisis"—to use the term "identity" in the new way, but that he also offered as a paradigm for the new sense the way in which someone presents himself or herself to others under one or another identity.

As has often been pointed out, Erikson never defined his term. He even acknowledged this himself. In his article on "Identity, Psychosocial" in the *International Encyclopedia of the Social Sciences*, Erikson indicates only that we will have to derive the new usage, that he introduced, from our usual idea of the identity of a person. He begins his article as follows:

> When we wish to establish a person's *identity*, we ask what his name is and what station he occupies in his community. *Personal identity* means more; it includes a subjective sense of continuous existence and a coherent memory. *Psychosocial identity* has even more elusive characteristics, at once subjective and objective, individual and social.[2]

In order to introduce his notion of identity in the psychosocial sense in this passage, Erikson proceeds through three steps. First, he invites

---

2. Erik H. Erikson, "Identity, Psychosocial," in David L. Sills, ed., *International Encyclopedia of the Social Sciences*, vol. 7 (New York: Macmillan, 1968), 61.

us to start from the question "Who is it?" in the sense of a roster or Who's Who: we know *who is who* when we know the names of the people as well as some of their social positions and distinctions, i.e., their *backgrounds* (family, education) and elements of their *résumés*. How might this sort of identity find itself in crisis? Perhaps if it were disputed or became impossible to establish after the annihilation of archives and witnesses. If such a thing happened to me, I would certainly be disturbed and disoriented, but my distress would not be, strictly speaking, due to an *identity crisis* or a *loss of identity*. It would be a difficulty in maintaining my own certainty—and, ultimately, my own mental health—in the face of the entire world's hostile skepticism.[3]

Next, Erikson moves from the third person to the first. Each of us may ask the question "Who am I?" in the sense of "How is it that I remain, in my own eyes, the same person throughout my life?" Erikson here alludes to a philosophical notion of personal identity. Such subjective identity assumes that the person should be defined above all through her psychological capacities and that her identity "as a person" is the one provided by the exercise of those capacities over time. In this case, an "identity crisis" might be an effect of a lapse of memory or, perhaps, a difficulty in finding a coherence to one's past life. It nevertheless seems to consist in a loss of the person's *unity* rather than a loss of identity. One might explain the distinction as follows: when a vase has been shattered into a thousand pieces, it is no longer in a state of wholeness or of physical unity; it is nevertheless *that* vase that has been broken and not another.

Finally, Erikson announces a third application of the question of identity. In asking the question "Who is it?" we are now seeking a *psychosocial* identity. Unfortunately, Erikson does not define it, speaking only of "even more elusive characteristics." All that he tells us is that the question of identity, taken in this third sense, will bring together the two preceding questions: one that the group may ask about an individual (e.g., What is his name? What does he do for a living?) and one that an individual may ask about himself (e.g., How is it that I am myself from my birth to my death?). What is missing is therefore an explanation of the key aspect of the notion of identity at work in a diagnosis of

---

3. Clément Rosset has described several situations of this sort and their unnerving effects in his essay *Loin de moi: Étude sur l'identité* (Paris: Les Éditions de Minuit, 1999).

an "identity crisis": the relationship between the subjective and objective senses, the connection between what the group thinks and what the individual thinks.

The only thing that this same article tells us is that identity in the psychosocial sense can give rise to crises. There is a pathology of psychosocial identity and thus a pathology of this relation between the objective and the subjective. According to Erikson, this pathology can take two forms: *not enough* identity or *too much* identity. Erikson usually refers to an "identity confusion." This term is surely infelicitous, since it strongly suggests a kind of mental confusion (along the lines of the stereotypical madman who thinks he is Napoleon). In fact, the term "identity confusion" was not his first choice. Erikson first summarized his clinical description by reference to *identity diffusion.* He tells of how some anthropologist friends pointed out to him that the term "diffusion" suggested to them the idea that cultural and behavioral elements are "diffused" from one society to another—i.e., through a kind of contagion from one individual to another.[4] A particular society's culture would then be nothing but an agglomeration of resemblances among individuals who had borrowed the characteristics of the culture from one another. This atomistic view of culture is diametrically opposed to Erikson's conception. Erikson meant that an "identity" becomes "diffuse" (not that it is "diffused") when it is not clearly demarcated, when no well-defined *Gestalt* of the personality can be established. This is why the pathology can just as much consist in a lack of such contours as it can in the inverse problem of an *overdefinition*—i.e., too great an insistence on what sets an individual apart. Moreover, such excessive self-definition does not result in any great self-assurance of the individual concerned—e.g., confidence in her own abilities—but rather in an uncertainty to which the subject responds awkwardly and with intransigence.

Thus, an identity crisis takes place on two fronts: one where the individual confronts others (who recognize her "objective" identity in the sense of what might be written in a Who's Who entry) and another where the individual confronts herself (at which point "subjective" identity comes into play). The conflict that gives rise to the identity crisis is therefore not just a purely internal disharmony, such as one finds in the Freudian representation of the individual as having an *ego* torn between

4. Erik Erikson, *Identity: Youth and Crisis* (New York: Norton, 1968), 212.

the drives of the *id* and the strictures of the *superego*. It arises because the individual will be unable to fit into the community on which she depends for as long as she fails to coordinate the two sides of what Erikson calls her "identity."

How Can Identity Be Subjectified?

Erikson asks us to conceive of psychosocial identity as a synthesis of "objective" identity (my identity according to the Who's Who) and "subjective" identity (my identity according to my personal experience). Yet before we can bring these two senses together, we will have to come to an understanding of what is meant by "subjectivity."

Today the term is used in everyday language but often means little more than a vague emphasis on individual freedom, the right to one's own opinions and tastes, or even the impossibility of justifying an assertion in any way other than through the testimony of one's feelings or the dictates of one's moral conscience. In philosophy, we cannot use this technical term in such a vague manner.

We want to *make the question of identity subjective*—in other words, to *subjectify* it.[5] What do we mean by "subjective"? It would appear to be easy enough to provide a definition that ought to command the assent of every philosophical school: what is subjective is, literally, *what is in the subject*. More precisely, what possesses a subjective mode of existence is what can exist within the subject (and, perhaps, can *only* exist within

---

5. One contemporary usage of the verb "to subjectify" [*subjectiver*] that is common among French psychoanalysts blithely conflates two different things: on the one hand, the subjectification of a property or a state, i.e., to make them dependent on the knowing subject rather than on the object known; on the other, to give or impose on someone or something the status of "subject" in one of the senses of the word. I will stick to the classical sense one finds in the *Littré* dictionary and according to which to subjectify something is to *render it subjective*. As for giving the status of "subject" to someone who did not yet possess it, assuming that we are not talking about *subjecting* [*assujettir*] someone to a sovereign will but rather of turning him into a being conscious of its own activity, such an operation would require further explanation. The literature that discusses "becoming a subject" offers little more than word play, as Étienne Balibar points out in his *Citoyen Sujet et autres essais d'anthropologie philosophique* (Paris: Presses Universitaires de France, 2011). The alternative is a trivial explanation: having regained consciousness (after, say, a coma), the patient becomes conscious once again and thereby also a subject of consciousness. By extension, in becoming conscious of the fact that the situation is serious, the individual makes progress in his consciousness of the situation and is thus *more* of a subject than he was before, since the scope of his consciousness has been extended.

the subject). However, we must still specify what "within the subject" means, and this is where our difficulties begin. For one thing, we do not mean "within the human individual." Within the individual, one will find a brain, a heart, guts, etc., but these parts of a person are in no way subjective (except perhaps metaphorically). We also do not mean "in the subject" in Aristotle's sense—that is, in the sense in which the color of a white horse is in the horse "as in its subject," meaning simply that this whiteness exists insofar as the horse is of this color, i.e., that it is the subject of predication of this quality.

The word "subject" is here clearly being taken in the modern sense of the self-conscious subject. And therefore I will also take it in this sense. Unfortunately, subjective existence—i.e., existence within the self-conscious subject—is currently understood in two entirely contradictory ways. There are, it so happens, two rival philosophies of subjectivity.

On one side, we can understand the subjective in the way in which it is understood by doctrines of *mental interiority*. For these doctrines, the subjective is defined as what exists within the subject in a mode that forbids it to emerge, to be made manifest or public. Interiority has an exclusive character: only the subject has direct cognitive access to its mental states.

On the other side, we might derive our concept of the subjective from the doctrines of *personal expressivity*, according to which the subjectivity of an individual corresponds to the capacity for expression that he might exhibit. What exists within the subject is whatever that subject on its own can cause to emerge—in other words, what it can *express*.

§§§ The theory of mental interiority derives its concept of the subjective from an epistemology, the principle of which is as follows. What is subjective is what is within the subject in the sense that it is not given to observation or inspection *in the world*. There are, in the world, phenomena that are accessible to any and all observers—for example, the presence (or absence) of a tree in my garden. There are also phenomena that are given only to a single subject: the phenomena of his mind. The subject is the only one in a position to perceive what is happening *within him*. Others can only form hypotheses regarding his internal state. Subjectivity thus defined by the private access to oneself assumes a doctrine of mind built on the principle of the interiority of mental states. If

I am the only one to be able to see and inspect something, I may well be able to talk to you about it, but I cannot *show* it to you. Subjectivity conceived as the interiority of private states therefore necessarily has a solipsistic cast: whatever my efforts to make known the states I experience, I remain the only one to *see* them (or to be in cognitive contact with them). You cannot do it, just as I cannot see your mental states. The fact of your mental life is thus *for me* of a hypothetical—or, if you prefer, analogically "constructed"—nature: I form the hypothesis that, when you are in the same situation that I am and seem to react as I do, you are also in the same mental state that I am. This nevertheless is only a hypothesis and, philosophically, one may still have doubts about the matter.

By contrast, according to the expressivist theory, the subjective is eminently accessible to all. Indeed, what is subjective is that which is within the subject in the sense that it can *emerge* in the form of an expressive act. For example, we may deem someone to possess within himself different information, memories, opinions, etc., if he is able to share them with us by expressing them. If we find that the discourse that comes out of his mouth contains the information or opinions in question, that is proof that he had them within himself. Generally, subjectivity is here the capacity for an expressive behavior. The difference between the subjective and the objective is then what separates a capacity from the exercise of that capacity, the capacity to say something from the activity of saying it.

Charles Taylor has shown how these two conceptions of mind gave birth, beginning in the late seventeenth century, to two different theories of language.[6] For the theory of mental interiority, linguistic signs can only be *inductive* signs. They cannot transmit the speaker's thought itself; they can only point to it indirectly, indicating that it is present within her. It is then the hearer's job to learn to associate a thought with the sign emitted by the speaker—a thought that he himself, as hearer, must find within his own mind—and subsequently to formulate the hypothesis that the two thoughts, his own and that of the speaker, are

---

6. See Charles Taylor, "Action as Expression," in Cora Diamond and Jenny Teichman, eds., *Intention and Intentionality: Essays in Honour of G. E. M. Anscombe* (Brighton: Harvester Press, 1979), 73–89, as well as the texts collected in his *Human Agency and Language: Philosophical Papers 1* (Cambridge: Cambridge University Press, 1985).

not excessively different from each other. Things are entirely different for the expressivist theory of language: the speaker's thought is her own because it is to be sought in her expressive behavior and her discourse insofar as they originate with her. The expressive behavior does not manifest a state of the subject in the way that redness might be a sign of fever, but in the sense in which a face can express a mood, or a hand gesture can indicate the way to go, or, above all, the way in which a linguistic sign *says* something in virtue of the subject's *articulation* of it.

In fact, Erikson derives his vocabulary from the philosophy of subjectivity as mental interiority when he sets subjective and objective identity in opposition: the difference between the two is that I have an *internal* perspective on my own person that does not necessarily correspond to the *external* point of view that others have on me. It is therefore conceivable for the question "Who am I?" to receive two answers: those of other people and my own. We should therefore begin with this first conception of subjectivity—the conception put forward by classical reflexive psychology—in order to determine whether it can account for the question of identity as something to which the subject must personally respond.

To Be the Same in One's Own Eyes

Why ask the question "Who am I?" in the first person? An entire philosophical tradition replies that it is indispensable to do this if we want to reform the concept of a person in a subjective direction.

Why, you might ask, would we want to reform our concept of a person in a subjective direction? Since John Locke, two motives have been put forward. The *metaphysical* motive is that the concept of a person must be freed from a metaphysical system that is indefensible on empirical grounds: because the concept of substance has not been derived from sensory experience, it cannot be used to conceive of the person. The *moral* motive is that the concept of a person must be made consistent with our conception of responsibility: I can only be responsible for what I know myself to have done.[7]

In France, this reform was vigorously defended by none other than Voltaire. One might even say that, through his promotion of Locke's

---

7. For an excellent presentation of the reasons for adopting a subjective definition of the person, see the account given by Stéphane Chauvier in his concise essay *Qu'est-ce qu'une personne?* (Paris: J. Vrin, 2003).

ideas, Voltaire introduced them into the French language. This can be confirmed by consulting the article on "Identity" in the nineteenth-century *Littré* dictionary. In it, we read as sense 3: "Consciousness that a person has of himself." Littré then cites Voltaire praising Locke in these terms: "He is the first to have shown what identity is and what it is to be the same person, the same self." Littré then adds this to the definition: "Personal identity, persistence of the self-consciousness that the individual has." This definition of personal identity, which is precisely the one that Erikson draws on in formulating his notion of identity in a "subjective" sense, assumes that the reform proposed by Voltaire has been established and has become the standard conception. Can this have been the case? This is the question I will seek to answer in discussing the two texts by Voltaire cited by Littré, before returning to Locke and his paradoxes.

§§§ In Voltaire, we find both motives for revising our conception of a person. In Chapter XXIX of his short essay entitled *The Ignorant Philosopher*, he moves from the *metaphysical* critique to the *moral* critique of the traditional conception.[8]

That conception of a person appealed to the concept of substance. According to the definition that has commonly been accepted since Boethius, a person is "an individual substance of a rational nature" (*rationalis naturae individua substantia*). But Voltaire takes on board Locke's view that the concept of substance gives us nothing to think about; substance is a "whatsit" that cannot be characterized or described, but only called upon as an ontological support for the thing's sensible qualities.

After attacking the notions of innate ideas and substance, Voltaire draws from Locke the lesson about personal identity. We must recognize, he writes,

> that I am only the same person insofar as I have memory and an awareness of it: for, not having the smallest part of my body which belonged to me in my infancy, and not having the least

---

8. The editor of the *Pléiade* edition tells us that Voltaire wrote *The Ignorant Philosopher* at the end of 1766. Voltaire, "Le philosophe ignorant" in *Mélanges*, ed. Jacques Van den Heuvel (Paris: Gallimard/Pléiade, 1961), 877–930. English translation: Voltaire, *The Ignorant Philosopher* (Girard, KS: Haldeman-Julius Company, n.d.).

remembrance of the ideas that affected me at that age,[9] it is clear that I am no longer that same child any more than I am Confucius or Zoroaster. I am reputed the same person by those who have observed me grow and who have always resided with me; but I have in no respect the same existence; I am no longer my former self; I am a new identity; and what singular consequences must hence arise![10]

We see here the opposition between two points of view on the person beginning to crystallize. On the one hand, the external point of view that others have on my person: *I am reputed the same person by those who have observed me grow and who have always resided with me*. On the other, the individual's perspective on himself, a perspective that I alone can have on my own existence and identity: subjectively, I am not that child, *I am no longer my former self; I am a new identity*.

Thus, if we follow Voltaire, who rightly claimed to be a disciple of Locke, we will have to draw a distinction between two questions:

1. Am I that same child?
2. Am I, *in my own eyes*, that same child?

The added condition suggests that I might be the same (for example, the same as the small child in a photo or a story) without being the same "in my own eyes." These words make up what might be called a *subjectivity clause*—i.e., a way of restricting the truth conditions on the answer one gives to a subjective fact: is it this way *for the subject himself*, that is, in the consciousness he has of it? This restriction is often expressed by the phrase "for itself" (*für sich*). Voltaire here shows that he has fully absorbed Locke's lesson: it is right to subjectify personal identity.

I am the same person as X if I am such in my own eyes. It follows that I am someone other than X if, in my eyes, X is someone other than me. As Voltaire admits, a subjective person thus defined has no childhood beyond his memories of childhood. His identity is not genealogical. In fact, as a subjective person, I was not born on the date of my birth as a human being.

---

9. Voltaire is speaking like an empiricist. The word "idea" does not here have its ordinary intellectual meaning, but is used to refer to any kind of mental event of which the individual is aware through his internal sense, including, it would follow, sensations.
10. Voltaire, *The Ignorant Philosopher*, 45 [translation modified].

What consequences! Voltaire exclaims. He had already derived these moral consequences in a chapter of his *Treatise on Metaphysics* in which he discusses the question of the immortality of the soul (and what it is that makes such an attribute desirable).[11] He inquires into what it is that makes a man into a subject of moral and juridical imputation who is responsible for his acts. Like Locke, he develops the question by asking us to imagine ourselves present on the day of the Last Judgment. He offers the following reasoning with regard to an individual he calls Jacques:

> What it is that comprises Jacques's person, what makes Jacques himself and the same as he was yesterday in his own eyes is that he remembers the ideas he had yesterday and that, within his understanding, he brings together his existence yesterday and his existence today. For, if he had entirely lost his memory, his past existence would be as unfamiliar to him as that of another man: he would no more be the Jacques of yesterday—the same person—than he would be Socrates or Caesar. Supposing, then, that Jacques dies of a disease that causes him to lose his memory entirely and therefore dies as a different Jacques than the one who lived his life: Will God restore his lost memory to Jacques's soul? Will He recreate the ideas that no longer exist? In such a case, will he not be an entirely new man, as different from the first as an East Indian is from a European?[12]

Voltaire begins by positing the Lockean definition of the person; then he imagines an individual falling prey to a total amnesia, asking us to conclude that such an individual could not be held responsible for the actions he carried out in his past life.

Voltaire unreservedly adopts Locke's conception: the amnesiac is no more the same person as the Jacques of yesterday than he is Socrates or Caesar. The person that, yesterday, *we* called Jacques is today as foreign to him as would be those figures from antiquity. It follows that the concept of the person is entirely subjectified, since there exists the same

---

11. According to the editor of the *Pléiade* edition, the *Treatise on Metaphysics* was written between 1734 and 1738. See Voltaire, *Mélanges*, 1366.
12. Voltaire, "Traité de métaphysique," in *Mélanges*, 185.

difference between the past and present lives of the amnesiac as between his own life and that of another man.

Voltaire then derives moral consequences from this definition of the person. His reasoning is as follows: if Jacques (present before us) has forgotten the deeds of Jacques yesterday, he does not see the behavior of Jacques yesterday as something for which he is answerable. The actions that he carried out yesterday seem to him to have been carried out by a stranger. This is *subjectively* the case, since what is at issue is not what Jacques did yesterday but what he is aware of having done.

Ordinarily, we describe such experiences of the loss of one's sense of self using the analogy of the difference between two people: *it is as if* he had become another man. Voltaire takes things a step further, moving beyond a mere description of an experience such as "Jacques regards the actions he carried out yesterday (when they are described to him) as those of someone else." Instead, Voltaire posits that Jacques has in fact *become* unfamiliar to himself, that from this day forth he *is* someone else. But how can he have become someone else while remaining—and nobody disputes this—the same man? Voltaire answers: from the point of view of his own consciousness, he is another person because he cannot identify himself as *the same self* as yesterday's Jacques. Thus it is that self-consciousness, in the form of the agent's memory, will henceforth be what constitutes the person.

If, then, we follow Voltaire, who is himself following Locke, we will have to adopt a dualistic conception of the person, according to which it will be one thing to be (and to continue to be) *the same human individual* living a human life and quite another thing to be (and to continue to be) *the same self*, the same subject of a conscious life.

§§ In truth, readers of this passage might come away with the impression that, by giving only one example of the dissociation between Jacques and his *self*, Voltaire is seeking to attenuate the philosophical revolution he appears to be celebrating. He stipulates that Jacques is a victim of amnesia. Voltaire seems to be saying that someone, like Jacques, who is no longer in possession of his entire memory nevertheless remains a person like us. He is a human person, but one whose diachronic surface has been reduced, since his identity is measured by the extent of his memory. Jacques is a person like us, but diminished.

This impression is reinforced by the fact that Voltaire narrates in the third person and so cannot refrain from *naming* Jacques's person. Jacques's name is the one that everyone around him uses, a name that was given to a human being. Yet the person in Locke's sense *is not* the human being but the subject of memory, as Voltaire makes clear. When Voltaire gives the name "Jacques" to a person, he does not bestow it upon a human individual. This is why one would normally have to posit a succession of multiple persons within the same body. Because there was someone called "Jacques yesterday" who disappeared at the moment his entire memory of his actions disappeared, there must also be a "Jacques today," precisely the one that is as distinct from "Jacques yesterday" as he is from the *persons* of Socrates or Caesar. But are we able to give proper names to such subjective persons?

This question arises because Voltaire does not limit himself to claiming that "it is *as if* things were this way." In fact, he takes the next step and attempts to follow the logic of the new concept of the person. In order to respect this logic, one must not say that *it is as if* the Jacques of today were (in his own eyes) someone other than the Jacques of yesterday. Rather, one is obliged to say that *it seems to Jacques*—or to *the Jacques of today*—that the person being spoken about (Jacques and his actions of the day before) is someone else. It is this subjective appearance that henceforth constitutes personal identity.

It goes without saying that Jacques can only be held responsible for an action carried out yesterday if he is the one who carried it out. This responsibility attaches to the fact of being a person and thus to the fact of knowing what one does. He is the one who carried out the action yesterday only on the condition that he is *the same person* as the agent of that action. Yet, thanks to the new definition of the person, Jacques only carried out *as a person* the actions done yesterday (here we should add: done *as a man*) if he remembers *today* having done them. The Jacques of today is not the same person as the Jacques of yesterday unless he is conscious of the actions of yesterday's Jacques as being his own.

§§ At root, Voltaire confronts us once again with Epicharmus's argument but transposes the argument from a metaphysics of living beings to a metaphysics of the flux of consciousness. In the Greek "argument from growth," a change in the material composition of an individual produces a new individual. In the psychological version, a change in psychic composition (the mind being made up of impressions, of "ideas") produces a new person. There then arise the same objections regarding the kinds of relations that would be possible with a person thus redefined. We can imagine all manner of comic episodes in which a character appeals to this subjective philosophy of the person.

Imagine that Jacques made a commitment to us yesterday: he promised that within twenty-four hours he would reimburse a loan we gave him. Today, he has forgotten yesterday's deeds. *In his own* eyes, he is no longer yesterday's Jacques. As a result and as a good disciple of Locke and Voltaire, he announces to us that he cannot be held *personally* responsible for the debts incurred by yesterday's Jacques. How can he be obliged to pay what yesterday's Jacques promised to pay if he is not the same person as that Jacques? He may as well be asked to pay the debts of Socrates or Caesar.

Will we accept such a claim? Will we accept it on the condition that it appears to us to be sincere?

It seems to me that we would have no trouble understanding a Jacques who denied being *the same man* as he who incurred the debt, and who claimed that he had been mistaken for someone else, that we had the wrong person (i.e., the wrong human individual). We would understand what he was saying, and we would know what to do in order to prove to him that he was indeed the man in question. But how would we react if, instead, he declared this? "I admit to being *the same man*, but I am not *the same person in my own eyes*, and philosophy has shown that only by being the same person in one's own eyes is one the same person at all."

And what about *the future*? What happens at the moment Jacques makes a commitment (for example, to repay tomorrow a loan taken out today)? It is clear that, in making this promise, he applies the concept of identity to his concept of the person. By committing himself, he declares that *he* is the one who will be obliged to repay the loan tomorrow. His use of the first person identifies the agent of the future repayment as *himself*. If that is so, it will matter to us what his concept of the person is. Who will be committed by Jacques's promise to personally repay the loan? Is it the *man* who made the promise or only the *subjective person* who remembers having promised? In the latter case, it will be as if the promise included a subjective restriction clause: e.g., I promise to repay the loan tomorrow and will therefore be personally held liable to repay, *provided that* I have not forgotten this commitment in the meantime.

In my view, we would insist that the man making such a commitment use the everyday concept of personal identity rather than the concept put forward by disciples of Locke. For us, the person who commits himself in a promise is the person that *is itself* insofar as it is this human individual and not the person that *claims to be itself* insofar as it is the subject of its memories of itself.

Let us nevertheless suppose that Jacques insists on his subjective concept of the person and that he makes the second sort of promise, one that commits the Lockean and Voltairean self and not the human being. Is it possible for a "self," taken subjectively in this way, to commit itself? What could we ask of him in order to truly bind him to the obligation he undertakes? Could we ask him to include within his commitment a promise not to forget? To do so would be pointless: even though he can promise to repay, he cannot promise *to remember* to have to repay. Such an additional commitment adds nothing. He would be freed from his promise to repay simply by forgetting that he promised *not* to forget. It follows that a promise that commits only one's self-consciousness is no commitment at all.

The Prince and the Cobbler

Voltaire presented Locke's doctrine in the perspective in which it appears most plausible and comprehensible. He did an excellent job as a propagandist for these new ideas.

In reality, the conceptual reform proposed by Locke in the *Essay Concerning Human Understanding* is much more radical. According to the subjective conception of personhood defended by Voltaire, to be the same man as Jacques is *insufficient* for being the same person as Jacques. There is a paradoxical consequence of the conceptual reform that Voltaire does not mention but that Locke spells out clearly: *it is not necessary* to be the same man as Jacques to be the same person as Jacques. One need only be the same *self,* i.e., to be constituted as a person by the same self-consciousness—in other words, to have the same memories.

The theory that bases personhood on self-consciousness includes within it a philosophical paradox. This theory seeks to maintain that

Jacques can become as unfamiliar to himself as Socrates and Caesar are to him. But in order to uphold this thesis, one must also accept the inverse theoretical possibility: that Jacques might remember having carried out the deeds of Socrates and also, moreover, those of Caesar and that he recognizes himself in their biographies. Indeed, the only reason that Jacques is presently not the same person as Socrates is that Jacques's self-consciousness does not allow him to claim Socrates's actions as his own. But what should we say if his self-consciousness *did* inform Jacques that he was the one who performed Socrates's actions? Locke stages precisely such a possibility in his fable of the Prince and the Cobbler.[13]

§§ This fable seeks to convince us that our ordinary concept of the person is indeterminate and will have to be made more precise. The scenario on which it is based involves two characters: one is the Prince, the other the Cobbler. Let us imagine a transmigration by which the soul and the consciousness of the Prince passed into the Cobbler's body. We might add that the transformation takes place at night while the two characters are asleep, so that, at first, the change is imperceptible. Of course, Locke is not asking us to believe that such a thing might happen, but only that we come to an understanding of the fable.[14]

When day breaks, someone wakes up in the Cobbler's bed. It has been established that it was the Cobbler who lay down in this bed the previous night. We may even give the Cobbler a spouse sleeping by his side. The philosopher then asks, "When the Cobbler's wife wakes the next morning, whom does she find next to her in the bed? Who is now in the Cobbler's bed?" According to Locke, our question is ambiguous. If we ask which person in the sense of *which man*, the response is that it is the cobbler. But if we ask which person in the sense of *which subject or self*, the

---

13. John Locke, *An Essay Concerning Human Understanding*, ed. Peter H. Nidditch (Oxford: Oxford University Press, 1975), II, XXVII, § 15 (340).

14. Nevertheless, according to Locke, the dogma of bodily resurrection requires something of this kind, since it is difficult to conceive of each of us being resuscitated in our own bodies, which may have long since disappeared. Today, the philosophers who uphold a neo-Lockean conception of the person prefer to imagine scenes of fictional surgery by which the Prince's brain could be placed in the Cobbler's cranium. The intention, however, remains the same. Just as it was in the past, the goal today is to raise the question of personal identity and to explore the consequences of a subjective definition of the person.

response is that it is the Prince. The human body of the Cobbler does indeed henceforth contain the subject of the Prince's consciousness.

Locke believes that the question "Who is it?" is ambiguous. Each of us has several identities and can be identified in several different ways, such that these identifications may in principle not coincide. This is what would happen in the case of the transmigration of the Prince's soul into the Cobbler's body.

> For should the Soul of a Prince, carrying with it the consciousness of the Prince's past Life, enter and inform the Body of a Cobler [sic] as soon as deserted by his own Soul, every one sees, he would be the same Person with the Prince, accountable only for the Prince's Actions: But who would say it was the same Man? The Body too goes to the making the Man, and would, I guess, to every Body determine the Man in this case, wherein the Soul, with all its Princely Thoughts about it, would not make another Man: But he would be the same cobbler to every one besides himself.[15]

Locke concludes that the notion of "the same person" remains indeterminate. It is incumbent on us to decide whether we will choose to identify someone by his human body or by his thoughts.

By maintaining that each of us has, in reality, several identities, Locke invents a new form of soul/body dualism, one that can weather every critique of Cartesian substantialism. Why is Descartes's dualism obliged to separate the soul as substance from the body as substance? Because, in the Cartesian meditations, there is a step at which the philosopher asks himself the question "Do I have a body?" Implicit in this is the idea that it is *conceivable* that I exist (as the argument of the *cogito* proves) but that the body that I thought I had does not exist (that it is nothing but a dream, for example). Locke, by contrast, does not ask us to believe that the thinking subject could exist without at the same time being a human animal. In this sense, his doctrine of the person is not a dualist one. Nevertheless, he does draw a *real* distinction between the identity of a man and that of a person (of a *self*). The identity of a man is biographical: the fact of being the same living being, identified by his

---

15. Locke, *Essay*, § 15 (340).

parents and the continuity of his life. The identity of a *self* is based in the *consciousness* of being the same thinking subject as someone in the past— i.e., in the memory of his successive conscious states.

By means of the argument of the *cogito*, Descartes establishes at first to his own satisfaction that he is a *self*, an *ego*. It then remains for him to confirm, by means of some arduous metaphysical reasoning, his own humanity and individuation as the man known by the name René Descartes. Locke in no way suggests that the person can exist as a pure subject of consciousness, a pure *ego*, without at the same time being endowed with a human body. His new dualism consists, therefore, in claiming this: at every moment of my *mental* life as a thinking subject, I am also a man, but not necessarily *the same man*. And conversely, at every moment of my *human* life, I am a *self*, a subject conscious of its mental operations, but not necessarily the same *self*.

Thus, Locke's bold idea is not that an individual like me can be *described* in multiple ways, an idea that no one has ever disputed. His idea is that I can be *identified* in multiple ways. This opens up the possibility of a discrepancy between my identity for others and my identity for myself. This is a discrepancy that every subsequent phenomenology will attempt to overcome, seeking some means to make these two points of view on the individual coincide: the point of view of others (the "for another") and the individual's own point of view (the "for itself").

Recovering One's Own Self

The subjective definition of the person upheld by Locke has the following consequence from which, in true philosophical spirit, Locke does not shy away: there is nothing illogical about the idea that I might, upon waking every morning, be anxious to verify that I am *in the same body* as I was the day before, that I am *the same man* as the one with whom I coincided yesterday. In a delightful passage from *In Search of Lost Time*, Proust makes an appeal to the same Lockean psychology in order to describe the momentary disarray of someone aroused from a deep sleep. The idea is that such deep slumbers are tantamount to a mental estrangement from oneself, not unlike a coma. But rather than presenting a *self* that sets about verifying that it has retained its body from yesterday, the passage calls to mind a body in search of its *self*. He has his narrator make the following reflection on the experience of waking:

How then, searching for one's thoughts, one's personality, as one searches for a lost object, does one recover one's own self rather than any other? Why, when one begins again to think, is it not a personality other than the previous one that becomes incarnate in one? One fails to see what dictates the choice, or why, among the millions of human beings one might be, it is on the being one was the day before that unerringly one lays one's hand. What is it that guides us, when there has been a real interruption?[16]

The experience to be described is that of a person who "comes back to himself" after an episode of confusion. He becomes himself again. The question raised, however, is troublesome: what does he do in order to become once again the person he was at the moment he fell asleep? How does he avoid taking on some other personality? The incongruous aspect of the question derives from the way a person's personality (i.e., his character as it manifests itself in his way of doing things and speaking) is represented as a kind of garment to be found lying next to one's bed.

The problem with which Proust concludes this philosophical sketch is one that psychology *would have to* confront if the fact of "coming back to oneself" or being oneself again (rather than disunited) were conceived as the establishment of an appropriate cognitive contact between me and my personality (i.e., between me, the sleeper, and the *self* that belongs to me, *my self*). I would have to be able to recognize, by certain of its traits, the *self* that belongs to me; I would need to make sure not to make a mistake about *its* identity. And this brings us to the real question: do we have an identity criterion that allows us to understand what is meant when one speaks about "the same self"?

Proust thus provides the key to this psychology: just as one can lose one's keys or one's papers, and in much the same way as one can grab the wrong hat or umbrella or coat (in the coatroom), or go to the wrong door (believing that one is visiting friends and ringing the bell), one can also make an error regarding one's "personality" or *self*. Just as there can be cases of mistaken identity regarding other people, it is also possible to make errors of mistaken identity regarding oneself.

---

16. Marcel Proust, *In Search of Lost Time*, vol. 3, *The Guermantes Way*, trans. C. K. Scott Moncrieff and Terence Kilmartin, rev. D. J. Enright (New York: The Modern Library, 1993), 110.

It follows that what this subjective definition of the person presupposes is the possibility of setting in opposition *my self* and someone else's, or of juxtaposing *the same self* with *another self*, in the way one might contrast the same garment (mine) with another (yours). In short, it must be possible to apply the concept of identity to the concept of the self. It must therefore be possible to provide an *identity criterion* for the person taken as a *self*.

§§ We already possess an identity criterion for our anthropomorphic concept of the person. The same person in such cases means *the same human being*, regardless of her age or whether she is in possession of her faculties (*compos sui*) or asleep, weakened, amnesiac, or even failing in every respect. Post-Lockean philosophy has defended the idea that a reform of the concept of the person was necessary and that a place had to be made for the person's subjectivity so that, in order to be the same person, the person must be so in her own eyes. As we have just seen, for such a subject, the question cannot be one of being *the same human individual* in her own eyes, since that would not require a new criterion. Rather, it is a matter of being *the same subject of consciousness*, the same *self*. Do we have an identity criterion for the same *self*?

Proust reveals the weak point of this entire construction. If we had such an identity criterion for the *self* or the "personality," we would be able to say upon waking, "Here is a *self*, but it is not the one I had yesterday." We would be able to talk about the *self* as we would talk about an object that one might lose. For that to happen, the concept of *self* would have to provide a principle of individuation; it would have to be what Quine called "an individuative term" in the way in which words such as "man" and "umbrella" are.

In reality, if the subjective reform of the concept of the person could provide an identity criterion, this criterion would be subjective. Jacques is not, in his own eyes, the same person as the man he was yesterday, because it does not seem to him that he was that person. Jacques would be the same person as Julius Caesar if a transcendental surgical operation placed Caesar's consciousness and memories within him, after which, if he seems to himself to be identical to Caesar, he is Caesar. But nothing other than a subjective criterion is provided. And, as Wittgenstein pointed out, to have a *subjective* criterion is much the same thing as having no criterion at all, since every application of the criterion leaves me in the realm of appearance:

> One would like to say: whatever is going to seem correct to me is correct. And that only means that here we can't talk about "correct."[17]

---

17. Ludwig Wittgenstein, *Philosophical Investigations*, rev. 4th ed., trans. G. E. M. Anscombe, P. M. S. Hacker and Joachim Schulte (1953; Oxford: Wiley-Blackwell, 2009), § 258 (99).

THE DISEMBEDDED INDIVIDUAL

The Right of Subjectivity

We are seeking to learn the correct use of the identitarian idiom. To do this, we are trying to understand how the question of my identity might become *subjective*, which means: how it might call for a response that can only be given by me, in person (*in propria persona*). A first solution presented itself and asked us to posit that the human individual in reality possesses two identities, one as a living being and the other as a subject given to itself in the experience of being itself. But we were forced to accept that this solution led to an impasse for lack of any real criterion that would allow us to determine what it is that makes a *self* the same *self* as my own. In reality, we have no idea what it would be to distinguish the same *self* from another *self*, in the way that we do when we distinguish one of our friends from another one of our friends.

There is nevertheless another meaning of subjectivity, one that we can look to Hegel to provide. In the *Outlines of the Philosophy of Right*, Hegel casts the affirmation of a "right of subjective freedom" as the watershed that divides universal history into two eras—the ancient and the modern. He writes:

> The right of the subject's *particularity*, his right to be satisfied, or in other words the right of subjective freedom, is the pivot and centre

of the difference between antiquity and modern times. This right in its infinity is given expression in Christianity and it has become the universal effective principle of a new form of the world.[1]

Hegel here brings together two considerations that are usually separated: considerations of historical philosophy and those of moral psychology.

Historical philosophy is concerned with deriving the differences among historical eras or ages of the world from a philosophical principle. According to Hegel, the principle in question is provided by the "right of subjective freedom," a right that was misunderstood in antiquity and only came to be recognized in modern times, which, for him, means: in the epoch following that of ancient paganisms. Hegel thus places himself among the thinkers who define modernity as the upholding of a constellation of values that are summed up by the term "individualism," even though Hegel was not yet in a position to use this term, as it only came into use later on, in the French political literature of the Restoration. As Tocqueville pointed out in a famous passage, individualism should not be understood as meaning *selfishness*—i.e., as a character flaw that consists in being concerned only with one's own interests even where this is to the detriment of others.[2] On the contrary, to adopt the individualistic point of view of the moderns is to accept that ancient morality—whatever its greatness—had the *flaw* of failing to grant to the individual the right to formulate his own conception of what he deemed to be good. This flaw is overcome in modern morality.

What is it that underlies Hegel's use of labels such as the "principle of particularity" or the "principle of subjective freedom" or, more succinctly, the "right of subjectivity"?[3] He explains what it is in § 185 of the same work in a remark on Plato's *Republic*: Plato accounted well for what gives the city its moral *unity*—the possibility of a "we"—but he left no place for the other principle, which is the possibility of a "self." Of

---

1. G. W. F. Hegel, *Outlines of the Philosophy of Right,* trans. T. M. Knox, rev. and ed. Stephen Houlgate (Oxford: Oxford University Press, 2008), § 124 (122).
2. "*Individualism* is a recent expression arising from a new idea. Our fathers knew only selfishness." Alexis de Tocqueville, *Democracy in America,* ed. and trans. Harvey C. Mansfield and Delba Winthrop (Chicago: University of Chicago Press, 2000), 482.
3. See Hegel's addition (*Zusatz*) to § 185 (184) of *Outlines,* where he writes: "It was in the Christian religion principally that the right of subjectivity arose. . . ."

course, this principle of a right of subjectivity had not yet appeared in antiquity other than as a cause of "ethical corruption" (given expression in sophistry). The excessively restrictive aspect of Plato's ideal manifests itself practically in the fact that a citizen of the Platonic *polis* is not free to establish his own familial household as he wishes and to be at home in it (in his private property), nor is he free to choose his occupation.

The principle of subjective freedom proved capable of redrawing the "form of the world." It is remarkable that Hegel formulates this in terms of the subject's *satisfaction* and thus considers it from the perspective of *moral psychology*. Normally, one would seek a moral psychology in authors that are called "moralists" because they write in a well-defined literary genre that includes *Characters* (La Bruyère), *Fables* (La Fontaine), *Thoughts* (Pascal), *Maxims* (La Rochefoucauld), or, as in Nietzsche, *Mixed Opinions and Maxims*. In this genre, morality is understood in the sense of the human customs that one might observe around one, in the diversity of personalities and social milieux. What are the motives that move men to act? That is the question to which the moralists of modern literature, from Montaigne to Nietzsche, are responding. These motives—for example, the concern with one's honor or glory—are brought together by Hegel under the inclusive concept of *Befriedigung*, of complete human satisfaction (which must, then, include a "subjective" satisfaction).

When an individual today speaks about her "identity"—in the sense of "ego identity"—does she not seek to assert precisely this right of the subject to find satisfaction in her action *as an individual*? Modern morality grants the individual the right to particularity, because it does not condemn the will to be oneself (as an individual) as a lapse into vanity or a form of selfishness. To accord a "right of subjectivity" is to see a moral attitude in the will to be oneself. The woman who asserts this right—the modern woman who subscribes to the values of individualism—wants to be responsible for herself. She can only be satisfied *with herself* if she can bestow upon herself—upon her own choices—the responsibility for what she is.

§§§ Hegel thus provides us with the meaning that we sought for the word "subjective." What is subjective is what, coming from an individual, says something about this particular subject because it *expresses* the subject—not in the sense of revealing (or betraying) it, but in the sense that the subject is what, by its actions or gestures, expresses itself, as if it were speaking in the first person. There is thus something that must come from the subject, that can come only from the subject, and that expresses the subject who thinks and speaks in the first person. This subjective something is its *decision*. Nobody can decide *in the subject's stead*, because doing so requires saying "I" in the place of a subject who is of an age at which it is his or her responsibility to say "I," where it is down to the subject to speak *for itself*. Until that time, it had been the parents' or guardians' responsibility to speak for the child.

We will therefore seek to find a subjective meaning to the question "Who am I?" by taking the word "subjective" in its expressivist acceptation. How can someone ask the question of his own identity and do so with the intention of making a decision? If he asks the question—if, therefore, he "does not know who he is"—it is not in the sense of lacking information but in the sense in which he has not yet decided among various possibilities. Can we envisage a situation of this kind?

§§ To tell the truth, if there is one thing that would seem necessarily to lie beyond the scope of the individual's freely taken decisions, it is his identity—or at least his identity *in the literal sense*, which consists in the fact that he is the human individual that he is, born on such and such a day to his parents, with his given anatomy, etc. None of that has ever depended on a choice that the individual might have made.

Could it be claimed that the decision to be taken bears not on the facts that individuate him but on their meaning? The identity that he must decide upon would then be a *narrative* identity. He would have to choose the narrative to be given to his life up to now. However, if the act of conferring an identity upon oneself consists in choosing a *satisfying* version of his biography, what would distinguish such a choice of an identity from a pure construction, one that presents the most favorable image of the person? Such a narrative construction of one's identity would be difficult to distinguish from the fabrication of an "individual myth," to use Jacques Lacan's terminology, and it would have a profoundly illusory and even neurotic character to it.[4]

The choice of an identity must therefore not bear upon a reconstruction of the past but rather on the *future* of the subject that expresses itself

---

4. Jacques Lacan, "The Neurotic's Individual Myth" (1953), trans. Martha Noel Evans, *Psychoanalytic Quarterly* 48 (1979): 405–425.

in its decision. Our problem then becomes this: what sort of decision must he make that concerns him personally and in such a radical way that it can legitimately pass for the question of *who he is*, the question of his identity? A first response immediately presents itself. The decision that the subject must take and upon which his subjective satisfaction (in the Hegelian sense) depends is that of a *radical choice* in the "existential" sense, one in which the entire existence of the subject is at stake.

I will therefore ask whether the term "identity crisis" can be understood as the stage in life during which an individual must confront herself in a radical choice of what her values will be and what the totality of her life will be. I will begin with the following remark: an identity crisis is, above all, a *crisis of indecision*. According to Erikson, Shakespeare provided the exemplary figure of such a crisis in the character of Hamlet.

To Be or Not to Be Oneself?

When Erikson seeks to explain the constitution of identity crises which, according to him, arise with varying degrees of seriousness among human beings at the moment of their entry into life at the end of adolescence, he does not hesitate to refer to the character of Hamlet. During such a crisis, it is as if a question had been asked of the individual, one that he alone can answer: to be or not to be? In his book on Gandhi, Erikson explains that the young Gandhi also had to confront the question "to be or not to be?" In this text, Erikson writes that Hamlet's question should end with the word "himself": "To be or not to be *himself*."[5] When completed in this way, Hamlet's question truly becomes the question of identity proper to the subject—i.e., in the Eriksonian sense that makes talk of an "identity crisis" possible.

What are we to make of the addition of "himself" to the alternative between "to be" and "not to be"?

§§ In evoking Hamlet, Erikson begins by discreetly brushing aside excessively reductive Freudian explanations such as that proposed by Ernest Jones. The "Oedipus complex" is not the key to Hamlet's drama.

---

5. Erik H. Erikson, *Gandhi's Truth: On the Origins of Militant Nonviolence* (New York: Norton, 1969), 195.

In fact, according to Erikson, the Danish prince is rather an "introspective late adolescent, trying to free himself from parents who made and partially determined him, and trying also to face membership in wider institutions, which he has not as yet made his own."[6] Nevertheless, in order to uncover Shakespeare's tragic argument, we will have to sketch out the historical context in which the action takes place.

How is it that Hamlet does not know "who he is"? Why is he in search of his identity? According to Erikson's reading, it is because he is subject to two moral systems, one that derives from his loyalty to the traditional order he comes from, the other from his adherence to the modern culture into which he was initiated in Wittenberg, the city in which he completed his studies and a center for the fashionable new ideas.[7] In the play, claims Erikson, other young men are quite certain of their identities, meaning that they know to whom they owe their loyalty (even if some will be led to betray those allegiances). Hamlet, though, does not know what he should remain loyal to, for he is torn between two requirements. Should he obey his conscience? Or should he carry out the duty that falls upon him according to the morality of his milieu and avenge his father's death?

Hamlet thus faces something like a modern crisis of values, one in which the individual is divided between two incompatible value systems and is in the uncomfortable position of being subject to contradictory imperatives. Hamlet has an identity problem because he cannot on his own fulfill the demands whose legitimacy he does not question but each of which requires the total commitment of a single man. He has an identity problem because he is required to split himself into multiple copies so as to be, at one and the same time, a good son according to the old morality and a brilliant young man according to the new one. It will be recalled that it was precisely this sort of contradiction that Erikson observed in the field when investigating the lives of Sioux adolescents on the Indian reservations of South Dakota and Nebraska.[8]

---

6. Erik H. Erikson, *Young Man Luther: A Study in Psychoanalysis and History* (1958; New York: Norton, 1962), 113.

7. See the passages devoted to Hamlet in Erik H. Erikson, *Identity: Youth and Crisis* (New York: Norton, 1968), 236–240.

8. Erik H. Erikson, *Childhood and Society,* 3rd ed. (1950; New York: Norton, 1986).

§§§ By completing Hamlet's question with the reflexive pronoun "himself" (i.e., "to be or not to be himself?"), Erikson suggests that an existential sense be given to the notion of an "identity crisis." In this he deploys the opposition that has defined every philosophical individualism from Rousseau to Heidegger: the opposition between the authenticity of *being oneself* and the inauthenticity of *being alienated*.

Here we can put to use some remarks by Ernst Tugendhat about Heidegger's thought.[9] Tugendhat suggests using Hamlet's question as a way of understanding the alternative expressed by this famous sentence from *Being and Time*: "*Dasein* always understands itself in terms of its existence, in terms of its possibility to be itself or not to be itself."[10]

Of *whom* is this proposition speaking? Who is *Dasein*? It is remarkable that the English and French translators of Heidegger ultimately gave up on translating the word *Dasein* by anything other than the word *Dasein* itself, as if the word had already entered into their languages. Of course this is not at all the case, and the word remains enigmatic. Moreover, as Tugendhat demonstrates, the same is true in German itself, since Heidegger's use of the word does not allow it to be placed in any syntactical category.[11] The reader must therefore try each time to paraphrase the sentence she has just read. In the case at hand, following Tugendhat, we can act as if Heidegger had written: *each of us* understands himself or herself in terms of the alternative between the possibility of being oneself and not being oneself.

Tugendhat explains that the thesis is obscure and even paradoxical if we understand the words "*sich verstehen*" in a cognitive sense—i.e., in the way we do when speaking of understanding the meaning of a text or of understanding the reasons for someone's hostile attitude. The thesis remains paradoxical for as long as it seems to lead to the question "How could it be that I am not me?" What could there possibly be for me to understand, having started from the strange hypothesis according to which it could be the case that *I* am not *I*? Things become clearer,

9. Ernst Tugendhat, *Self-Consciousness and Self-Determination,* trans. Paul Stern (1979; Cambridge, MA: MIT Press, 1986), 27, 156.
10. Martin Heidegger, *Being and Time: A Translation of "Sein und Zeit,"* trans. Joan Stambaugh (Albany: State University of New York Press, 1996), 10 (12 in original pagination).
11. Tugendhat, *Self-Consciousness,* 151–152.

though, if we give the words "to understand" a practical meaning, so that they no longer involve correctly *grasping* a meaning as opposed to making a mistake or being in error. Understanding in this sense will also not involve making *hypotheses* about what I am or am not. Rather, it is about *giving* a meaning to what one is going to do and to give this meaning by adopting a practical attitude toward oneself. In other words, it involves recognizing what I *can* make of myself and thereby responding to the practical question "What should I do?"

Once we do that, the thesis is that each of us has a *practical* relation to himself or herself and that this manifests itself in the "existential" meaning included in the verb "to be" when it is used in a *first-person attributive sentence*. Such a sentence generally presents itself in the form "I am A," where the letter "A" stands for any of the subject's attributes. The thesis is then that, if I *say* that I am A, it is because I agree to be A, for I could stop being A if it happened that I was no longer satisfied to call myself A. In a third-person statement ("that man is A"), the sense of the verb "to be" is constative. By contrast, the meaning of the verb "to be" in "I am A" is existential, i.e., practical. This clearly goes without saying for attributes that have been the objects of the subject's choices. Can we say the same thing about attributes that were never subject to a decision on his part? According to Tugendhat, Hamlet's question shows how this *responsibility for oneself* can be expanded to every one of the subject's attributes. Of course, the subject cannot choose *not to have been born* or *to be individuated in a different way* (in another body), but at every moment she has the choice whether *to be or not to be*.

§§ We may nevertheless have doubts about the *practical* character of Hamlet's question if we accept Erikson's diagnosis: the claim that the young man is passing through an identity crisis means that he is attempting to avail himself of a *moratorium* before deciding to enter into life (in one direction or another). Erikson stresses that it is not unusual to see a young man or woman arrange a time for reflection or indecision for themselves by stepping outside of the pressures of family life and the immediate environment. This is exactly what the young Martin Luther did when he took refuge in the Augustinian convent. In Hamlet's case, we observe him pretending to be insane, which allows him to avoid the demands of those around him (e.g., the pressing insistence that he take a bride).

§§§ Is Hamlet's question really a practical one? Is the subject who asks the question faced with a choice? In order to understand what is at stake in Hamlet's *to be or not to be*, we have the good fortune to be able to make use of a reading that is both scholarly and refreshing: the rhetorical interpretation offered by Francis Goyet.[12] In his great work on the art of oration in the sixteenth century, Goyet examines the orientation given to the study of rhetoric by Melanchthon, the founding father of the German university. With Melanchthon, the principal end of the art of rhetoric ceases to be political and practical (*movere*) in order to become homiletic and theoretical (*docere*).

Goyet begins by emphasizing that Hamlet is a student and that he has just returned from Wittenberg, precisely the city where one finds the famous university that Melanchthon headed. Hamlet must therefore have learned rhetoric there and have learned it through the exercises that at that time were part of how the discipline was taught. Among these exercises, which come from Latin rhetoric, there is one that consists in moving from the *quaestio finita* to the *quaestio infinita*. Cicero explains the distinction as follows: according to Greek authors, a discourse may bear upon a question that is highly determinate (in the circumstances) or on a general question.[13] A "finite" question is limited to particular people and circumstances—for example, "Should we now engage in an exchange of prisoners of war with our enemies, the Carthaginians?" An "infinite" question does not bear upon anyone in particular, but is, rather, a question of principle: e.g., "In general, what must be decided about prisoners of war?" As Goyet explains, the orator moves to the general question in order to "elevate the debate" and thereby give a depth to one's treatment of the subject. For Melanchthon himself, according to Goyet, the usual example of a particular question is "Should war be waged against the Turks?"; the example of a universal question is "Should a Christian wage war?"[14]

This distinction can be made clearer by looking at Quintilian's

----

12. Francis Goyet, *Le sublime du "lieu commun": L'invention rhétorique dans l'Antiquité et à la Renaissance* (Paris: Honoré Champion, 1993), 568–570. See also his article "Hamlet, étudiant du XVIe siècle," *Poétique* 113 (1998): 3–15.

13. Cicero, *De oratore*, 3.109. Cited by Goyet, *Le sublime*, 273.

14. Goyet, *Le sublime*, 276 n 3.

explanation of the "commonplace."[15] In school, the pupil will engage in increasingly difficult exercises: after having practiced doing *narratives* and *proofs*, he will be able to practice *invective*, followed by *commonplaces* and then the *quaestio infinita*. Then, at the end of this long initiation, he will practice defending a *thesis* by casting the "infinite question" in the form of a choice between two alternatives. For example, one might begin with this question limited to a particular case: "Should Cato marry?" Then one will learn to deal with the corresponding unlimited question by generalizing it: "Should man marry?" Finally, one arrives at the point of defending either the *thesis* or the *antithesis* of the question: "Is it better to live as a married man or an unmarried man?" The technique of the "thesis" here corresponds more or less to what is today called, in French, the art of the *dissertation*.

Goyet then takes up Hamlet's question, *to be or not to be*? Hamlet proves himself to have been a good student when he transforms his personal, and therefore finite, question into an infinite question. It is no longer about just him but about any human being. But Hamlet goes further. We see him move to a new generalization of the question by refraining from attaching an attribute to the verb "to be." This makes the question doubly infinite, as it were. It is "infinite" first in the sense of Cicero and Quintilian in that it is of a general character. But it is also infinite in the sense of incomplete, for there is now a blank in the interrogative sentence. The first unlimiting of the question takes us from "Should *Cato* do what must be done in order to be married?" to "Should *any man whatsoever* do what must be done in order to be married?" Then, a second unlimiting takes us from "Should any man whatsoever do what must be done in order to *be married*?" to "Should any man whatsoever do what must be done in order *to be* . . . ?" And this question amounts to asking whether it is better for someone *to be something, whatever that something may be*, than *not to be something, whatever that something may be*.

It is quite clear that, if this is its meaning, Hamlet's question can have no answer for as long as an attribute to which it applies has not been reestablished—for example, *to be* married or *to be* single, *to be* here or *to be* elsewhere, etc. How can he possibly determine what he must choose if he has not yet determined what he imagines himself being? According to

---

15. Quintilian, *Institutio Oratoria,* Book 2, Chapter 4.

Goyet, Shakespeare is playing here by presenting the comic character of the young intellectual who has truly taken on board the art of holding forth, postponing a decision by raising endless preliminary questions. His interpretation on this point thus agrees with Erikson's: Hamlet has provided himself with a *moratorium*, setting things up so that the response to the practical question at hand—"what can I do now to attain my ends?"—is indefinitely *deferred*. One might well use Jacques Derrida's term and say that Hamlet seeks to establish himself, by means of the ploys of feigned madness and of radical existential questioning, within a regime of *différance*, of a postponement of the moment of decision to an indefinite "later."

Of course, we know the "infinite question" that Hamlet puts off until later. It is the question he evokes immediately afterward when he asks:

> Whether 'tis nobler in the mind to suffer
> The slings and arrows of outrageous fortune,
> Or to take arms against a sea of troubles,
> And by opposing end them?

The topic given for the exercise must therefore have been something like this: is one right to revolt? Is it better to be rebellious or to be resigned? And, finally, as the end of the soliloquy suggests: act or endure? Not, as the existential interpretation suggests, to be or not to be *alive*, whether to live or to die. Indeed, as Goyet emphasizes, death is not evoked in the soliloquy as one of the alternative ends, but as a possible consequence of the attitude that would consist in "taking arms against a sea of troubles, and by opposing end them."[16]

Moreover, the question "Is it better to be alive or not?" is little more than the subject of a thesis defense as long as it heralds a mere choice between values rather than a decision to do x instead of y in the present circumstances. At the end of his discourse, the speaker comes to a conclusion that is a value judgment and, if you will, a radical choice of values. But it is one thing to recognize a value *in principle* and quite another to act *here and now* in accordance with it. It is entirely possible to defer to the higher nobility of a form of life without necessarily desiring to adopt it for oneself (or at least without desiring to adopt it immediately).

---

16. Goyet, *Le sublime,* 570 n 1.

However one takes it, Hamlet's question is not a practical one. When he asks it, Hamlet does not adopt a practical attitude with regard to himself, since he does not ask, "What should I do?"

§§ According to Erikson, Hamlet's drama is the illustration of an "identity crisis," because it presents a young man trapped in a personal contradiction that renders him incapable of making a decision. In order to get out of it, he must choose between two possibilities. He can decide to accept the fact of being his dead father's son (and with it the obligation to fulfill the duties of a son). Or he can choose to be resolutely modern by forging another place in the world for himself, another identity. But how, whatever he decides, is it possible for the son not to be the son? And how can the young intellectual who has been convinced by the new morality not listen to his conscience? In order to decide, Hamlet would have to be able to duplicate himself.

"To be or not to be . . . ?" is not the formulation of a practical question. Moreover, it is not yet a question at all, or, at the very least, it is a *suspended* question, for *it remains to be decided what the decision will bear upon*. Hamlet must still decide whether he will make a decision, and he will decide to make a decision if he manages to decide *what* he is going to make a decision about. But to take this decision about the decision to be made would imply that he was in a state to exit the moratorium. It would mean that he had managed to give himself an identity.

Does Hamlet's question become a practical one if we adopt Erikson's formulation and turn it into an "existential" interrogation: *to be or not to be myself*? Does this alternative have a practical meaning? No doubt the question now seems complete, because the empty space has been filled by adding the attribute "myself." However, the question is still not of the same type as "What should I do?" In order for the question "to be or not to be myself?" to confront the subject with a practical decision, he would have to be able to derive from some goal or another a reason to choose one line of conduct rather than another. The choice would have to be between, on the one hand, an action that would embody the practical content of "to be myself" and, on the other hand, a different action that would embody the practical content of "not to be oneself." Yet the young man's entire "identity problem" is that he is divided between two possible ways of being himself. His choice is therefore, rather, "Will I be myself by being my father's son, or will I be myself by being a modern intellectual?" Each of these options could just as easily be characterized as a decision to be himself as they could a decision not to be himself. It follows that, in envisaging the two options that present themselves to him, Hamlet must envisage himself as *being as yet neither the one nor the other*. But it is precisely this step back—that ought to take him to the root of all choices, toward a primordial "choice of himself"—that is a step too far for him. By shedding every practical identity, Hamlet deprives himself of any reasons he might have for preferring one possibility to the other. He has taken one backward step too far, arriving "behind himself," as it were. Whatever he chooses, he will not have chosen it *for his own reasons*, since, having become unlimited and indeterminate in his identity, he no longer has reasons to prefer anything to anything else. His choice will not be an expression of his person for as long as he dwells in indifference. In order to cease being indifferent, Hamlet must succeed in defining himself once again.

The "Apprenticeship Years"

To speak of an "identity crisis" is to speak of a conflict between the *subjective* identity in which the individual recognizes herself and the *objective* identity that society attributes to that individual. We have seen that this sort of conflict cannot arise out of a discrepancy between the information held by some and the information held by others. This is why we now seek the subjectivity of personal identity in a practical self-relation, which means that the subject has room to decide and do something about her own identity. But what can there be to decide and to do? Existential philosophy responds thus: each of us must make a radical choice of self, the choice to be or not to be oneself. Yet we have just established that there is nothing practical about such a question: it says nothing about what one would have to accomplish to arrive at such an end. And it cannot say what those actions are, because, as we have just seen, the subject must *already* possess a self-definition to have reasons for doing one thing rather than another *with an aim to being herself*.

§§ At this point in our enquiry, we should no doubt seek to give our moral psychology of identity a more historical form, since the subjectivity that we have been discussing is not one that can be observed in all humans in all circumstances, but is, as Hegel claimed, an idea that is proper to modern times.

It is remarkable that Erikson chose to rename the Oedipus complex the "generational complex."[17] By doing this, he sought to displace the internal conflicts of the young man to the surrounding milieu (*Umwelt*). The crucial point is that Erikson does not limit the phenomenon to a struggle for others' recognition. In his analyses, an individual's human milieu is not reduced to the indistinct presence of others (or, as the philosophies of the *Ego* would say, the Other-than-Ego). Erikson brings in the *succession of generations* and thereby also the law according to which children follow their parents. From American cultural anthropology, he retained the idea that human sociality should above all be sought within *culture*—i.e., in the fact of the transmission of ways of doing and thinking from one generation to the next. Each new generation must undergo an apprenticeship.

In a study on the German notion of *Bildung* (education or formation of oneself) and its utilization in the *Bildungsroman*, Louis Dumont discussed Erikson's ideas from a comparative point of view.[18] He asks what societies very different from ours might have that would correspond to our notion of a crisis of adolescence.

In "tribal societies," he notes, the relation between generations is organized by a structural principle that generally sets contiguous generations (e.g., father/son) in *opposition* to each other while *bringing together* grandchildren and grandparents (through kinship terminologies). In "modern individualistic societies," an analogous phenomenon can be found, but instead in the personal biography of each individual. This properly modern phenomenon is what is called a "crisis of adolescence." Dumont writes:

> An identity crisis is under way during adolescence when the subject must either define himself within the boundaries of the societal role he is assigned, or else find another role altogether, thereby

---

17. Erikson, *Gandhi's Truth*, 132.

18. Louis Dumont, *German Ideology: From France to Germany and Back* (Chicago: University of Chicago Press, 1994), 165–166.

rejecting his relatives' expectations, his father's especially. In the latter case a transitional period opens, characterized by maladjustment, irresponsibility, and even rebellion, which can be lengthy and will close only upon the readaptation of the subject to society in a role he accepts.[19]

Dumont explains that every society must in one way or another make it possible for a new generation to enter into adult life. He sees this as a cultural invariant. The transmission of the society's ideals cannot be carried out through a simple handover from one generation to another. They especially cannot be transmitted from father to son or from mother to daughter in the way suggested by an altogether too-crude representation of tradition as the mere movement of a trust from one hand to another. What one instead observes is the organization of such transmission according to a schema of alternating generations and the clamorous staging of generational conflicts. It is the grandchildren who take on board the ideals and values of their grandparents, and they do this through a confrontation with their parents.

Traditional societies organize the transformations of the adolescent's self-image that are required by the passage into adulthood and the entry into the life of the society: they impose *rites of passage* on the young man. Modern societies leave it to the individual to carry out the necessary transformation from the status of *his parents' child* to *parent of his own children*. According to this interpretation, the cultural schema of the "identity crisis" is what provides the foundation on which Bildungsromans are constructed. Dumont then refers us to Hegel's astute analysis of the Bildungsroman in his lectures on aesthetics.[20] This analysis is found at the end of a section that bears upon the representation of individual characters in "Romantic" art (by which Hegel means from Cervantes and Shakespeare right up to writers contemporaneous with Hegel). The section ends with reflections on the contemporary Romanesque, which for Hegel means the Bildungsroman.

Hegel first notes a turnabout in the representation of the hero. In chivalric romances, the hero is a dispenser of justice who rises up to defend

---

19. Ibid., 166.
20. G. W. F. Hegel, *Aesthetics: Lectures on Fine Art,* vol. 1, trans. T. M. Knox (Oxford: Clarendon Press, 1975), 592–593.

and avenge the weak in a chaotic world; by contrast, in the "modern" novel (which here means: contemporaneous with Hegel), the world in which the action unfurls includes institutions that serve to safeguard justice and the social order. As a result, the character of the dispenser of justice becomes comical because he is devoid of purpose. *Don Quixote* inaugurates this stage. After *Quixote*, the conflict between the hero and the world is transposed into a conflict within the hero himself, thereby becoming "subjective." Romanesque heroes are henceforth *individuals* for whom the subjective aspirations of the heart are set against the prosaic reality of the world and the conventions of a milieu that seems stifling to them.

The plot of a Bildungsroman, according to Hegel, is sketched on a fixed canvas. It includes a love story: the hero is enamored with a young woman that he must rescue from the prevailing mediocrity (and not, as in the chivalric novel, from monsters or cruel sorcerers to be vanquished in an extraordinary battle). The hero—who has ambitions to do great things, for example to become a great poet—finds that his love interests are inevitably in conflict with "the will of a father or an aunt," as Hegel puts it.[21] The hero's great expectations are contradicted by the hard realities of life, and especially by his own inadequacies. The story finally ends with the reconciliation of the hero to the prose of the world. He ends up establishing a household, having children, and practicing an honorable profession devoid of glory. He becomes, says Hegel, "as good a Philistine as others" (*ein Philister so gut wie die anderen*).[22] This matter-of-fact judgment—a philistine like any other—says it all. Erikson would no doubt add: he ends up becoming a philistine just as was the man he feared coming to resemble, his father, a father who had of course lived through his own similar crisis of ambition during his youth before becoming reconciled to the way things are.

Hegel adds that this trial is an obligatory stage in the personal development of a modern individual. It is *normal* for young people to harbor ill-defined "aspirations" and illusory ambitions that result in them being thrust into a conflict with their milieu and, first and foremost, with their parents. This test is the path that the subjective aspiration to the satisfaction of "subjective particularity" must

---

21. Ibid., 593.
22. Ibid.

take—the path of the "education of the individual" (*Erziehung des Individuums*).[23]

§§ According to Hegel's analysis, the Bildungsroman stages an ordeal that is inevitable in a world that has conceded a "right of subjective particularity" and that thereby burdens the individual himself with the responsibility of entering adult life through the choice to marry (or not) and the choice to take up one profession or another. This ordeal always seems unique, but it is implied by the very notion of a subjectivity that is free to seek fulfillment in the world.[24]

Hegel, of course, cannot yet use the word "identity" to characterize the years of apprenticeship undergone by a young man in an individualistic society. Yet his analysis reveals many of the ingredients of an identity crisis understood as a dilemma that confronts young men and women: one either maintains a certain idea of oneself (an "identity") and undertakes to struggle against society, or one consents to modify this representation or to interpret it in a way that is compatible with the requirements of life. In both cases, work on oneself is necessary. In order to describe this work on oneself, we must, like Hegel, bring together the perspective of a historical philosophy and that of a moral psychology.

Modern Identity

Charles Taylor, harking back to his Hegelian roots as he often does, insists on the modern character of the phenomenon that we call an "identity crisis." Of course, it can happen in any era and in any sort of social milieu that someone becomes disoriented or no longer knows what to do as a result of going through a phase of mental confusion or amnesia. But such "personality disorders" are cognitive disorders, not identity crises.

Only a modern individual can experience an "identity crisis" and emerge from it by "constructing his identity." Taylor speaks of our

---

23. Ibid.
24. Dumont remarks that Hegel's "sarcastic tone" suggests that he is alluding to personal experiences and not just to texts he may have read. Dumont, *German Ideology*, 166.

"modern identity."[25] To refer to "modern identity" is to require that the notion of identity (taken in the sense of moral psychology) be explained from a *comparative* point of view: it will have to be demonstrated how moderns provide a response *that is their own* to a question that arises for *every human*. This is precisely what Taylor does in an analysis of what he calls "The Great Disembedding."[26]

The question that arises for all humans is the question of self-definition expressed as a response to the question "Who are you?" How does it happen that there is a properly modern way of responding to this question? We will have to construct a comparative perspective. Taylor here appeals to Karl Polanyi's idea that Western societies, beginning in the eighteenth century, entered into a process of becoming "disembedded."[27] Polanyi is referring to the fact that economic activities that, until that point, were considered social relations (i.e., as participating in social life in all of its dimensions, be they familial, political, religious, etc.) are progressively separated from social life in the name of the supposed rationality of the market. They are thereby removed from any sort of social control.

Where Polanyi wrote about a dissociation between market-based activities and the social fabric, Taylor speaks about a disintrication of individuals, a *desocialization*. Needless to say, becoming modern did not lead human beings to cease living in society. What has been desocialized is the *conception* that a human being has of himself, the model that he naturally follows in answering the question "Who are you?" Taylor's thesis is thus that we are modern from the time that each of us finds it normal to define himself or herself in desocialized terms.

To put it another way, we became modern—and thus in search of our own identities—when we began to conceive of society as *made up of individuals*. From that point on, each of us defines himself or herself as an individual in a world "constituted by individuals."[28] Our conception of society has become *individualistic*.

25. This notion of modern identity, which Charles Taylor has discussed in several works, appeared alongside a reference to Erikson in an article from 1981 entitled "Legitimation Crisis?" and reprinted in his *Philosophy and the Human Sciences: Philosophical Papers 2* (Cambridge: Cambridge University Press, 1985), 248–288.
26. Charles Taylor, *A Secular Age* (Cambridge, MA: Harvard University Press, 2007), 146–158.
27. Karl Polanyi, *The Great Transformation: The Political and Economic Origins of Our Time* (1944; Boston: Beacon Press, 1957).
28. Taylor, *A Secular Age*, 155.

Here we are obliged to answer an objection that is invariably made to this thesis: what is new about this? Of what would society be made up if not individuals? There is nothing especially modern about it. Wherever there is society, there must also be individuals.

True, but what is in question is not the *material* out of which society is made—which is, of course, particular human beings—but rather the normative *form* of its composition. How do we explain the fact that people think of themselves as having duties to one another and common aims simply because they belong to the same group?

This point requires some clarification. It is the word "individual" that trips us up here. Since we are seeking to construct a comparative, or synoptic, perspective on what it is to *present oneself as who one is* or to *define oneself*, we will have to clarify our use of the word "individual" in a comparative way. This is what Taylor does when he borrows some conceptual distinctions from social anthropology.

Every society is indeed made up of individuals, but in what sense of the word "individual"? Louis Dumont, who endeavored to provide a comparative scope to the sociological term "individual," observed that the word is used in two different ways in the social sciences and contemporary philosophy, respectively.[29]

If we take the word "individual" *in its empirical sense*, the proposition according to which "society is made up of individuals" is nothing more than a platitude. Wherever there are human societies, there are human individuals. Moreover, in every society, these individuals will have personal relations among themselves: they will bear proper names, they will have forms of language for addressing one another, they will have ways of distinguishing what is mine from what is yours, etc. They will have, as they must, a sense of the identity and personality of each of them.

---

29. Dumont asks that we distinguish between "(1) *The empirical agent, present in every society,* in virtue of which he is the main raw material for any sociology" and "(2) The rational being and *normative subject* of institutions; this is peculiar to us, as is shown by the values of equality and liberty: it is an idea that we have, the idea of an ideal." Louis Dumont, *Homo Hierarchicus: The Caste System and Its Implications,* trans. Mark Sainsbury, Louis Dumont, and Basia Gulati (1966; Chicago: University of Chicago Press, 1980), 9. By making clear that the normative individual is the "subject of institutions," Dumont is stressing that the individual taken in this sense is not a natural reality, but an institutional being, a being of the sort represented in the juridical and political system.

But if we take the word "individual" *in its individualist sense*—i.e., in the sense of a normative ideology—we are no longer considering an empirical individual, an example of the human species. The word now designates the human being as individualistic thought conceives of it and as the individual conceives of herself insofar as she thinks, as Dumont puts it, "as an individual"—i.e., as we ourselves in fact think. Thinking as an individual is here opposed to thinking as a social being. The human being defines herself as an individual when she posits herself as *independent* of the social ties she might also happen to have.

The "great disembedding" is precisely this passage from a human being and empirical individual who conceives of himself as a social being to a human being who defines himself in a desocialized way. Traditional man is in fact incapable of conceiving of himself as an individual in the normative sense. Ultimately, that is Taylor's thesis. In order for it to have become normal to conceive of self-definition as the definition of an individual, there first had to have been the movement by which minds were modernized, *the great disembedding.*

The thesis initially seems implausible, for we believe that anyone can make a distinction between his own person and the various bonds he has formed or the various dependencies he falls under but did not choose. The distinction seems basic to us, one inseparable from self-consciousness itself. How can such a basic intellectual ability be denied to human beings, whatever the form of their social life?

The answer is that we are not imputing to part of humanity an intellectual inability to make the distinction that we make. The difference does not lie in the intellectual ability to draw distinctions but in the *desire* to draw such distinctions and in the possibility for the *imagination* to give them life and meaning for the subject.

Consider the question "Who are you?" In a traditional world such as that of a Homeric hero, to ask who someone is amounts to asking about his family, his native land, his affiliations. In *The Odyssey*, when Circe wants to know who the man is who was able to withstand her magic potion, she asks Odysseus "Who are you? From what family? What city?"[30] In the Homeric world, the hero answers the question of his identity by indicating what he is called, the country of his birth, and who his

---

30. Homer, *The Odyssey*, trans. Allen Mandelbaum (New York: Bantam, 1991), X:323.

parents are. He could not imagine giving an answer that would properly be called subjective or "in the first person." The only conceivable response he can give is one that positions him among other humans through his place in a genealogical line and his status as defined within the group to which he belongs.

But that must mean that people in the Homeric world do not conceive of themselves *first* as individuals and *only subsequently* in relation to their life circumstances, as son or father, daughter or mother, warrior or merchant. Between them and us, a sea change must have occurred. When a man in a traditional society is called on to present himself, he defines himself as the point of intersection of relations among various complementary statuses (e.g., parent/child, husband/wife, master/servant, eldest/youngest, countryman of his fellow countrymen, etc.). A modern man, on the other hand, presents himself as an individual, as someone who *happens to* have various social statuses but who can think of himself *independently* of these statuses. For example, he is from his native country, but he could have been born in another country, or he might yet change his country of residence.

Exercises in Self-Definition

Traditional man is "imbricated" or "intricated" within the social fabric; modern man is "disimbricated" or "disembedded." We must admit that the thesis initially appears implausible since we tend to believe that every human being can think of himself "in the first person," subjectively. Every human being can, if only in thought, liberate himself from his de facto identity. To do this, it is enough to think of it as being precisely that—a mere de facto identity. We therefore see the "disintrication" of the individual from social life as going without saying. It seems entirely natural to us to dissociate the *person* from the *social milieu* in which he was born and raised, by imagining circumstances that would have given him a different biography.

Charles Taylor wants to make us aware of the fact that we *learned* to consider ourselves individuals and to think of society as a society of individuals. To be an individual (in the normative sense) is not an inherent status of every human being. Each of us has become (more or less) an individual through a labor of self-fashioning that consists in desocializing one's idea of oneself. No doubt this conception that each of us has of himself or herself has become like a "second nature." Nevertheless, it is cultural in origin.

In order to reveal this cultural dimension, Taylor asks that we consider an imaginative exercise that each of us can carry out regarding his or her own identity.[31] The exercise consists in asking ourselves what we would be if we had been born into another milieu or in other historical circumstances. What sort of person would I be if . . . I had married someone else, chosen another profession, adopted another religion, emigrated to America?

When I use my imagination retrospectively upon my past in this way, doing so may take the form of a pleasant reverie, but the exercise takes on a more serious cast if it becomes forward-looking. As Taylor points out, in doing this, one moves from an "abstract exercise" that commits one to nothing to an existential exercise that transforms me into a subject who is responsible for the totality of my social attributes. The exercise stops being a mere imaginative game when it becomes self-fashioning work of the subject upon herself, work by which she seeks to alter the idea she has of herself, to alter it by desocializing it, by disembedding it from the social fabric. The *right of subjectivity* of which Hegel spoke is here transformed into a *duty to be oneself.* The individual must turn every element of her biography in the Who's Who into the result of a choice. She will have to ask herself "Should I not emigrate?" Indeed, if her nationality is truly to be her own, it will have to be because she decided not to change it. If she is married, she will have to ask herself every morning whether she ought not instead to get divorced, so as never to forget that persisting in the bonds of matrimony is entirely down to her. If she has a tendency to lead a sedentary life, that is all the more reason to interpret herself as a virtual nomad who has temporarily come to a stop where she currently is. And so on.

In principle, desocialization should allow the individual to separate entirely his "identity"—what he is when he is himself—from every contingent social tie, by representing all of these ties as optional. Yet, like someone from a traditional society, we also come up against a limit in our attempts at *disembedding.* The difference between us and a traditional man is that we do not set the limit in the same place.

What would my life and my self-conception be if circumstances were

31. Taylor, *A Secular Age,* 149.

different? The exercise teaches me that some possibilities are easy to imagine, while others remain impossible. Compare these two possible lives:

1. In another life, I have a different job, a different spouse, a different nationality. We find it easy to imagine such possibilities.
2. In another life, I am of the opposite sex. Here, according to Taylor, for most of us, our thoughts become confused and nothing presents itself to our imagination. Why do our thoughts become confused? Because the imagination runs up against a limit, and we cannot determine if it is cultural, and therefore arbitrary, or logical, and therefore inescapable.

It is here that Taylor takes up as an example a question that children invariably ask: what would I have been like if I had been born to different parents?[32] What if, for example, I had been born to the parents of my friend Arthur, who has exactly the same birthday I do?

The question seems to elicit a confused response: I would have been me, because it is about me, but, at the same time, I would have been Arthur, because I would have been born to Arthur's parents on the same day Arthur was born. The answer is necessarily muddled because the question itself is muddled. In fact, the question's vertiginous effect is the result of its ambiguity. But this ambiguity will teach us something about our normative idea of the individual and his identity.

What is meant by the reference to *different* parents? My parents would have been different than what they were if they had followed different paths in life than they did. Clearly, they might have taken up different professions, emigrated to other countries before my birth, or joined a religious cult, and my own life would have been different as a result. Yes, but in that case we are talking about *my* parents, with the aim of the exercise being to imagine them making other decisions at various points in their lives. For as long as the parents that we are to imagine as different remain *my parents*, the question bears upon me, their son. The answer is then trivial. What would I have been if my own parents had been *like* those of my friend? Answer: I would have been *like* my friend. In this imaginative game, my biography varies along with the biographies of my parents, but the fact of my individuation remains untouched.

---

32. Ibid.

If, on the other hand, imagining different parents means that I would have actually been born to my friend's parents, then the question is altogether different and leads to only one response: if my parents were really those of my friend Arthur, then what I call "my birth" would have been Arthur's birth, so that the child thus born would have to say of himself "I am Arthur." But how can I imagine myself being me while also being my friend Arthur? Such a thing is impossible. The absurdity here consists in bestowing upon a human being an individual essence that is *independent* of its actualization in a particular empirical figure, detaching personal identity from every genealogy.

§§§ One way of bringing out the incoherence of this hypothesis is to follow the advice of the logician Arthur Prior and to *temporalize* the counterfactual question of what I might have been in other circumstances.[33] Prior asks us to compare the following two questions:

1. Could Julius Caesar have had a name other than "Julius Caesar"?
2. Could Julius Caesar have had different parents than he had?

It is a useful exercise, Prior explains, to ask *when* it would have been possible for Caesar, so as to account for the fact that the possibilities that are available to us are so available on particular occasions *in time*. For example, once I have reached adulthood, it ceases to be possible for me to have had a studious adolescence rather than a dissolute one, or vice versa. These possibilities henceforth present themselves in the past conditional: *I could have . . .*

Certainly, Caesar could have been given another name. He could have been given it, as long as he had not yet been given the name Julius Caesar, if it had been decided at the moment when he was to be named to call him something else. But when could he have had different parents? The mere asking of the question reveals the sophism:

After his birth, indeed after his conception—indeed, *at or after* his conception—it was clearly *too late* for him to have had different parents. But why not before? . . . My difficulty here is that *before* Caesar existed (whether we suppose his conception or some other event to

33. Arthur N. Prior, "Identifiable Individuals," in his *Papers on Time and Tense* (Oxford: Clarendon Press, 1968), 70.

constitute the start of his existence) there would seem to have been no individual identifiable as Caesar, i.e., the Caesar we are now discussing, who could have been the subject of this possibility.[34]

To temporalize the possibilities that are available to Caesar is to consider Caesar as the *subject of his own possibilities* in the sense that we can only attribute them to him by saying, "Caesar could have . . .," "Caesar could not have . . ." This clears things up. *After* his birth, Caesar no longer has the possibility of having other parents; it is too late. *Before* his birth, Caesar does not yet exist, there is no person in the world that is Julius Caesar, and there is therefore nobody to whom one might attribute the (future) possibility of having these parents rather than those others. In order to be able to evoke the possibilities of which Julius Caesar is the subject, Caesar must already be an (empirical) individual that can be named, a human being present in this world with his own identity.

One might be tempted to say this: before his birth, Julius Caesar did not exist as an actual individual, but he always existed as a *possible individual*. Julius Caesar as a possible individual would then be Julius Caesar and everything that constitutes him *except* his actual existence. But Prior has put his finger on what ruins every theory of possible individuals: they lack an *identifiable subject* to whom these possibilities can be attributed. In reality, what there was before Julius Caesar was born was the possibility for a particular couple (Caesar's parents) to one day have a son to whom they would give the name "Julius Caesar." But the possibility for a couple to have a son is not a possibility for a being that would *already* have been individuated on its own in virtue of his singular timeless essence to enter into existence as the son of the couple in question (as if one could conflate the *birth* of Julius Caesar with the *adoption* of a possible individual by his actual parents).

In reality, it is therefore impossible to entirely dissociate—as some sort of "individual essence"—what constitutes me as a distinct individual from the (contingent, yes) fact that my parents brought me into the world on a given day in given circumstances. Prior suggests that we locate the practical possibilities of an individual—Julius Caesar, say—within the order of time. But the same is true when an individual asks

---

34. Ibid.

such questions about herself from a practical point of view. If her question of identity is truly practical, she will have to ask, "What am I going to do *now*, knowing that I must choose between these two given possibilities?" In order to be, in her own eyes, the subject of such possibilities—for example, she can accept or reject an offer *by tomorrow*—she must already have been able to situate in time her thoughts about herself, thereby agreeing to recognize the various consequences that flow from the ontological fact of her individuation.

§§ What have we learned from this exercise? That I can certainly imagine myself having lived another life, but only on the condition that this other life would have been *mine*. At the root of what I call "my identity," there necessarily lies the genealogical fact of my birth. Thereafter, what is it that distinguishes the way in which a modern asks the question "Who am I?" from the way in which it would have been asked in other cultural contexts? What distinguishes the modern man is not that he has ceased to owe his individuation to the fact of having been born, and therefore escaped having his actual genealogical and social position in the world as his identity in the literal sense. What distinguishes him is his refusal to invest this literal identity with a normative function. At this point he must replace the literal identity, which is for him a simple factual identity, with another self-definition that he will henceforth call his true identity.

Taylor has shown that this conception is not natural. It is no more natural for us than it is for other cultures. Imaginative work is required in order to create a desocialized idea of oneself. We must *learn* to conceive of ourselves as individuals, in the normative sense of the term. This apprenticeship is called an "identity crisis."

Becoming a Modern Individual

The comparative perspective on our modern notion of identity allows us to resist the undeniable attraction of a historical philosophy that Taylor calls "a 'subtraction' account of the rise of modernity."[35] We ask the question "How is it that Western culture has proved to be dominant all over the world, sending off into obsolescence ways of doing and

---

35. Taylor, *A Secular Age*, 169.

thinking that had previously been dominant? Why do modern ideas and tastes prevail?" The "subtraction theory" answers that it is because it is *simpler* to be modern than to preserve ancient customs. In order to become modern, one need only get rid of everything superfluous in our forms of life. To be more modern than one's parents or neighbors is, for example, to have more informal relations with people. Entry into modernity requires nothing more than that one turn back to oneself—i.e., a withdrawal toward the "fundamentals" of the human condition. Each of us, by looking into himself, ought to perceive that he is an individual linked to his various titles and attributes only by virtue of social conventions.

In reality, to become an individual in the normative sense is an operation that is both complex and demanding. It requires the person who carries it out to engage in profound work on himself. The man who conceives of himself as a normative individual is a *more complex* and perhaps more fragile being than one who sees himself as a being defined by his social ties. Indeed—and this is the result of Taylor's analysis—the definition of oneself as a normative individual is *necessarily second*: it presupposes a first definition of oneself as a social being. A human being *cannot* spontaneously conceive of herself as a *self* detached from her social context. Her first definition of herself is *embedded*, representing her in her social positions: as a mother, a daughter, member of her particular tribe, etc. In order for her to be able to think of herself in the first place as independent from others and only subsequently bound to them by personal commitments, she will have to have already had the thought that her social existence is, in principle, optional.

In order to defend this thesis, I will have to introduce a distinction between two kinds of individuals—a distinction that Dumont and, following him, Taylor had themselves borrowed from the sociology of religion. In order to characterize the puritanism of Calvin's disciples, Max Weber distinguished it from the traditional religious attitude that prescribed the rejection of the world and its values through retreat from it. The puritan must reject the world and its seductions by combatting it where earlier spiritual masters were content to ignore it. Puritanism constitutes an "asceticism in the world," an attitude that seeks to be successful in the world as opposed to the "asceticism outside of the world" of recluses and anchorites. Generalizing this distinction, Dumont sets up an opposition between "individualism-outside-of-the-world," which seeks to develop individuality within a spiritual interiority, on the one hand, and modern individualism, which is an "individualism-in-the-world," meaning that it seeks to transform the existing world in order to make it accommodating to the individual in the normative sense.[36] But this transformation is never finished; it requires a never-ending struggle, for the world continues to resist it.

The Indian renouncer and the early-Christian anchorite were unable to individualize themselves within the world, because the societies into which they were born left no place for a "right of subjectivity." They could become "individuals" (in the normative sense) only by *materially* withdrawing from society. More precisely, they "abandoned the world," as one might say in religious language, settling into a retreat, away from other men. Henceforth, they would be "outside the world," not, needless to say, because they had somehow found a way to live without food—they lived from alms—but because they had decided to remove themselves from the social cycle of duties and obligations. The modern individual, by contrast, has as his project to live an individual life within the world. This requires him to redefine radically his normative relations with other individuals.

In order to become a normative individual in the modern sense, one must dedicate oneself to work on oneself. The individual must learn to detach himself *using his thought and imagination* from the contingent place that he occupies within society. He does this by applying to himself scenarios constructed along the lines of the kinds of exercises in self-definition described by Taylor. I am what I truly and authentically am independently of my social positions. Let us consider an excellent example of such an exercise on one's identity, one provided by Pascal.

§§ The *Discourses on the Condition of the Great* is not a text written in Pascal's hand, but rather Pierre Nicole's transcription of three discussions that Pascal had with a young nobleman (the fourteen-year-old son of the Duke of Luynes, according to historians).[37]

---

36. Louis Dumont, "World Renunciation in Indian Religions," Appendix B to *Homo Hierarchicus*, 267–286.

37. Nicole writes in his preamble that, having been present for these conversations, he was so impressed by what Pascal had to say that, even though he was setting their substance into writing at ten years' remove, he could guarantee that these were Pascal's thoughts (if not his exact words). Pierre Nicole, preamble to "Trois discours sur la condition des Grands" by Blaise Pascal in his *Pensées et opuscules*, ed. Léon Brunschvicg (Paris: Classiques Hachette, 1990), 232–233.

What is the tenor of the ideas that Pascal hopes to communicate to his pupil? He presents them to him as follows: the young nobleman must learn his "true condition," which means that he cannot remain content with the condition he derives from the fact of being his father's son.

In the first of the three *Discourses*, Pascal uses an analogy to illustrate what he calls "recognizing one's true state," which is nothing but what we have been calling "defining oneself," forming an idea of oneself—in short, building an "identity" for oneself in the moral or normative sense of the term. Thus, even if he does not yet use the word "identity," Pascal makes use of the paradigm of answering the question "Who are you?" in order to introduce a morality based in the subjective relation to oneself. Who better than Pascal to guide us along the path we have been attempting to follow from the beginning, a path that leads from the *literal* sense of the question of identity to its *figural* sense?

Pascal invents a short fable in which a man, shipwrecked on an unknown island, becomes the king of the islanders after a misunderstanding. It happens that the man in question bears a very close physical resemblance to the king of the island, who had disappeared some time earlier and had never been found, despite all of the islanders' efforts. When they come upon the castaway, they imagine they have found their king.

The castaway resembles the king, with the result that he is taken for the king. A mistake has thus been made regarding the castaway's identity *in the literal sense*. Now, Pascal explains, the castaway would be quite insane if he were to make the same error about himself that the islanders have made about him. He is in a position to know that he is not really the king. How will he act, then? Pascal concludes his apologue as follows:

> Thus he had a double thought: the one by which he acted as king, the other by which he recognized his true state, and that it was accident alone that had placed him in his present condition. He concealed the latter thought, and revealed the other. It was by the former that he treated with the people, and by the latter that he treated with himself.[38]

---

38. Blaise Pascal, "Discourses on the Condition of the Great," trans. O. W. Wight, in *Thoughts, Letters, Minor Works* (New York: P. F. Collier & Son, 1910), 382–383.

The question raised is precisely that of the normative scope of an identity. How should our castaway act? It depends on *who he is for whom*, since his experience has split him in two. *With others* the castaway will act as if he were the king. *With himself*, he will let his behavior be guided by the opposing thought—i.e., the certainty that he is not the king.

Is this, then, an early version of our "question of modern identity"? Does our castaway have what we would call an "identity problem"? In fact, the fable stages an "identity confusion" in the most literal sense. When the man acts with the islanders in accordance with the thought that he is the king, this simply means: as if he were in fact the same person as the king, as if that were his "true state." As a result, the identity problem that the castaway has to resolve is the same as that confronted by all impostors and usurpers. He must make sure not to confuse his roles—not to "treat with himself" as if he took himself to really be the king, and not to reveal himself when he "treats with the people."[39]

However, we can see in this story how one can move from such identity in the literal sense to the notion of a moral identity that concerns us. First of all, the question "Who am I?" can easily take on a normative sense. If the castaway were the legitimate sovereign by birth, he would have no need to divide his thought, since he would not have to maintain a false identity for the benefit of others while also making sure to retain his real identity in his encounters with himself. For all of the other people in this fable, their de facto identity is also their normative identity, in that the answer to the question "Who am I?" determines the appropriate conduct in the presence of whoever is asking the question. Since they know who they are, these people know how to behave in a meaningful way with regard to one another. This means: they know how to behave in a way commensurate with what may be expected of them.

In this fable, circumstances have as a result that the castaway can no longer rely on his native identity to know how to behave. The others do not have this problem: they are (for others) who they are (for themselves), and therefore they have no "identity problems." But Pascal will go on to teach his young pupil that we must all perform an analogous doubling of ourselves.

---

39. Ibid., 383.

§§§ In the rest of this first *Discourse*, Pascal proceeds to his real argument in his interview with the young nobleman. The latter is not an impostor and has nothing to hide, since he is in fact the duke's son and therefore certain of his status in society. He has a right to this identity that everyone recognizes him as having, whereas the castaway's proper place is not on the throne. Nevertheless, according to Pascal, his right is grounded in human conventions and not "a title of nature."[40] In natural law, there are no social distinctions. Just as the castaway is king only as a result of the imagination of the islanders (who were fooled by the physical resemblance), so the duke's son is vested with greatness only in virtue of human imagination (in this case, the imagination of the anonymous legislators who established these conventions).

It is therefore a "human institution" [*un établissement humain*], as Pascal puts it, that attaches a given social status to the fact of having been born to the appropriate set of parents in the right circumstances. The fact of being a duke is the result of a series of chance occurrences: the accident of being born (his parents might not have ever met), the accident of living in a society in which there are dukes (the institutions might have been different), etc. The young nobleman would be deluding himself if he thought that the consideration he is shown because of his hierarchical rank is consideration for him personally, in virtue of what he is in himself. The signs of respect addressed to him are addressed not to him but only to his condition as nobility. He will also have to become accustomed to having *doubled thoughts* with regard to his own condition:

> What follows from this? that you should have a double thought like the man of whom we have spoken, and that, if you act externally with men in conformity with your rank, you should recognize, by a more secret but truer thought, that you have nothing naturally superior to them. If the public thought elevates you above the generality of men, let the other humble you, and hold you in a perfect equality with all mankind, for this is your natural condition.[41]

40. Ibid.
41. Ibid., 384.

The exercise that Pascal proposes to his pupil is precisely one of self-definition through disembedding. It involves learning to stop thinking of oneself as being naturally—and thus legitimately—what one is as a result of one's genealogy. Pascal goes on to explain, in the second of his *Discourses*, that there are two sorts of human greatness. Indeed, one must distinguish two sorts of qualities. One sort is constitutive of the person. Pascal calls these qualities "natural greatness." The others, which are external to the person, Pascal calls "greatness of institution."

> Greatness of institution depends upon the will of men who have with reason thought it right to honor certain positions, and to attach to them certain marks of respect. Dignities and nobility are of this class. . . . Natural greatness is that which is independent of the caprice of men, because it consists in the real and effective qualities of the soul or the body, which render the one or the other more estimable, as the sciences, the enlightenment of the mind, virtue, health, strength.[42]

It is not obvious or easy to practice having such a double thought. It is all the more difficult given that, viewed from without, there will be no evidence of one's doubled identity. Indeed, there is nothing revolutionary about Pascal's idea. There is no question of denying the Great the "respects" that they are owed; it is rather about qualifying and doubling those respects. There are *natural* respects and there are *institutional* respects, which Pascal explains as follows:

> It is not necessary, because you are a duke, that I should esteem you; but it is necessary that I should salute you. If you are a duke and a gentleman, I shall render what I owe to both these qualities. I shall not refuse you the ceremonies that are merited by your quality of duke, nor the esteem that is merited by that of a gentleman. But if you were a duke without being a gentleman, I should still do you justice; for in rendering you the external homage which the order of men has attached to your birth, I should not fail to

---

42. Ibid., 385.

have for you the internal contempt that would be merited by your baseness of mind.[43]

How should the young duke carry himself if he has taken Pascal's lesson on board? At the end of his exercise in self-definition, what sort of individualism will he practice?

It will not be an individualism-outside-of-the-world in the strict sense, since there is no question here of withdrawal from or renunciation of his condition as a nobleman. Pascal sought to teach him how to conduct himself as a duke without being unjust; he is not concerned here with his salvation (as he stresses at the end of the third *Discourse*). The young duke therefore will maintain his position within the system of *who owes what to whom* that is defined by his birth. He is therefore by rights entitled to require that others accord him the "respects of institution"—i.e., the "external ceremonies" that result from his position as a duke. Before a duke, one must remove one's hat, bow, give way, etc. But if he wants to be respected for himself or be recognized for his value as a particular individual, he will have to demonstrate that he merits being so treated by his individual qualities—for example, by showing himself to be a "greater geometrician" than others.[44] Even so, this quality will grant him only a "preference of esteem" but no "external preference":

> M. N. . . . is a greater geometrician than I; in this quality, he wishes to pass ahead of me: I will tell him that he understands nothing of the matter. Geometry is a natural greatness; it demands a preference of esteem; but men have not attached to it any external preference. I shall therefore pass ahead of him, and shall esteem him greater than I in the quality of geometrician.[45]

This is why the subjective position described here by Pascal retains an element of individualism-outside-of-the-world. For natural respect and natural contempt must remain *internal*. They take place within *thought*. On the one hand, the duke will have to consider himself *internally* as

---

43. Ibid., 386.
44. Ibid.
45. Ibid [translation modified].

being—in accordance with his true condition—equal to all other men (even if it is better that he not reveal this thought to the people, who imagine that his greatness is "natural"). On the other hand, Pascal explains how he himself practices the necessary doubling when he encounters the nobility of this world: externally, he bows, but this is only an "external duty"; internally, he grants others esteem or contempt according to either the real qualities (for example, that of being a superior geometrician) or the lack of personal merit that he discerns in them.

§§ So it is that the individualism advocated by Pascal is not yet one that calls on each of us to develop his individuality *in the world*. The young nobleman is meant to have the idea that all men are equal. However, nothing yet flows from this within social life. The thought of such equality—which is a revolutionary thought if ever there was one—must remain a hidden thought. At root, Pascal has adapted the individualistic spirit of ancient stoicism, which was an individualism-outside-of-the-world, to the needs of a young nobleman of his time. Through spiritual exercises, the wise stoic could become independent without as a result having to take leave materially of the society of men or consider himself discharged of the duties incumbent upon those in his position (*officia*).[46]

The Future of Individualism

Pascal asks that we lead doubled lives, since we will have to judge people and things using two different hierarchical scales. The solution Pascal offers therefore seems unstable as a result of the tension it cannot avoid creating within each individual. The castaway was acting as an impostor in allowing the islanders to take him for the king. But the subject seeking to develop a "double thought" regarding his own identity may well also appear to be an impostor, especially to himself. He may suffer from not being able to comport himself externally in a way in conformity with his internal feelings. He may then aspire to a more "authentic"

---

46. On the question of Stoic spiritual exercises, see Pierre Hadot, *Philosophy as a Way of Life: Spiritual Exercises from Socrates to Foucault*, ed. Arnold Davidson, trans. Michael Chase (Malden, MA: Blackwell, 1995).

existence, one that is more in accordance with the demand for a match between the internal and the external (which is how one might define the demand for *Eigentlichkeit* or authenticity). What reality can there be in a "natural respect" that is in no way marked in one's external conduct toward others? Similarly, what value can there be in an "institutional respect" if it may be contradicted by an internal contempt?

Moreover, as we are about to see, Pascal does not believe for a moment that one can stay within this compromise. At this point, and from a philosophical point of view, the question is raised of what future modern individualism can have. By proposing this doubling, Pascal is asking the future duke to accomplish an internal "night of August 4."[47] The abolition of privileges takes place, but only in the interiority of the subject. It is in no way made manifest in the performance of his "external duties."

Of course, one can maintain that the abolition of privileges had to be carried out in two stages, and that before one can destroy the ancient order of justice in reality, one must first put an end to its legitimacy within people's minds—and that this is precisely what Pascal accomplishes. But if that were the case, things would be entirely different for those of us living after the real, *external* "night of August 4." For us, there should now be but a single hierarchical scale for measuring the tokens of esteem that we owe to various people: the scale of real qualities. Is someone a better geometrician than we are? If she is, she is entitled to our external recognition, and this idea provides the principle for a liberal order of justice: "careers open to talents."[48]

So how does it happen that the establishment of a meritocratic order based on personal talent does not result in each of us being assured of our moral identity—i.e., our entitlement to others' esteem and, based on that, to our own self-esteem? The liberal hierarchical regime ought to have put an end to "identity crises." Even if such crises were understandable during the period of transition from the old order to the new one (i.e., in Pascal's era), they ought to have since come to an end. What

---

47. [Translator's note: *La nuit du 4 août* refers to the moment in 1789 when the Constituent Assembly abolished all feudal rights and privileges.]

48. [Translator's note: "My maxim was: *careers open to talents*, without distinction of birth or fortune." Napoleon, cited in Barry E. O'Meara, *Complément du Mémorial de Sainte-Hélène: Napoléon en exil*, vol. 2 (1822; Paris, Garnier Frères, 1897), 6.]

reasons could an individual today have for doubling himself and thereby having to choose from among his possible identities the one that will govern his actions?

The only conceivable explanation is that we have not yet moved out of the transition period. And we have not yet done this because it is not possible for us to enter the world as normative individuals who are already disembedded and desocialized. It is a matter of principle that we are born free and equal. This principle is the formulation of a demand to which we strive to conform. But this means that it is just as much the case for man in modern times as it was for his ancestors that he comes into the world within a human milieu from which he receives his genealogical identity, which fortunately holds a normative meaning for his parents and educators. This is why modern man must also learn to become a modern individual. He finds himself confronted in his youth with the question of identity in Louis Dumont's Eriksonian formulation: *either* to define himself so as to be able to feel that he is in his place if he takes up the place set up for him by those around him (parents, teachers, well-meaning friends), *or* to define himself in such a way that he is only satisfied with himself if he manages to construct another place for himself (thereby, at least initially, failing to meet the legitimate expectations of all those who looked after him). This conflict is precisely the moment of a "double thinking."

The definition of oneself as a desocialized individual is necessarily derived, given that we moderns, like all those who came before us, have not ceased to be social beings. This is why it cannot be said that individualism-in-the-world has purely and simply replaced individualism-outside-of-the-world. That would be the case if humanity were able not only to enter into the process of its modernization but also to settle peacefully into a stable state of modernity. That is not possible, however; instability is constitutive of the very idea of an individual who means to be fully self-sufficient.

Here again, Pascal perhaps provides the deeper reason for this. He shows how a spiritual danger threatens the individual who is in search of himself. From the point of view of moral psychology, the search for oneself means the search for full satisfaction (Hegel)—being esteemed and appreciated as an individual. At that point, however, a difficult question arises. If I want others to esteem me for my value, I will have to be able to claim that there is something estimable in what makes me an individual. The question is then one that the Port-Royal editors gave as the title to one of the most disconcerting of Pascal's *Pensées*: "What is the self?"[49]

In this short text, Pascal carries out the spiritual annihilation of what he calls the "self" [*le moi*]. He seeks to show that nobody can claim a right to the respect of others in virtue of his "natural qualities." In order to come to this conclusion, Pascal need do nothing more than radicalize the exercise in self-definition used in the *Discourses*. As we have seen, this imaginative exercise consisted in the subject asking, "What would I have become if my circumstances had been different?" The exercise aims to separate those of the subject's attributes that are constitutive of his person from those that are only contingently his and that could therefore be removed. A subject who applies such thoughts to himself, imagining that he *could have* had a different place in the world, is thereby meant to discover his true self, the kernel of qualities that constitute his individual being. However, in this fragment, Pascal demonstrates in three steps the inanity of anything one might take to be a true self at the end of such a process of divestment.

In the *first* of these steps, Pascal imagines a scene that allows him to introduce a distinction between two comportments others might have toward me.

---

49. Here is the text:

> What is the self?
>
> A man who sits at the window to watch the passers-by; can I say that he sat there to see me if I pass by? No, for he is not thinking of me in particular. But someone who loves a person because of her beauty, does he love her? No, because smallpox, which will destroy beauty without destroying the person, will ensure that he no longer loves her.
>
> And if someone loves me for my judgment, for my memory, is it me they love? No, because I can lose these qualities without losing myself. Where is the self, then, if it is neither in the body nor in the soul? And how can you love the body or the soul except for its qualities, which do not make up the self, since they are perishable? For would we love the substance of a person's soul in the abstract, whatever qualities it contained? That is impossible, and would be unjust. Therefore we never love a person, only qualities.
>
> So let us stop mocking people who are honored for their appointments and offices. For we love no one except for his borrowed qualities.

Blaise Pascal, *Pensées and Other Writings,* trans. Honor Levi, ed. Anthony Levi (Oxford: Oxford University Press, 1995), 130 (Sellier, § 567; Brunschvicg, § 323; Lafuma, § 688).

A man who sits at the window to watch the passers-by; can I say that he sat there to see me if I pass by? No, for he is not thinking of me in particular.

Someone has sat at the window to watch the passersby. I pass by his window. He sees me while I am passing, and, as a result, he has seen what he wanted to see. Yes, but what exactly did he want to see? With what intention did he sit at the window? At this point, a distinction seems to be required. For there is a logical difference between the following two possibilities:

1. A man sits at the window because he wants to *see me pass by*.
2. A man sits at the window because he wants to see a passerby pass by, regardless of who the passerby is.

What is the difference between these two situations? *Materially*, there is no difference. If the man has sat at the window and looks out on the street and if it so happens that I am passing by his window at that moment, he will see me pass by; in other words, I am the one that he sees passing by. Thus, it is this man's *thoughts* that make all the difference. Today, we express this distinction by appealing to the logic of intentionality, which allows us to bring out the distinction that is introduced into a mental act by the *way* in which the thought targets its object. The intentionality of an act is the *respect* in which the act gives itself an object. To better understand the intentional difference that concerns us here, imagine that there are two men at the window, one (man A) that wants *to see me pass by* and another (man B) who merely wants to *see passersby*. The logic of intentionality allows us to distinguish their intentions by determining the conditions under which each of the two men will attest to having seen what they wanted to see once they have seen me pass by. Here are these respective conditions:

a. Man A wanted *to see me pass by*; his intention is satisfied if he sees me pass by; it is not if he sees someone other than me.
b. Man B wanted to *see passersby*; his intention is satisfied if someone passes by and he sees him or her, whether that person is me or someone else.

The first step of Pascal's demonstration therefore reaches the following conclusion: a man sitting at the window casting his gaze upon me thereby enters into a relation with me. But there were two ways for the man to establish this relation, because there were two ways for him to conceive of me: either as the very person that he wanted to see pass by, or as any passerby whatever, if he is not particularly interested in the identity of the person he sees. In the latter case, it is only my quality of being a passerby that interests him, not me as a particular individual. There are thus two ways for someone to have a relation with me: the first is personal and the second impersonal. Man A wants to see me in person. Man B only relates to me in an impersonal way: what interests him is not that *I* am passing by but that there is someone who is passing by, regardless of who it is.

In the *second* step of his demonstration, Pascal considers a relation between one person and another that he calls "loving someone." He will go on to show that it is not really personal in the aforementioned sense. By the verb "to love" he does not here refer to the amorous passion that links two lovers to each other but, rather, the feeling of attachment that arises from the esteem for or appreciation of a person's qualities. In this fragment, "to love someone" must be understood in a sense close to that of "to esteem this person." Taken in this sense, the verb "to love" behaves much as does the verb "to esteem." Pascal here applies the logic of intentionality derived from his example of the man at the window. One cannot esteem someone purely and simply or in an absolute way; one can only esteem someone for something or another—for example, for being a notable of the state. The same is true of the love that Pascal is discussing: one loves someone for a quality that renders him lovable and on condition that he possesses this quality or, more precisely, on condition that one believes him to possess this quality. If he stops having it, or if we stop believing that he has it, we stop loving him for it. Pascal then asks what it is that makes me lovable to others. And he answers: my qualities. But what do we mean by my qualities? The same thing is true of the qualities I consider to be personal as was true of my quality of being a passerby in the street: they are not constitutive of my person. Pascal writes: "And if someone loves me for my judgment, for my memory, is it me they love? No, because I can lose these qualities without losing myself." The subject is therefore wrong to say, "my judgment, my memory, my qualities"; none of that truly belongs to him, since he can be denuded of them at any moment without it resulting in his disappearance.

Finally, Pascal arrives at the *third* and last step of the demonstration.

What had until this point been a speculative discussion concludes as a kind of spiritual exercise—i.e., work on oneself by which the individual seeks to improve himself by correcting the false conception of himself that he had hitherto embraced. There is no self-definition that is conceivable in the language of "qualities" or in terms of the reasons for others' esteem.

> Where is the self, then, if it is neither in the body nor in the soul? And how can you love the body or the soul except for its qualities, which do not make up the self, since they are perishable? For would we love the substance of a person's soul in the abstract, whatever qualities it contained? That is impossible, and would be unjust. Therefore we never love a person, only qualities.

This is why Pascal is able to conclude by placing on an equal footing the reasons for loving someone and the reasons for esteeming someone: "So let us stop mocking people who are honoured for their appointments and offices. For we love no one except for his borrowed qualities." In the language of the *Discourses*, one might say that there is no difference between *natural respects* and *institutional respects*, for natural qualities are every bit as external to someone's individuality as are institutional qualities. It is absurd and unjust to ask to be loved for oneself, for there is nothing lovable in the fact of being oneself.

§§ Pascal's exercise is therefore an example of an ascetic morality conceived as an active refusal of the world and of that which allows one to be loved and esteemed within it. Such an asceticism consists in freeing oneself from the world (through divestment) and not in transforming the world. Pascal, on the threshold of our modernity, thus refuses the perspective of an *individualism-in-the-world*.

We may certainly reject this Jansenism and hold that an individual has the right to see as her own those "qualities" that she has cultivated out of her natural gifts. If someone is a good geometrician, she may owe it to luck or to nature, but she also had to change her natural gifts into an ability through hard work. By cultivating her talents, she made them her own, at which point there is nothing unjust in her saying, "This quality is part of my identity, of the moral identity that, in each of us, serves as the basis for a just self-esteem."

It is nevertheless the case that the man who wants to define himself beginning with himself and entirely by himself may well find himself, like Hamlet, suspended in a state of indecision. Indeed, how does such a man proceed in order to transform himself into a modern individual? In order to do this, he must cancel out the normative consequences that every social order attaches—at least during childhood—to genealogical identity. He must pass through an adolescent identity crisis and ask himself whether he will stick to his native identity or, instead, give himself another one, taking on board in each case the concomitant duties. Philosophically, the operation consists in invoking as an incontrovertible principle the formula that is sometimes referred to as "Hume's Law" (or putative law). As a result of the logical chasm separating factual judgments from value judgments, it is held to be impossible to derive from a description of my status (e.g., "I was born into such-and-such a family," " . . . in such-and-such country," etc.) a conclusion saying what I ought to do (a value judgment), let alone a conclusion about what I am obliged to do.

But when someone seriously applies "Hume's Law" to herself, she puts herself in the position of a radical choice, meaning that she suppresses the normative fact of her individuation and thus loses every given practical identity. She thereby denies herself any reasons that she might personally have to make one choice rather than another. By relegating the various aspects of her natural individuation into the realm of insignificant facts, she transforms herself into a latter-day Hamlet or a pure Pascalian *self*, neither of which bears within itself reasons to prefer one thing over another.

In fact, in seeking to be a modern individual and deciding that "Hume's Law" is logically beyond question, the subject has already chosen. Yet, if she is lucid, she will have to conclude that she chose her modern identity (to the detriment of her genealogical identity) without having any reasons for doing so. The dichotomy between facts and values rests on a *choice of values*, which is the epitome of an individualistic choice. The subject is then surprised to learn that she can discover the reasons for choosing to be modern only on the condition that she has already chosen—and *without reasons*—this modern identity.[50]

---

50. Here I must refer the reader to Alan Montefiore's book, *A Philosophical Retrospective: Facts, Values, and Jewish Identity* (New York: Columbia University Press, 2011), in which he

Expressive Identity

In conclusion, it behooves us to ask whether we have answered the question we asked at the outset. We sought to understand how to ask the question "Who am I?" in the first person and in a subjective sense. This question is asked in a subjective sense when the subject is asked to *identify himself* by saying not just who he is "for us" (e.g., his name, etc.) but who he is "for himself." In this way, Erikson drew a distinction between identity in a literal or "objective" sense—the "identity of the person" according to his official documents—and an identity in the subjective sense, a "personal identity" that is that of a *self*, at once subject and object of a consciousness of being self-identical.

Erikson's distinction suggests that the meaning of identity *for oneself* ought to be sought in classical reflexive psychology. The question would then bear upon the subject's private knowledge. As we have seen, this interpretation would open the door to some disturbing possibilities: does your consciousness of being yourself confirm that you are in fact the same human individual as the person called by your name in the past? Or, rather, that in the more distant past you were a different human individual from the person called by your name—for example, Julius Caesar? However, as we have seen, these possibilities depend on the possibility that we could use the word "self" as an individuative term. To be the same person would be to be the same *self*. Now the only conceivable identity criterion for a *self* would be a subjective criterion—i.e., a merely apparent criterion (Wittgenstein).

This is why we have sought the meaning of subjective identity within a moral psychology—i.e., a psychology of the human being insofar as he is liable to be contented or discontented, satisfied with what he has done, or at odds with himself. What is involved, then, are the feelings the subject may have about his own value as a particular being. As Hegel put it, man in modern times is someone who lays claim to being able to derive legitimate satisfaction from what he does in being himself. Consequently, the fact of asking the question "Who am I?" would

---

describes the path that led him from a first position that was orthodoxly modern (when he still believed that the gap between facts and values was of a rational or logical sort) to a more complex modern position (when he concluded, after having reflected upon his own personal identity and also upon what "Jewish identity" might be, that the gap in question was a mark of our sociality, a culturally given fact).

become a way of emphasizing what Hegel called the "right of the subject" to be satisfied as a *particular* individual.

If we understand the subjective in this subjectivist sense, the question "Who am I?" will have to take on a practical sense, one in which I seek my identity in the expression that I, as the subject of my decision, give to it. This also means: as the subject of my possibility of being or not being this or that (Arthur Prior). The question then becomes "What must I decide in order to be satisfied with having taken the decision and to be able to take it on board as something that expresses me?"

It was tempting to seek this practical sense of identity "for oneself" in an existential theory of "radical choice." According to that theory, the condition for subjective satisfaction would require the subject to be entirely responsible for the entire set of her attributes, including those that she happens to possess from the facts of her birth or her "situation" in a world that she found as it happened to be.

Yet we have seen why the path of radical choice leads to an impasse. Hamlet says that the question that must be asked is "to be or not to be . . . ?" Unfortunately, this sequence of words fails to articulate a question, since it is missing an attribute. Hamlet is not yet in a position to replace the blank that he left within his question (between the verb "to be" and the question mark) by an adjective that would allow him to transform a question that is doubly infinite (both unfinished and general) into a finite question. However, the only practical questions are those that are *finite*: what should I do, here and now, knowing that I have this or that possibility open to me? Standing at the crossroads, I can take the road to the left or the one to the right. Before I arrived at the intersection, I could do neither. Therefore, these two paths are available only to *me*, as I am individuated in this spot on earth. As Prior points out, one can attribute possibilities only to an *individuated* agent, and this is why the purported subject of a radical choice is in fact a "vague individual," an indeterminate agent. He is incapable of asking finite questions because he has no reason to envisage one possibility as preferable to another from the perspective of the ends that he would have if he were an individuated agent. He has no reasons that are his own, reasons that, by indicating what he should do, allow him to think of his decision as an expression of himself, of what he is and of what he wants in life.

The result of our discussion, then, is this: *practical* questions—i.e., *finite* questions—can be raised only by an agent who is sure of the conditions of his choice, conditions that result from his individuation in a particular place in the world. Consequently, the theory of radical choice will not be able to provide us with subjective identity in an expressive sense. The only choice that can express a subject is a *deliberate* choice—i.e., one that he makes for his own reasons. But in order to make his choice after having considered the reasons he might have for doing or not doing something, the subject will have had to accept the ontological fact of his individuation. He will have had to accept that his identity is defined by his human origins rather than by pure subjective fiat.

§§ In order to philosophically situate the concept of expressive identity, I will end on an Aristotelian note. In a passage from the *Nicomachean Ethics* (IX, 1167b34–1168a9) in which he discusses friendship, Aristotle points out that artists are attached to their productions by a feeling that reminds one of the love parents have for their children. The same is true of benefactors with regard to those they have helped. More generally, man as the agent who produces handiwork loves it as he loves his offspring; that is, he loves himself within his handiwork. So it is that the artist *takes on board for himself* the compliments that are made about his work, just as parents are proud of their children's successes, treating them as if they were their own. For artists as for parents, love of oneself extends to other beings outside of oneself.

Is it an aberration to love oneself in something other than oneself?

It would turn out to be an aberration if we relied on reflexive psychology to provide us with the meaning of love of oneself, for in such a case the subject would have to find his *self* within and not outside of himself.

Things are entirely different, though, if we derive our moral psychology of identity from an expressive conception of subjectivity. How does it happen that the subject seeks herself outside of herself? The answer is that she does not seek herself in just anything that may be outside of herself, but only in those that she can claim in one way or another as manifesting in actuality what had only been in potentiality within the subject. Aristotle puts it as follows:

> The explanation of this is that existence is an object of desire and love for everyone; that we exist by being in actuality (since we do so by living and acting); and that in a way, the work *is* the maker in

actuality; so he loves his work, because he loves his existence too. And this is a fact of nature; for what he is in potentiality, the work shows in actuality.[51]

The crucial point for us is Aristotle's observation rendered quite literally by the translator as "in a way, the work *is* the maker in actuality" (*energeia de ho poiēsas to ergon esti pōs*). By putting the verb "to be" in italics, the translator emphasizes that Aristotle is here stating an identity between the artist and the work. In Sarah Broadie's commentary to this translation, she stresses that the explanation of this claim should be sought in lines 8–9: "for what he is in potentiality, the work shows in actuality." The idea is obviously not that a sculptor is identical to a statue or a novelist to his novel. The identity in question must be understood in an expressive sense: what it is that constitutes the individuality of a particular artist should be sought in what constitutes the individuality of her particular work. What the former is capable of (her artistic "capacity") is shown in actuality in her artistic expression.

This idea has an important consequence for art criticism and literary stylistics, which is essentially one brought out by Proust in his *Contre Sainte-Beuve*: one ought not look for the artist in his biography, in his (often banal) conversations, in his strategies for social advancement. One should look for him in his work. Stylistic analyses do not consist in a movement that goes from the clues that the work contains toward the artist's personality; they consist in looking for the individuality proper to the artist in what is his being in actuality (*energeia*), his expression in the form of an *ergon*.

Consequently, there is nothing incongruous or unjust about an artist who says, "If you do not like my work, that means that you do not like *me*" rather than, as an application of the Jansenist exercise in the denudation of the self would require, "If you like me for having produced this work, that means that you do not really like *me*."

---

51. Aristotle, *Nicomachean Ethics*, trans. Christopher Rowe, ed. Christopher Rowe and Sarah Broadie (Oxford: Oxford University Press, 2002), 1168a5–9 (233).

PART III

"WHO ARE WE?"

5

COLLECTIVE IDENTITIES

"Who Are We?"

The question "Who are we?" often comes up in contemporary public debate. Controversies arise among various groups regarding collective identities—for example, regarding our national identity or our European identity. These notions are often the subjects of fierce polemics. For example, it might be asked whether the fact of European identity is the result of having a *common history* (which would make it akin to a national identity) or of having *common values* (which would make it akin to the identity of a religious denomination or philosophical association). Or might European identity be a *political* identity? In this case, one would have to ask the Europeans to define the territory over which they intend to exercise their sovereignty, since a claim of sovereignty not accompanied by the setting of external borders is a claim to deploy a global *imperium*. These are some possible responses to the question of our European identity, different conceptions of what is too-imprecisely referred to as the "European project."

However, it is not just the *answers* to the question "In what does this or that collective identity consist?" that are controversial, but also the question itself. When we inquire about the identity of a group, what are we looking for? Is it a list of family resemblances? Or is it a matter of applying the elementary concept of identity to collective entities so as to be able to distinguish them from one another—i.e., to individuate them (in the logical sense)? And how do we move from identity in the sense of the *identical* (e.g., "it is the same group") to identity in the *identitarian* sense (e.g., "this group exhibits in its conduct an acute sense of its own identity")?

Does philosophy have any contribution to make to these debates? The answer is that it does, since the difficulties that the notion of collective identity confronts us with are above all linguistic difficulties. We ought to be able to easily explain what we mean by the words "our identity," but our explanations invariably become muddled such that we feel betrayed by the very words we use. It suddenly seems impossible to say what we want to say without, at the same time, also saying things that we had no intention of saying, let alone of taking on board.

Here again, we will therefore have to *act as if* we had to relearn the identitarian idiom. And in order to learn to speak about the identity of a group in the identitarian sense, there is only one possible starting point: we will have to begin with our understanding of trivial assertions such as "it is the same group" or "it is a different group."

A Linguistic Difficulty

I will start by sketching out the various critiques to which the very notion of collective identity currently gives rise.

What is in question is the identity of a group of humans *over time*, and it is this aspect that explains the vigorous objections that have arisen among professional historians. Pierre Nora writes, for example, that many of his fellow historians feel that the expression "national identity" is to be avoided because it suggests permanence, as if a nation were an inalterable substance rather than a historical entity.[1] He also notes that the historians' objections have been naturally extended into a political critique: the mere fact of speaking of a "national identity" for any purpose other than that of denouncing the illusion of such a thing is itself a sign of one's adherence to a *nationalistic* representation of history. Finally, he amusingly observes that some authors have condemned the very idea of a "group identity" when it is supposed to be the identity of a nation but have no trouble accepting and even exalting the notion

---

1. Pierre Nora, "Les avatars de l'identité française," *Le Débat* 159 (March-April 2010): 5.

when the identity in question is that of a regional, linguistic, or other minority within an overarching national community. At the same time, other authors maintain just the opposite view: minority identity amounts to closing oneself off in an oppressive and closed community, while national identity represents individual emancipation guaranteed by republican universalism.[2] It would therefore seem that the critique emanating from historians can be developed on two levels, as if there were two possible degrees of rejection of this notion of a collective identity.

§§ A *historical* critique of collective identity has as its primary object, naturally enough, assertions of a historical kind. For example, one might encounter in political literature or in basic history textbooks statements such as this one: "We have a national dish, one that our ancestors also ate" (for example, apple pie or roast chicken); or "We have a national language, which was also that of our ancestors." Similar things are claimed for national literatures, national musical forms, etc. These are historical statements and are therefore vulnerable to historical critique based on investigations into the archives and the monuments of the past. Such investigations often result in negative conclusions. The historian shows how, in fact, all of these customs and monuments were put in place by policies aiming to "nationalize" the past.[3] Consequently, according to some historians, collective identities (national identities, say) are not the reliable products of collective memory that they seem to be but are, rather, fabrications—i.e., inauthentic; for the historical process of their fabrication can be described.

What is the scope of such a critique? In what follows, I will refer to *first-degree* historical critiques, which are those that are only valid for a particular case because they only bear upon factual matters (e.g., "Since when have people engaged in this practice?" "In what era did people wear this dress?" "For how long has this festival been celebrated in this way?"). This type of critique is one that aims to invalidate baseless claims. But to attack a baseless claim is to denounce a *false* claim, which implies that there can also be true claims. Consider, for example a social

---

2. Ibid., 16.

3. Anne-Marie Thiesse, *La création des identités nationales: Europe XVIIIe-XXe siècle* (Paris: Les Éditions du Seuil, 1999).

climber's claim to be descended from an illustrious family. Imagine that this false noble, in order to bolster his claim, has acquired a gallery of ancestral portraits. The gallery is made up, then, of false portraits. Another possibility is that the portraits are real but are not of his relatives. Here again, in order to be able to apply the term "false portrait" to a painting, one must be able to give meaning to the notion of a true portrait. There cannot be forged Titians if there are no real ones, nor false noblemen if there are no real ones. You may well claim that, contrary to what is often repeated, such and such a tradition is in fact a recent invention. Yet to make that claim is also to accept that some traditions may be authentic. This possibility must be accepted *in principle*, even when it turns out that none are *in fact*. It so happens that the poet Ossian was a fabrication, but we are well aware of what it would have meant for the Scots to have been able to refer to an ancient national epic poem worthy of Homeric ones.

First-degree criticism is limited in another way as well. Using the same terms of comparison, we would say that people who claim to be of noble stock when in fact they are not do not have the genealogy that they claim. That, however, does not mean that they have no ancestors. Similarly, one might say that when it has been established that the collective identity claimed by a particular people is in fact a recent invention, this means that these people do not have the prestigious collective identity that they would like others to recognize today, but that does not mean that they do not in fact have a (less impressive) collective identity.

Historical critique can be carried out in a more radical way, however, putting into question the very idea of a "collective identity" and not merely the claims of certain individuals to have one. When a historian explains that history textbooks transmit nothing but a "national fiction" or even a "myth," the objection is not focused on this or that apocryphal fact but becomes a matter of principle. In that case, we would have to call it a *second-degree* critique. These two sorts of objections can be compared with the two possible critiques that might be leveled at a list of saints. A first-degree critique will claim that some of those on the list are figments who never existed. The conclusion would then be that they should be struck off the list. But one can also mount an entirely different critique that goes beyond the verification of a particular historical episode. Such a critique would consist in pointing out that sainthood is *necessarily* imaginary because one cannot be a saint without having been credited with carrying out miraculous cures and supernatural interventions—i.e., operations that are impossible according to our natural philosophy. There is therefore no person whose name can really appear on a list of saints. According to this second sort of critique, *every* list of this sort is necessarily legendary or mythical.

In the case that concerns us, this radical critique invokes a social philosophy. It thereby becomes sociological and puts into question the validity of the very concept of collective identity. "Of course," the critique runs, "people believe in their collective identities, but these ideas are false. They are even misleading, for they mask not only the scale of the changes that are constantly modifying their social life, but also the persistence of the conflicts and divisions that cut across their society." It is in similar terms that Peter Berger and Thomas Luckmann advise us to avoid the notion of "collective identity," which they deem dangerous.[4] To use the term, in their view, is to progress down a slope that leads to the *reification* of one's subject.

> The danger is present in greater or lesser degree in various works of the Durkheim school and the "culture and personality" school in American cultural anthropology.[5]

Berger and Luckmann speak a great deal about identity in their book, but they understand the term in the interactionist sense, which, as we know, goes against the way Erikson used the term. It is then not surprising to see them challenge the positions of the American anthropological school from which he derived some of his ideas.

The second-degree critiques put forward by historians see themselves as political. They mean to *unmask* a relation of domination that is *unnoticed* by those who are subjected to it. In doing so, they hope to reestablish a true awareness of the interests for which individuals ought to mobilize themselves. In this view, talk about collective identities has a

4. Peter L. Berger and Thomas Luckmann, *The Social Construction of Reality: A Treatise in the Sociology of Knowledge* (1966; New York: Penguin Books, 1971), 194.
5. Ibid., 233 n 40.

delusive effect, distracting people from the real conflicts.[6] What are these real conflicts? For some, those of the class struggle. For others, those of the individual struggle for survival. But whether this political critique sees itself as on the extreme left or on the extreme right, it rests on a social philosophy that is well summarized by Margaret Thatcher's famous declaration in a 1987 magazine interview: "Who is society? There is no such thing! There are individual men and women and there are families."[7] However, if human groups have no historical identity, then they have no historical existence, which means that they also cannot constitute objects for historians' investigations.

§§§ It is at this point that the question becomes philosophical. By becoming more radical, the critique has moved beyond the realm of empirical demonstrations. It will no longer be asked, "Is this claim confirmed by the work of historians?" (e.g., the claim that our nation was already in existence in antiquity or that the Moldavians are not Romanians, etc.). Instead, the question is, "Do we have a concept of group identity?" The radical critique claims that we have never needed such a concept.

In Chapter 1, I spoke about a linguistic trap that gave rise to a *sophistical refutation*, a form of self-refutation in which one falls into a sophist's trap all on one's own. Some historians have done exactly this—for example, the critics of national or regional identity mentioned by Pierre Nora. Such historians tell us that we must avoid speaking of the identity of a nation because to do so would encourage a static view of its history. They thereby set identity into opposition with *change*. But if they think that identity means a *quality* of permanence or invariance, then they have already surrendered to the sophists, who will not hesitate to point out to them that they will then have no right to say things such as "France has changed a great deal in the past ten years." Such a proposition purports to be about a single, selfsame country while at the same time maintaining that it has changed. It will then have changed while nevertheless remaining the same.

This sophism will no doubt appear ridiculous to you, but that is the

---

6. See, for example, Gérard Noiriel, *À quoi sert "l'identité nationale"?* (Marseille: Agone, 2007).

7. Margaret Thatcher, "Aids, Education, and the Year 2000!" (Interview by Douglas Keay), *Woman's Own* (October 31, 1987), 10.

case with every sophism once it has been fully revealed. This is why it is embarrassing to find it within the arguments offered by certain theorists who seek to debunk the myth of collective identity.

Historians who practice such second-degree critique will perhaps claim that history has become reflexive such that what concerns them is not the history of France but, rather, the history *of the history* of France. This amounts to seeking refuge in idealism, along the lines of the witty remark attributed to Léon Brunschvicg that "the history of Egypt is the history of Egyptology."[8] Yet this maneuver can only delay their eventual "sophistical refutation." If one cannot speak of what makes a country the same country, if the words "the same country" are meaningless because they are meant to *fix* a reality whose mode of being is historical—i.e., fluid and changing—then one can also not discuss what it is that people who think they are speaking about a selfsame country are really discussing. If the history of France has no object, neither does the history of the history of France.

The same sophistical trap ensnares *inconsistent* nominalist sociologists. What I am calling a nominalist sociologist is one who makes no distinction between a *nominal* group—for example, an administrative social category (such as the set of candidates for the *baccalauréat* this year or the set of people who made use of the lost-and-found service of the Paris metro last year)—and a *real* group. Of course, even for a nominalist sociologist, a human group is real in one way: it is made up of real people. But that does not make the group itself real *as a group*. For such a sociologist, there is nothing more in a human group than a plurality of human individuals. If this nominalist sociologist is consistent, he will refuse to say that certain groups are endowed with a group identity. To do so would be to reintroduce in disguised form what was to have been evacuated from his descriptions of the real: authentic groups that would be more than mere collections of individuals brought together within our representations. Indeed, Quine's golden rule—no entity without identity—can also be stated as "no identity without entity." This was the tenor of Karl Popper's condemnation of what he called the "essentialism" of holist historians, who believe it possible to write

---

8. Cited in Raymond Aron, *History and the Dialectic of Violence: An Analysis of Sartre's "Critique de la raison dialectique,"* trans. Barry Cooper (1973; Oxford: Basil Blackwell, 1975), 177.

histories of *historical totalities*. Because these historians are historians, they want to speak about changes that affect these human groups. But, they claim, such changes are attributable to the human groups whose history they reconstruct. In order for them to be able to attribute the changes to the groups whose history is made up of these changes, they will have to be able to find something in these groups that does not change: it must be the case that the history of a group does not alter its "essential identity."[9] And it is true that it is troublesome to have to say that a group can have a history and change only on condition that it does not change "in its essential identity." Consequently, for a nominalist thinker who rejects "essentialism" as stipulated by Popper, the history of a group is not strictly speaking *its* history in the way that my biography recounts *my* history; it is, rather, the history of the individual elements that we bring together within our representation under the label by which we designate the group.

However, there are also *inconsistent* nominalist sociologists who would ask us to accept the possibility of conceiving an impossible entity: a *nominal* group that would nevertheless have the mode of existence of a *real* one. Indeed, such a group, although it is in fact nominal, could have a history of its own. But in order to have a real history of its own, it must possess a diachronic identity. This is the lesson that the ancient Greeks derived from their discussions of the "Growing Argument": if a totality is nothing more than a collection of the elements of which it is composed at a given instant, this totality will disappear each time its composition changes. In fact, the inconsistent sociologist accepts this conclusion, claiming that the group has a *changeable identity*. As a result, if the identity of the group is changeable, then with each change the group in question will change into *another* group (of the same nature). Generally, a nominal group has no history, since the identity of a purely taxonomical class is a function of the identity of its members, such as can be set forth in an itemized list or inventory of the collection's elements. By contrast, a real group can have a history, since its identity is not given in the list of its members, allowing it to be maintained across generations. To speak about changeable identities is to inflict upon oneself the sophistical refutation made possible by the preposterous expression "an identity that is subject to change" that one nonetheless insists

---

9. Karl Popper, *The Poverty of Historicism* (1957; New York: Routledge, 2002), § 10 (28).

remains the identity of the group in question, allowing it to be continuously identified as being itself rather than another.

The notion of a "changeable identity" is indefensible for *logical* reasons. Of course, logic is not answerable for questions of existence. It cannot tell us if there are or are not human groups that are concrete totalities endowed with a history in the same way that nominalist sociologists think that each individual has his or her own history. On the other hand, logic can tell us what we will have to do in order to designate and refer to such groups if there turn out to be any.

The Analogy between a Person and a People

Contemporary social sciences present collective identity in various forms (cultural, religious, professional, national, etc.), but this proliferation serves to hide a lack of clarity in the very logic of the concept. To whom does such collective identity belong? Is having, say, a political identity an attribute *of the individual* (for example, the fact of being a citizen of a particular country)? Or is it an attribute *of the group* (for example, the fact that a certain group wishes to define itself in political rather than religious terms)? In fact, the question of a collective identity ("Who are we?") is raised by analogy with the question of personal identity ("Who am I?"), and it is this analogy that ought to serve as our guide. Pascal puts this analogy to use when he writes:

> Time heals pain and quarrels, because we change: we are no longer the same person; neither the offender nor the offended are the same. It is like a people whom we have angered and have come back to see after two generations: they are still the French, but not the same.[10]

In this fragment, Pascal indulges in a variation on a well-known rhetorical theme in the genre of the *consolation*: time heals all wounds. He develops this theme in an original way, though, by reversing the meaning of the equally classic analogy between a person and a people. Here, the

10. Blaise Pascal, *Pensées and Other Writings*, trans. Honor Levi, ed. Anthony Levi (Oxford: Oxford University Press, 1995), 146 (Sellier, § 653; Brunschvicg, § 122; Lafuma, § 802) [translation modified].

change in generations is used to illuminate the changes in personal feelings.

The ground for this analogy is the possibility of attributing feelings to a people. It is possible to *anger* a people and even to *offend* one. Is Pascal claiming that peoples have a psychology, that they experience feelings of pride or humiliation, that there are phenomena of collective memory and forgetting? If so, one would have to grant peoples not only a diachronic identity, but something like a personality in the psychological sense of self-consciousness. Is Pascal's attribution here literal or metaphorical?

Of course we understand perfectly well the sentence that tells us that this people has been angered and has taken offense. So it is with Rousseau recounting the difficulties caused by his *Letter on French Music*: "The *Letter on Music* was treated seriously and raised the whole nation against me, for this attack on its music was taken as an insult."[11] He writes, "the whole Nation," but of course only men of letters, musicians, and the "public" are concerned, and certainly not the heart of the country.[12] It is thus not a matter of numbers but rather of collective identity. The great minds who took offense at the *Letter* were offended as Frenchmen, not as musicians or as men of letters.

We are more accustomed to seeing the analogy move in the other direction; a people is in some regards like a person and has feelings of pride. Normally, we *personify* a people. Here, Pascal is doing the opposite: he is *collectivizing* the individual person by presenting it as a succession of generations. *It is like a people whom we have angered and have come back to see after two generations: they are still the French, but not the same.* The key to the comparison is clearly in the last sentence. After many years, we run across someone with whom we once had a dispute. In one sense, the person is not the same; he has changed so much that you would think him *another* person. Yet it is in fact he, because we call him by the

---

11. Jean-Jacques Rousseau, *The Confessions*, trans. J. M. Cohen (New York: Penguin Books, 1953), 358.

12. In *Rousseau, Judge of Jean-Jacques*, Rousseau invents a character, *the Frenchman*, who is supposed to represent the nation. This fictitious interlocutor will have "the traits that his whole nation eagerly displays toward me." Jean-Jacques Rousseau, *Rousseau, Judge of Jean-Jacques: Dialogues*, ed. Roger D. Masters and Christopher Kelly, trans. Judith R. Bush, Christopher Kelly, and Roger D. Masters (Hanover, NH: University Press of New England, 1990), 5.

same name. In short, it is the same person, and this is why the change in his feelings is so striking, since he reacts as if he had been replaced by an entirely different person.

§§§ When one returns to France after two generations, the name that is appropriate for the inhabitants of the country remains the same: they are *the French*. This is the question then: is it the identity of the name that creates the identity of the thing named, with the result that collective identity is a linguistic effect? This hypothesis would satisfy nominalist sociologists. We may speak about "seeing the same people again," but, the nominalist will claim, this is only because we *act as if* there were a continuity. When one sees a people again (one that is still referred to as "the French"), not one of the individuals who played a role in the first encounter still remains. It is the observer and his way of speaking that produces the linguistic appearance of the permanence of the French nation. Allowing the attribute of nationality to be transferred from one generation to the next creates the illusion of a people who never leave the stage.

Or should we not rather recognize that, in saying that those newly encountered are still the French, we mean exactly what we seem to be saying—namely, that we are dealing with a selfsame people? We will then make clear that a people is defined precisely by the fact that generations follow one another and that these generations, through the effect of such succession, are but a single people. When children replace their parents and their grandparents, it is not a case of a new people that comes to replace the group that was previously occupying the place but, rather, precisely the way in which a people persists in existence. This sort of renewal of the generations therefore cannot be likened to the mutations by which a particular people become *a different people* than what they once were. One should instead be reminded of the way in which a river maintains its existence through the uninterrupted renewal of its waters.

Pascal does not come down on the side of either of these hypotheses. He nevertheless indicates the way forward. In order to understand the logic of the attribution of a collective identity, we will have to examine the way in which we designate the collective entity to which we either attribute (in the view of a realist sociologist) or pretend to attribute (according to the nominalist sociologist) an identity of its own. We will therefore have to examine the way in which we give proper names to collective entities and historical totalities.

The Logic of Collective Bodies

I turn now to the *Port-Royal Logic*, a work in which our problem is broached in an altogether remarkable way. Arnauld and Nicole first take up the Greek paradoxes about the diachronic identity of material things in order to come to an account of the logic of historical propositions concerning such things. Their conclusion is a radical one: *material individuals have no history*. After reaching this conclusion, they derive from it consequences concerning the moral psychology of collective identities—i.e., regarding the way in which individuals bizarrely find their self-esteem fulfilled by their belonging to what they believe to be a historical community.

As one would expect, Arnauld and Nicole approach the question of collective identities from the logical point of view that is provided by the analysis of the propositions we formulate about entities (here, collective entities). In two chapters of the work, the authors discuss the discrepancy that can sometimes be observed between the grammatical and logical forms of a proposition.[13] In logic, a "singular proposition" is one in which the subject of predication is designated by name or identified in one way or another by a "singular term" that serves to identify it as an individual (for example, by its proper name, if we know one for it, or by an indexical expression such as "this body," "this animal," etc.).

Certain sentences in ordinary language seem to be singular propositions yet are not singular from a logical point of view. Other sentences do not appear to be singular because they are in the plural, but must be analyzed by the logician as having the form of a singular proposition. There are thus two separate cases to be considered.

The first case: a proposition that *seems* singular but in reality is not. Arnauld and Nicole give an example here that comes directly from the discussions about Epicharmus's arguments. We say of an animal that it has grown, that it has put on weight; we therefore speak of it as if it were, from one moment to the next and from its birth until its death, the

---

13. Antoine Arnauld and Pierre Nicole, *Logic or the Art of Thinking*, trans. and ed. Jill Vance Buroker (Cambridge: Cambridge University Press, 1996), Chapters 12–13 (111–119).

same body. However, the authors point out, we know that the matter of this body is constantly being renewed. We know this yet have not reformed our way of speaking to reflect it.

> For ordinary language allows us to say: the body of this animal was composed of certain particles of matter ten years ago, and now it is composed of entirely different particles. There seems to be a contradiction in this way of speaking, for if the parts are all different, then it is not the same body. This is true, but we still talk about it as the same body.[14]

This animal is a material totality. At every moment, this totality changes in its composition (such that, after a certain time, its matter will have been entirely replaced). Yet our proposition is constructed such that it seems to bear on a single individual even though it in fact bears upon several distinct individuals. Whence the logical problem. If one remains within appearances, the proposition is singular—i.e., it tells us about *this animal* in particular. Yet the predicate that we want to apply to the subject excludes this very possibility, "for if the parts are all different, then it is not the same body." The authors conclude that the logical subject of such a proposition—"this animal"—is equivocal, that it is a "confused subject" that takes the place of two distinct subjects.

They propose that we consider the proposition to be singular only in appearance. In reality, the proposition bears upon two subjects: an animal that existed ten years ago and another animal that is today its distant successor. They write, "What makes these propositions legitimate is that the same term is taken for different subjects by being applied differently."[15] In other words, the phrase "the body of this animal" is not really a singular term, but rather a term for a succession of entities. It is as if, when attending a parade of brass bands at a votive festival in the village, I point out the passing groups one by one while saying in turns "This band is from Plougonvelin," "This band is from Locmaria-Plouzané," and so on.

The authors then derive from this what we would today call a "thinking of difference" whose application they nevertheless restrict to

14. Ibid., 112.
15. Ibid.

the material world (thereby leaving intact the diachronic identity of souls and minds). How does it happen that we speak about two bodies as if there were only one? The reason is that their succession does not happen all at once but is gradual and imperceptible. The critique of the concept of identity carried out by the Port-Royal logicians therefore amounts to saying this: in ordinary language, a sufficient resemblance between two successive objects in the same place is enough for us to say that we are dealing with a single, selfsame object.

The consequence is that physical bodies have no history because their only diachronic identity is that resulting from the identity of their material parts. The authors illustrate this by taking the example of the Emperor Augustus's aphorism about Rome:

> Augustus said that he found the city of Rome made of brick and left it made of marble. Similarly, we say about a city, a house, or a church, that it was destroyed at a certain time and rebuilt at another. So which Rome was once made of brick and another time made of marble? Which cities, houses, or churches were destroyed at one time and rebuilt at another? Was the Rome made of brick the same as the Rome made of marble? No, but this does not prevent the mind from forming a certain confused idea of Rome to which it attributes these two qualities, namely being made of brick at one time and of marble at another.[16]

A city (or, for that matter, any building whatsoever) is the epitome of a composite body whose material components do not persist through time. Yet we use the same word "Rome" for the various momentary urban wholes that follow one another in the same place. And here, unlike in the previous examples, Arnauld and Nicole contend that our ordinary way of speaking reveals an intellectual confusion. The mind formulates a "confused idea" of an entity that admits of the two predicates. The idea is confused because one cannot conceive of a city being entirely made of brick and at the same time entirely made of marble.

The authors' metaphysics has as a consequence that a material body cannot be the subject of a change in its material composition. If this is the case, it seems that one is forced to conclude that the only

---

16. Ibid.

individuals that are able to have a history of their own are *spiritual* individuals. If Rome were to have a history, it would have to be more than a material entity; there would have to be something like an immaterial identity of Rome that would maintain the city as itself throughout its material history.

§§ Let us now take up the second case of a proposition whose logical and grammatical forms are discordant—a proposition that does not *appear* to be singular when, in reality, it is. The authors give this example of a proposition bearing on an entity presented as being collective: "The Romans conquered the Carthaginians."[17]

In this case, the logician confronts a difficulty that is basically the opposite of the one in the previous example. In the case of the city that is first demolished and then rebuilt, the proposition seemed to be referring to a single object, but the meaning seemed to require that it be considered to be two objects sequentially occupying the same location. The proposition about the Romans and the Carthaginians has exactly the opposite difficulty. The sentence is grammatically in the plural, yet, for the logician, it must be understood as a proposition in the singular that refers to a single individual. Consequently, the authors point out, the subject is in reality in the singular.

> The nouns "body," "community," and "people," when taken collectively as they usually are for the entire body, an entire community, and all the people, cause the propositions they occur in, properly speaking, to be neither universal nor, even less, particular, but rather singular.[18]

The reasoning of the Port-Royal logicians is incontestable. First, the proposition cannot be held to be *universal* because it does not speak of each of the Romans, as if one could claim, "Gaius is a Roman citizen and therefore he conquered the Carthaginians" and claim it even though Gaius was not yet born when the battle took place. The proposition does not say that if someone is Roman then he was present at the victory over the Carthaginians. But it also cannot be taken to be a *particular*

---

17. Ibid., 119.
18. Ibid.

proposition, as if it said that there are *some* Romans who conquered the Carthaginians. *The Romans* are being discussed, not some particular group of Romans. They are not being discussed as they would be in a universal proposition, but rather as a historical totality, for they are brought together within a singular subject of predication that Arnauld and Nicole call a "moral person." When one makes such statements, according to our logicians, "each people is considered as a moral person who endures for several centuries, which subsists insofar as it makes up a state, and which acts at all times by those who compose it, just as people act by the members of their bodies."[19]

Thus, the logical form of the proposition excludes the possibility that it is speaking, in the plural, about several people. It requires that we understand it as bearing on a single entity, a single object bearing a collective name such as "the Romans," "Rome," "the Roman people." This name is used as the proper name of a *moral person* (a term whose history will be of great interest to us and to which I will return below).

It is only because the proposition is singular that we can conceive of the individual about which it speaks—the Romans—as having a history that is common to multiple successive generations. The authors explain this:

> As a result, we say that the Romans, who were conquered by the Gauls who took Rome, conquered the Gauls in Caesar's time. Thus we attribute to this same term "Romans" both being conquered at one time and being victorious at another, although there were no Romans living at one of those times who lived at the other time.[20]

For the Port-Royal logicians, it goes as a matter of course that it is only as a fiction or a linguistic convention that we speak of the Romans as a single moral person endowed with a diachronic identity. It is only by imagining Rome with an immaterial body that the history of Rome can be told as that of a single people, of an immortal person able to persist over centuries thanks to the successive generations of Romans.

It might be claimed that the authors give up any possibility of Rome having a history—for example, the history of its *expansion*, the history of

19. Ibid.
20. Ibid.

its *embellishment*, etc. For them, that is the price to be paid in order to avoid a confused conception of Roman "narrative identity," one that seeks to maintain that a change in the material composition of a collective body is a *change in its identity* while also retaining the possibility of there being a history of the Roman people. Is it the same people from one century to the next? In one sense no, because it changes in its composition. Is something preserved? Yes, but what is preserved can only be an immaterial body (whether it is called the soul, the self, or "identity"). Only a dualistic conception allows for the combination of discontinuity and continuity in this way. Yet this dualism is confused, for the immaterial element that survives the succession of generations appears to be an immortal body—in other words, a body made of an immaterial material.

§§ Having come to this *logical* conclusion—that the proposition in question is singular and bears on a moral person—the authors then become moralists, deriving a second lesson about the feelings of vanity one might derive from belonging to a people. They draft a moral psychology of identity.

> This exposes the grounds of vanity people derive from the fine actions of their nation in which they took no part, which is as foolish as for a deaf ear to glory in the eye's liveliness or in the skill of the hand.[21]

It would be a mark of mental confusion, on the part of Romans today, to consider themselves to be the Romans of yesteryear who triumphed over the Carthaginians. Such a confusion boils down to taking literally what is only a manner of speaking: attributing to an entity called Rome—rather than to a few men in particular—the credit for a victory. This is an illusion that our authors, had they lived in the twentieth century, would no doubt have called, following Jacques Lacan, an *imaginary* identification—i.e., a form of self-satisfaction.

According to the authors, this illusion is the basis for the feeling of pride experienced by those who continue to celebrate a past victory today as if they could appropriate it. Someone may delight in the victory

---

21. Ibid.

of one group over another, but it cannot be a source of pride or glory for him if he had nothing to do with it. Indeed, it is a logical condition for feelings such as pride or vanity that the subject must have appropriated for himself the events that elicit these feelings. I can only be proud of myself or of what in one way or another is part of me. How can today's Romans appropriate for themselves the result of a battle that they could not have participated in, as it took place before they were born? The absurdity is reflected in the authors' comparison: it is as if the ear congratulated itself for the qualities of the eye or the hand.

Yet this comparison reveals precisely the limits of a critique of identity that does not go to the crucial logical point, namely these questions: to what was the proper name "Rome" given? How do we use these names that are "taken collectively" ("Rome," "the Romans," "the Roman people")?

Arnauld and Nicole compare the pride of today's Romans in the glory of their ancestors with a deaf ear that wants to take credit for the operations of a sharp eye or a nimble hand. The identification that they condemn is the result of a mental confusion: individual A is the victim of an illusion about himself when he takes himself to be another individual, B, and believes himself to have carried out the actions of B. The denunciation is thus limited to identifications among different parts of a body. Yet the representation of a people as a body persisting through time much as a river does, through the succession of individuals replacing one another, should be analyzed by identifying both the Romans of yesteryear and those of today with *a single, selfsame people* that both groups call "Rome." The relation that the victors' descendants have with their fathers passes through the unity of the people considered as a single body. It is because *Rome* was victorious when the ancestors were victorious that the Romans of today—to the extent that they see themselves as having the collective identity of the Roman people—can derive sentiments of pride from the history of that people. They are therefore like a deaf ear that is happy to belong to a body whose eye is sharp and whose hand is nimble, qualities that allow this body to see and grasp objects well, even if it does not hear well.

It follows that the criticism of misplaced vanity collapses: when Romans are proud of Rome, they attribute to themselves no other quality than that of being members of that city (and certainly not qualities that belong to their ancestors). It is possible that some frivolous Romans treat such membership as a source of vanity, but normally they will instead feel obligated to live up to the model provided by the ancients and to communicate to their descendants what they themselves have received from those who preceded them.

There is an important difference between the examples of the growing animal and the rebuilt city, on the one hand, and that of the Romans who remember the great deeds of their past, on the other. Fido the dog clearly exhibits a will to live and sometimes also, at least during puppyhood, a joy in living, but it is only figuratively that we might refer to any attachment on his part to his "identity" (by which we might perhaps mean the feeling he has of belonging to our family). Fido the dog does not say, "I am Fido." By contrast, the Romans say to us in their speech, in their monuments, in their ceremonies, "We are the Romans." Arnauld and Nicole interpret this affirmation as a sign of self-deception, one that metaphysical critique must eliminate. Yet if one takes into account the fact that the moral person's proper name is used in the first person, one will see it rather as manifesting a *will to be oneself*, a will to name oneself in conformity with a collective representation of oneself—one that allows each Roman to envisage a collective history in which her own individual existence participates.

Consequently, one must ask the people who give themselves a collective name what the identity criterion is for the application of this proper name. I will examine in turn two ways of conceiving of collective identity through the determination of such a criterion: first, a medieval conception of an identity through time of the "moral person"; then, the Aristotelian conception of an identity of the political community.

The Moral Person as Fictive Person

In the course of his investigation into the British concept of the corporation, an investigation that led him to write his great book on the king's two bodies, Ernst Kantorowicz was led to draw up the genealogy of the concept of a "moral person."[22] Medieval glossators and jurists drew from three sources in elaborating this concept, of which only the

---

22. Ernst Kantorowicz, *The King's Two Bodies: A Study in Mediaeval Political Theology* (1957; Princeton: Princeton University Press, 1981).

theological source is properly medieval. The two others are Roman law and the Greek metaphysics of physical bodies.

The theological notion of a "mystical body" gives content to the maxim that the church never dies, *Ecclesia nunquam moritur.*[23] The universal church is a mystical body. Kantorowicz stresses that this does not mean that the community of the faithful is represented as an organism, i.e., a "natural body." What is distinctive about a "mystical body" is that it can act at all times (as we have seen, the *Port-Royal Logic* will make that a feature of the "moral person"). As Thomas Aquinas put it, the members of a natural body are contemporaries of one another, while the members of a mystical body exist in succession, which assures this body's perpetual existence.[24] It follows that a mystical body only has its future members in the mode of potential beings. Indeed, the Church has a universal vocation: all future generations are called to join it. This requires us to conceive of a totality *endowed with a future.* This totality includes in advance human beings who are not yet born and who, for the most part, will not be born for centuries. There can therefore be no question of identifying these future individuals. They are not individuals who are *already constituted* and for whom present existence was all that was missing. Rather, they are future possibilities that can only be specified vaguely. And because these "possible individuals" cannot be identified, one cannot reduce such a social totality to a collection of individuals in the way the nominalist sociologist would have it.

The Roman legal source furnishes, through the idea of the *lex regia*, the idea of a prerogative or a *dignitas* that can never come to an end, thereby assuring its holder of the same perpetuity: *Populus romanus non moritur.*[25] The reference to the *lex regia* will have to be supplemented by another to which I will return, for Yan Thomas has shown how medieval

---

23. Ibid., 292.

24. Thomas Aquinas writes: "The difference between the natural body of a man and the mystical body of the Church is that the members of a natural body all exist together, whereas members of the mystical body do not.... So people can be classed as members of the mystical body because of their potentiality, and not merely when they are actually in it" [... *haec est differentia inter corpus hominis naturale et corpus Ecclesiae mysticum, quod membra corporis naturalis sunt omnia simul, membra autem corporis mystici non sunt omnia simul.... Sic igitur membra corporis mystici non solum accipiuntur secundum quod sunt in actu, sed etiam secundum quod sunt in potentia.*] Thomas Aquinas, *Summa Theologiae*, vol. 49 (3a. 7-15), *The Grace of Christ*, ed. and trans. Liam G. Walsh O. P. (Cambridge: Cambridge University Press, 1974) 3a, q. 8, a. 3 (60-63). Cited by Kantorowicz, *The King's Two Bodies*, 308 n 85.

25. Kantorowicz, *The King's Two Bodies*, 294-295.

glossators drew from the Roman law of succession in the construction of the notion of a "moral personality" of organized collectivities.

But our topic here is not a historical one. What matters most to us is the philosophical source. We know where the subtle metaphysical distinctions used by the medieval glossators come from, since they are the very ones that arose out of the "Growing Argument" in both Epicharmus's version and the version known as the Ship of Theseus. They applied to their problem a hylomorphic distinction: the *matter* of the people is constantly changing, but the *form* is maintained. This distinction allows one to refer to the same Ship of Theseus even though all of the wooden parts have been replaced. Kantorowicz cites an author (Baldus, himself glossing the work of the glossator Accursius) who explicitly states the principle of the solution: *ubi non mutatur forma rei, non dicitur mutari res* [where the form of a thing does not change, the thing itself is said not to change].[26] The texts of the gloss refer to the series of canonical examples in discussions of diachronic identity: the identity of a city, a tribunal, a legion, a boat, a herd of sheep, etc.

What can this unchanging form be? The Scholastics of the time provided two solutions, and it would appear that the jurists availed themselves sometimes of one and sometimes of the other, depending on the cause they were defending. Kantorowicz presents these two solutions as follows, taking as his example the city of Bologna, which at the time was a main center of juridical thought.

The *realist* solution (in the medieval sense of a realism of universals) is one that they might have derived from Scotism. This would have involved explanation through what Duns Scotus called "formalities," thereby positing an individuating form, meaning not just an *individual* essence of the city of Bologna, but an essence *individuated by itself* independently of any material reality. Indeed, Duns Scotus's doctrine allows for the following reasoning: just as Socrates is and remains himself (after the complete replacement of all of his corporeal matter) because he possesses *Socratitas*, so the *populus Bononiensis* is and always remains the same people (after the complete replacement of its population) because it possesses *Bononitas* ("Bolognity").[27] The theory is thus one of the individuation of entities through individual differences in form. There then remains the task of providing a content to the abstract

---

26. Ibid., 295.
27. Ibid., 303.

notion of a form that is somehow meant to confer individuality upon a city. For the invocation of *bononitas* risks being as empty a gesture as that by which people today invoke a *Frenchness* or *Britishness* or *Japaneseness* or *Turkishness* in order to give substance to the affirmation of a national identity. In fact, it is exactly the same doctrine of collective identity that is condemned (and with reason) by those who see it as an "essentialist" conception. If there is no other way to provide Bologna with an identity over time than to make it the empirical vehicle of *bononitas*—i.e., of the formal and ineffable difference that explains the fact that there is but one city of Bologna in the world—then it would seem that, for want of any less abstract diachronic identity, we will henceforth have to forgo saying that Bologna has a glorious history and that one can still find there the famous university that was founded in the twelfth century. We are thus stymied.

Here is the *nominalist* solution: human communities as such are intellectual fictions, creations of language. The *personification* of a collective being is nothing but a manner of speaking. Nevertheless, the fictions put forward by jurists may give rise to illusions, and we run the risk of taking such purely fictive hypostases seriously and of behaving toward them as if they were real. As Kantorowicz reminds us, Pope Innocent IV was forced to issue a serious clarification and to solemnly declare at the First Council of Lyon (1245) that it was impossible to excommunicate colleges and other human groups taken as bodies—a *universitas* is only a *nomen intellectuale*, not a real person.[28] A moral person cannot be punished, because it is nothing but a "fictive person" (*persona ficta*).

Kantorowicz underscores that this medieval personification of a city is distinct from both ancient personification and modern personification. Properly speaking, ancient cities were not personified but rather associated with the personal figure of a god that the city worshipped.[29] Moreover, in the Middle Ages, historical communities were not represented as human persons with anthropomorphic traits as would become common in modern times.

§§ There was never a question of granting a *persona ficta* the psychological faculties of a real "natural person": self-consciousness, personal

---

28. Ibid., 305–306.
29. Ibid., 303–304.

feelings, and thus an entire psychology of identity. But what happens when this notion of a collective person enters into the common consciousness? How is the collective person represented in the consciousness of the individuals who are its members? The affirmation of a collective identity—e.g., "we are the Romans"—presupposes that an individual can *identify* with a group. Is such an operation an illusion, indicative of some confusion on the individual's part, as the Port-Royal logicians believed?

In order to answer this question, I will rely on an example of a juridical difficulty that Yan Thomas discusses in a study of Roman laws of succession, which is one of the sources of the notion of a "moral person."[30] I will begin by summarizing Thomas's presentation of the difficulty. One might begin with the following juridical event: it so happens that a collective entity—a city, a monastery, or a university, for example—has borrowed money from individuals or other cities. The jurist must explain how it is that flesh-and-blood individuals can enter into juridical relations with collective entities and how the latter can have juridical relations among themselves. It was in order to resolve this problem that medieval glossators turned toward Roman law.

The Romans never dreamed of conferring moral personhood on collective entities such as cities. Nevertheless, they recognized the possibility for such entities to possess, acquire, or dispose of goods and to borrow money and repay debts. From the creditor's point of view, a city appears to be the subject of a juridical relation. Such a creditor will want to know exactly who is in debt to him. Roman jurisconsults attempted to clear up this point. Who is obliged to pay the city's debts? Their answer is that the creditor cannot have recourse against the city's citizens, because the money was lent to the city itself and not to the citizens of that city. The city's debts are not the debts of the city's citizens.

In order to refine their thinking on the matter and to bring out clearly the distinction in question, Roman jurists imagined the hypothetical case of a city all of whose inhabitants have disappeared save one.[31] Is it the case that this last citizen inherits the assets and debts of the city, much as does the last living member of a group that jointly owned a

---

30. Yan Thomas, *Les opérations du droit* (Paris: Gallimard/Seuil, 2011).
31. Ibid., 110–111 and Chapter 8.

property? Is he, as the last survivor, the last legal successor? Not at all, according to the jurisconsults. In that situation, it will not be said that a human plurality has been reduced so as to consist in a single human unit. Rather, it will be said that the city now has only one spokesperson, that there is now but a single surviving citizen to bear the *nomen universitatis* (the name of the social totality). If this last survivor must uphold the city's rights or honor the city's debts, he does it not as a particular individual but insofar as he is the only one able to act in the city's name.

Medieval glossators took up this hypothetical example of a collectivity whose members have all disappeared bar one. How can a collective entity (for example, a monastery or a college) survive when it has been materially reduced to a single natural person? To the Roman idea of *nomen universitatis*,[32] medieval jurists add the idea of *representation*. The city is a *moral* person that is *represented* by natural (flesh and blood) persons. The difficult cases raised above are ones where there is a shortage of natural people. In the case cited, there is but a single representative. The same glossators extended their thinking to a case in which the collective persists in the absence of any surviving member. As Yan Thomas shows, these juridical speculations are at the origin of our juridical—and subsequently political—concept of the representation of a collective by a person.

§§ How does one move from medieval "moral personhood" to our notion of "collective identity"? We would have to be able to question the last survivor of a collective—the last citizen, the last monk, the last of the Mohicans, etc.—in order to ask him how matters appear to him. How does he distinguish between what falls to him as an individual (in virtue of his personal identity) and what falls to him insofar as he bears the *nomen universitatis*? One thing is clear: the group of which he is the representative must have an identity *independent of him* for him to be able to claim to be the (last) member and act in its name. Thus the notion of a collective identity is well and truly that of the identity of a group. Indeed, the name of the collective body (whether Rome,

---

32. Yan Thomas cites the solution reached by Ulpien (Ibid., 299 n 13). In the Middle Ages, the word *universitas* refers to any kind of human collectivity, regardless of its unifying principle (e.g., a city, a religious order, a university, etc.).

Bologna, the University of the Sorbonne) is given to a group and not to particular individuals. This name continues to serve to designate the group even where this group has been reduced to a single member or no members at all.

We must therefore once again return to the logic of the proper name (*nomen universitatis*). When we sign a contract by which we make a commitment to the city of Bologna (for example, to lend it money), it will be important that we agree on the semantic value of the proper name. Is the name of the city given to the set of its inhabitants or to the city as such? In the first case, the community of Bologna would be nothing but a *societas*, which is dissolved (perhaps in order that another be formed) as soon as one of its members retires or disappears in some way or another. In the second case, the identity of the city does not depend on the personal identity of its members. We want to know how we are to use the name "Bologna" in the future. We therefore require an identity criterion in order to provide a content to the phrase "the same city." And this identity criterion cannot be derived from the simple notion of a *bononitas* understood as an ineffable individual form. On this point, Aristotle's thinking will allow us to go further.

The Historical Identity of a City

In Book III of the *Politics* (1276a10–13), Aristotle asks this question: is a city-state that has undergone a change of regime responsible for the debts of the old regime? At the time, the subject was a topical one, since the Athenians were discussing whether they should pay back the loan made by the Spartans to the Thirty Tyrants (who were expelled in 403 BC). Reducing the issue to the main juridical point, the question was: is it the city itself that incurred the debt, or should one instead decide that democratic Athens has nothing to do with the oligarchic regime? It is important that the city here appear to be able to accomplish juridical operations such as going into debt, signing contracts, repaying, etc. Here we again find the juridical idea highlighted by Yan Thomas according to which the city must be assured of having the juridical status of a discrete agent such that a distinction can be drawn between the debts of the citizens and those of the city itself.

Should democratic Athens pay the debts of the Athens of the tyrants? Aristotle does not answer the legal question in this text, indicating only that it will have to be taken up later. Instead, he treats it as an opportunity to raise a more general question, specifically one in social metaphysics: how do we distinguish a city that is the same as it was before—a city that has persisted—from a new city that has replaced the one that preceded it in a certain spot (1276a17–19)? What is our criterion?

Aristotle considers several conceivable criteria that he rejects in turn. First he has to dispense with a purely topographical criterion according to which the identity of the city results from the identity of the territory. The territory cannot be sufficient to confer an identity on the city because, according to Aristotle, even if one surrounded the Peloponnese by a wall, that would not make a *polis* of it. He illustrates the point by citing the case of a putative city that does not merit the word *"polis,"* drawing a distinction between mere "peoples" or "tribes" (*ethnē*) and true "cities" (*poleis*). During the taking of Babylon by the army of Cyrus the Great, it took three days for news of the enemy's entry into peripheral neighborhoods to reach the neighborhoods in the center. In other words, such a collectivity lacks the moral and political unity characteristic of cities (1276a27–29).

One must also set aside a purely associative criterion according to which "the same city" means the same associated individuals. Aristotle rejects this atomistic criterion for two reasons. First, the city remains the same even when citizens are born and die. The city in this regard is like a river, which is still the same river despite the water's flow (1276a37). Second, the same individuals can form different collective entities, as would happen, according to Aristotle, if the same people sometimes formed a tragic chorus and sometimes a comic chorus (1276b5). The same people would be involved, but they would constitute two different choruses.

As a result, the question asked in this chapter is reduced to the question of what we understand by the word "city" (*polis*). This word is used in several senses (1276a23–24). To determine which of these senses we will make use of is thereby to determine an identity criterion for judgments such as "It is the same city." Aristotle has rejected the criterion of the material identity of the constituent units of the city. He therefore derives his criterion from what he calls the city's "form of composition" (*eidos tēs syntheseōs*, 1276b8). What makes up the "community of citizens" is the way in which those citizens are positioned or arranged relative to one another by the *politeia* of the city.

We translate the Greek word *politeia* as "constitution." But for us the word "constitution" calls to mind questions of constitutional law: is our regime parliamentary or presidential? What are the prerogatives of this or that public authority? We therefore think first of political institutions in the narrow sense of the term. The questions taken up by Aristotle when he discusses constitutions are considerably more vast. Today, one would not expect a professor of constitutional law to take up questions such as those Aristotle discusses in Book VII of the *Politics*: the relation between our constitution and our idea of happiness. The concept of *politeia* is inseparable from a concept of the public good. Here, it would be a mistake to set in opposition the idealizing perspective of ancient philosophers (who ask, for example, "What is the best conceivable political regime?") and the scientific or descriptive perspective of the moderns. Aristotle's position is not so much "normative" as it is anthropological. Aristotle is here adumbrating a program for a comparative sociology (which of course does not prevent him from also asking the practical question of what the best regime is for us). He is looking to determine what it is that the laws and institutions of a people *tend toward* (1324b5 and following), noting that some peoples valorize domination in war, while others valorize wealth, etc. On this occasion, he does not shy away from including in his philosophical reflections on the *politeia* an examination of customs and pedagogical institutions (*paideia*). In Carthage, he observes, the men wear decorative bracelets that indicate the number of military campaigns they have participated in. Among the Scythians and Iberians, a man worthy of the name is a warrior who has killed enemy warriors, an act that is marked by various demeaning procedures meant to indicate to those who have not yet killed anyone what it is that remains for them to do.

When Aristotle makes the identity of the *politeia* the identity criterion of the *polis*, the former should not be understood in the narrow sense of a political regime but in a broad sense as the entire set of laws and customs, a "disposition of the city" (*diathesis poleōs*, 1324a17) that expresses its general conception of the good. One might here follow Montesquieu in speaking of "the purpose of a state," a concept with which, in *The Spirit of the Laws*, he introduces his encomium to what he calls "the constitution of England," whose purpose, according to him, is liberty.[33]

But to invoke *paideia* and customs—i.e., what today we would call the cultural identity of the city—is to make reference to citizens as the agents of their own identity. At the outset, the question was what parts of its historical past the city would be responsible for. The response seems to be as follows: it is for the Athenians to decide in what sense they name themselves Athenian citizens, and the burden is on them to make other peoples—especially their external creditors—accept the criterion that they have set down for the identity of their city. Aristotle thus gives to the question of the *identity criterion* the added dimension of a question asked in the first-person plural. It is not enough to ask, "What is it that makes the city of today the same as that of yesterday?" The city would have to *accept* being the same city. What is therefore required is for the Athenians themselves to ask, "What is it that makes us Athenians?" And the Athenian *polis* will have to get the peoples that surround it to accept it as what it wants to be.

A Sociological Definition of the Nation

Is the distinction that Aristotle draws between a *polis* and an *ethnos* not typical of an ancient Greek's way of seeing the world, one that exalts his own form of society and disparages others as mere "tribes"? Is the *identity criterion* that sets down the meaning of the concept of a civic political community (*polis*) not somewhat anachronistic? According to this criterion, a *polis* presents the unity of an independent whole toward the external world, a unity lacking in the case of Babylon, for example. Babylon does not rise to the level of a city, as it is nothing but a wall

---

33. "Although all states have the same purpose in general, which is to maintain themselves, yet each state has a purpose that is peculiar to it. Expansion was the purpose of Rome; war, that of Lacedaemonia; religion, that of the Jewish laws; commerce, that of Marseilles; public tranquility, that of the laws of China; navigation, that of the laws of the Rhodians; natural liberty was the purpose of the police of the savages; in general, the delights of the prince are the purpose of the despotic states; his glory and that of his state, that of monarchies; the independence of each individual is the purpose of the laws of Poland, and what results from this is the oppression of all. There is also one nation in the world whose constitution has political liberty for its direct purpose." Montesquieu, *The Spirit of the Laws*, ed. and trans. Anne M. Cohler, Basia C. Miller, and Harold S. Stone (Cambridge: Cambridge University Press, 1989), Book 11, Chapter 5 (156).

sheltering an *ethnos*. This is illustrated by the anecdote according to which an entire part of the population was unaware that Babylon had fallen two days previously and continued on as if nothing had changed.

It is noteworthy that Marcel Mauss takes up this criterion and this example for his own use in his important essay on *the nation*.[34] Mauss's aim in this text is to put forward a *sociological* definition of the nation. This sociological view should serve both to enrich political theory and, especially, to eliminate various intellectual mystifications concerning the political form of a modern society.

Underlying Mauss's reflections on this subject, there is of course the entire experience of the nineteenth century, culminating in the Great War. Can such conflicts be explained through the political phenomenon of the nation-state? According to Mauss, this viewpoint is too cursory and based on an inadequate understanding of the sociological characteristics that are proper to the political arrangement called "a nation." Our talk about the nation-state remains too abstract, which does not help us understand the conflicts, difficulties, and crises that arise whenever one attempts to apply the "principle of nationalities" and accede to claims of national independence. Not all contemporary states are national states in the sociological sense of the term, even where they are such for the diplomats and political scientists who hold to the juridical criteria for national independence. Mauss defines his aim in this essay as follows: "to determine what sorts of society merit the name 'nation.'"[35] To say this is to announce that not every independent society merits this description, even in the case of its having been admitted to the League of Nations or the United Nations. All previous and current human societies have had and do have a unity, but only modern societies locate this unity in a *political* definition of what distinguishes them from others.

How should the national form of a society be defined sociologically? The sociologist's definition will have to be a comparative one—i.e., one that brings out a distinction between those political societies that merit

34. Marcel Mauss, "La nation," *L'Année sociologique*, 3rd series (1953–1954), 7–68. Reprinted in Marcel Mauss, *Oeuvres*, vol. 3, *Cohésion sociale et divisions de la sociologie*, ed. Victor Karady (Paris: Les Éditions de Minuit, 1969), 573–625. This text was probably written in 1920 but published for the first time in 1953–1954 according to the editor of the Minuit volume, to which I will refer.
35. Ibid., 577.

being called "nations," on the one hand, and those that are equally political but are of a different character, on the other. Mauss refers to Herbert Spencer's classification, which is based on degrees of integration: on the one hand, societies with no state; on the other, societies endowed with a central power. According to this classification, all societies that are unified by a central authority are of the same type. Mauss deems such a classification inadequate. To adopt it is to lose sight of a crucial difference:

> With this name we conflate societies that are very different from one another in their degree of integration: on the one hand, what Aristotle called "peoples" (*ethnē*) and, on the other, what he called cities (*poleis*) and which we call States or nations. Distinguishing the latter group is the aim of the present work.[36]

He then comments on Herodotus's anecdote to which Aristotle alluded. This allows him to put the emphasis on all that depends on a collective consciousness.

> Aristotle claimed that Babylon was hardly to be described as a *polis* but, rather, as a people, an *ethnos*, since it is said that, three days after it fell, part of the city had yet to notice. National solidarity is still merely potential and, basically, loose in such societies. They may allow themselves to be divided, pushed around and even decapitated; they are attuned to neither their borders nor their internal organization; among them one finds foreign tyrants and colonies that are assimilated or to which the nation is assimilated or simply subjugated. They are neither vertebrates nor highly conscious; they find no difficulty in doing without their political features and are rather willing to accept the benevolent tyrant as they do not have the desire to govern themselves.[37]

Thus the sociological distinction that Mauss seeks to draw rests on the form that consciousness of its collective individuality takes within

---

36. Ibid., 581.
37. Ibid., 582.

a particular society. Babylon does not define itself as a political entity and manifests no desire to govern itself. Mauss eventually comes to the following formulation of a sociological conception of the nation:

> By "a nation," we understand a materially and morally integrated society with a stable and permanent central power; with fixed borders; and a relative moral, mental, and cultural unity of its inhabitants who consciously adhere to the State and its laws.
>
> In the first place, the word "nation" defined in this way applies only to a small number of known societies throughout history and, for a certain number of those, has only been applicable in recent times.[38]

The sociological definition of the nation is superior to the usual definition, because it allows us to take into account a crucial fact: many contemporary societies—Mauss was writing in 1920, remember—are not yet nations (in the sociological sense) and will not be able to become nations (in the way that they hope) without a profound internal transformation of their systems of solidarity and their collective consciousnesses. In order to become nations in the sociological sense—that is, in order to govern themselves democratically—they will have to *nationalize* their sense of themselves, i.e., to set greater store by a sense of national solidarity than by more traditional forms of mutual assistance. And, according to Mauss, it is precisely in these European societies that *recently were not or have not yet become* nations in the sociological sense that we observe the phenomenon that is appropriately called a "nationalism." A nationalism here is, above all, a "revolt against the foreigners" by a group that is or believes itself to be oppressed, thereby showing that it is nothing but a "nationality" that aspires to its own emancipation.[39]

§§ Mauss's views here are the kinds of reflections that one might make after the experience of the First World War. Are they still valid today? Louis Dumont showed that they were entirely current in a text from 1964 that he devoted to the partition of the ancient Indian empire into

---

38. Ibid., 584.
39. Ibid., 576.

two independent states—the Indian Union and Pakistan.[40] The observer who expects to explain this brutal conflict as a clash of nationalisms would miss a decisive point and would fail to understand why this conflict was not fully resolved by partition, as subsequent events made clear (in particular the haste of both states to acquire nuclear weapons). What is expressed in this partition is not exactly a *nationalism* in the European sense, but a "communalism." Communalism closely resembles nationalism, but is not to be confused with it, since communalism seeks to ground the political unity of the group upon the "group religion" rather than upon the free adherence of the citizens to their political institutions. It is as if "the allegiance that should normally go to the nation were given by the communalist to his [religious] community instead."[41]

Dumont emphasizes the intellectual advance represented by Mauss's distinctions. He summarizes the contrast by setting in opposition the commonly received definition of the nation (*a*) that is not comparative and a sociological definition (*b*) that is. Political scientists and jurists generally define the nation as follows:

> (*a*) a group of people united in accordance with their own will and having certain attributes in common (territory, history, and others which are optional).[42]

According to Dumont, this definition (*a*) is not false but has the drawback of leaving an essential difference implicit: a society may be constituted as an independent state but will not be a nation (in the modern sense) unless it reforms its institutions in an individualistic way. The flaw of definition (*a*) is that it fails to register the role of religion in the representation of the group as a political entity. In traditional societies, the political sphere remains circumscribed within the group's religion. In modern society, "the religion of the individual" allows the political sphere to become autonomous and assert its own values.[43] A *nation*

---

40. Louis Dumont, "Nationalism and Communalism," Appendix D to *Homo Hierarchicus: The Caste System and Its Implications*, trans. Mark Sainsbury, Louis Dumont, and Basia Gulati (1966; Chicago: University of Chicago Press, 1980), 314–334.
41. Ibid., 315.
42. Ibid.
43. Ibid., 316.

implies the *principle of secularism*, which in turn implies that there cannot be a state religion. In other words, Pakistan is not a nation in Mauss's sense. A society cannot define itself as a nation for as long as it does not agree to abide by the individualist requirement for *freedom of conscience*, which means that religion must no longer appear to be a group practice, so as to become a personal practice. In a modern nation, religion speaks of the individual's salvation [*le salut de l'individu*] and leaves concern for public welfare [*le salut public*] to the people.

The sociological definition of the nation thus highlights the individualist values that this political form expresses. Here is Mauss's preliminary definition as reformulated by Dumont:

> (*b*) The nation is the political group conceived as a collection of individuals and, at the same time, in relation to other nations, the political individual. It is therefore incompatible with the religion of the old type.[44]

In general, the aspiration to national independence and to a form of government of the people by the people is not yet the desire for democracy in the sense in which we understand it—i.e., in a sense that is ordered by the normative idea of the individual.[45]

The Enigma of Collective Individuality

In order for a definition of the nation to be *comparative*, it will have to bring out the link between this political form and the values of the people who find their collective identity within it. Dumont summarizes Mauss when he writes, "For the sociologist, the nation is in the first place the society which *sees itself* as made up of individuals."[46] This definition posits that the nation is the political form corresponding to individualism-in-the-world. One might be tempted to raise here the objection that this explanation completely misses the political meaning of individualism. Should the politics of "individualism-in-the-world"

---

44. Ibid., 317.
45. The recent upheaval along the southern shore of the Mediterranean, which has been called the "Arab Spring" (in reference to the "Spring of Nations" of 1848), only confirms this diagnosis.
46. Dumont, *Homo Hierarchicus*, 445 n 19.

not instead be sought in the cosmopolitanism of the Enlightenment or in twentieth-century internationalism?

The objection is worth our attention, for it is undeniable that internationalism is the perfect expression of the value of individualism in its ideological purity (as Dumont himself stresses in his text). Indeed, as a purely ideological matter, there is no reason for an individual to be more attached to one particular society than to another (if both of them abide by the Declaration of the Rights of Man). In particular, she need not be particularly tied to the society in which she came into the world. The *normative* individual, by definition, has no social bonds others than those she assents to and from which she can always free herself in the conventional ways by which one terminates a contract. The real "society of individuals" can only be—potentially, at least—a global society.

The sociological definition of the nation, unlike the formal definitions given by political scientists, makes the (territorial) particularity of a political society into a condition of its national form. Why should such an importance be accorded to particularity, which seems to contradict the universalist aspiration that defines the republican ideal?

On this subject, Mauss made several useful remarks. He wondered whether the nation-state was not a transitional arrangement between the orders of the *ancien régime* and a society still to come. Without answering this question, he calls our attention to the sociological conditions for the formation of a supranational social unit:

> A society is an individual; other societies are also individuals. Among them it is not possible—for as long as they remain individualized—to create a higher-order individuality. Utopians generally lose sight of this factual and common-sense observation. But, conversely, societies are not irreducible individualities. . . . This possibility for societies to fuse together is generally scorned by those who seek to preserve the societies of their time.[47]

What is true of an *animal* individuality—whether that of a horse or a human being—is also true of a *collective* individuality. In contrast to certain material entities such as most fluid bodies, animals cannot fuse with one another. The waters of a tributary might be subsumed within those of a river, but two horses cannot fuse together in order to produce

---

47. Mauss, "La nation," 606.

a super-horse (though one can, of course, bring them together in a single harness).

Mauss draws our attention to the price to be paid if one seeks to "create a higher-order individuality" out of societies organized into nations. It is not that such a fusion of highly individuated societies is inconceivable; that is what conservative minds fail to see, in the process forgetting the history of all nations, their own included. But the price to pay is always the *destruction* of what constituted the *individuality* of the small countries, eclipsed within a more expansive political entity. What is therefore ruled out is for nations—that is to say, *collective individuals*, in their relations with one another—to come together so as to form a group endowed with an individualized form (with a territory and borders) while at the same time each continues to maintain its own collective individuality.

Are nations ready to dissolve themselves within a larger whole? Some philosophers of history believe there to be an irresistible historical dynamic that drives toward the creation of ever-greater human groupings. The uniformity of ways of life and of thinking would play a powerful role in such amalgamation. The construction of the European Union is often adduced as an example of this putative dynamic law. Yet those who expound this theory need to be reminded of Mauss's observation: modernity is also the idea of the individual whose conscience and vote are both free. This kind of individualism found its political form in the organization of the nation within the limits of a territory. Once a society has been established long term in this national form, it identifies itself based on its existing borders. Projects for territorial expansion (or, for that matter, the division or loss of territory) do not arise for it. As for the idea that the resemblance among various ways of life ought to provide an impetus for political unification, it would seem difficult to defend. If such an irresistible dynamic were at work in history, pushing societies to merge whenever they felt sufficiently close in their beliefs and customs, the harmonious union of the United States and Canada ought to have taken place long ago. Yet both of these nations are quite partial to their national sovereignty and show no signs of wanting to join together to form an even more formidable nation.

§§ Louis Dumont discussed Mauss's sociological perspective on this question, pointing out that Mauss's view is general in scope. Mauss drew a comparison between societies and human individuals: considered in their individuality, neither a human society nor a human individual can merge with others of its kind. Nevertheless, unlike people, the individuality of a human group is not irreducible. Two groups can merge, provided that each of them accepts the loss of its own individuality in favor of a new, higher-level collective individuality. Conversely, a group can divide into two components, as was recently seen in the case of Czechoslovakia. The general law is that one cannot produce a collective individual while retaining the (normative) individuality of its components. But in that case, the difficulty is this: if, as we see every day in relations among nations, an *individual* cannot be made up of *independent individuals* (but only of *parts* subordinated to a *whole*), how can a particular society conceive of itself in its composition, given that it is in fact made up of particular human individuals? This contradiction would evaporate if we understood the concept of an individual in an empirical sense and then agreed to treat a *collection* of such individuals as "a higher-order individual." However, we are here using "individual" in the normative sense. By definition, a normative individual can do no more than associate with other individuals; it certainly cannot become a part of a whole distinct from itself.

Recall the sociological definition of the nation according to Dumont: "The nation is the political group conceived as a collection of individuals and, at the same time, in relation to other nations, the political individual." How can the contradiction be avoided? It can only be avoided by emphasizing, contrary to the internationalist utopian view, that other nations have no desire to join with us in forming some great universal nation. There is a *particularism* inherent in the will to stand together within a *political* community—i.e., one that intends to govern itself. The desire to govern oneself implies the refusal of anything involving submission to a government felt to be foreign as well as any sort of "governance" by invisible authorities, even under the highly improbable hypothesis in which it could be shown that these foreign or anonymous authorities were exceedingly benevolent and efficient.

Is such particularism the mark of an inability to open oneself to others? Does it carry within itself the seed of selfishness and conflict, as the partisans of supranational political formations maintain? I assert that it should instead be seen as the counterpart of a *modern* definition of sovereignty. If sovereignty is to be democratic, it will have to be *territorial* and not *universal* as it was in a more archaic conception of the political domain. It is out of such considerations that Dumont concludes his analysis with the following definition of the nation:

> (c) [T]he modern nation is characterized in the first place by a People (a group of people possessed of a common will) as the political subject, and a territory as its inalienable attribute.[48]

In this portrait of the nation in the political sense, the notion of territory must not be understood in the *empirical* sense of a space under the effective control of the political group, but in the *normative* sense of a condition of the consciousness that this group has of itself. Dumont means by this that "the image of a territory of a certain shape" allows the citizens of a modern nation to represent their country as *individuated* and thereby overcome the representation of society as a mere collection of individuals.[49] This is why "the notion of a common territory appears so necessary in the modern consciousness of political identity."[50] What is therefore at issue is not some mythology of the soil or of rootedness that one finds in nationalist ideologies. What is at issue is the very possibility for a group to identify itself in a political form and therefore in the language of the will and self-consciousness rather than in the form of a group religion.

How can individuals imagine the society that they comprise as possessing a "political identity"? The answer given by political philosophy is well known: they do this by constituting a *general will*. The individual who participates in the general will is not subject to the will of someone else, because she is a part—on equal terms with her fellow citizens—of the sovereign and can therefore say of any enacted law "this law is nothing but the expression of our will."

The first act of this general will—at least according to the theory—is the act by which (normative) individuals conclude the social contract among themselves. The description of the social contract that Rousseau provides in the first book of *The Social Contract* is particularly abstract. It postulates the complete alienation by particular individuals of their persons and their goods to the community, an alienation that is

---

48. Dumont, *Homo Hierarchicus*, 332.
49. Ibid., 331.
50. Ibid.

immediately followed, however, by a restitution to them of what they have given up. These two operations come across as some sort of philosophical alchemy whose secret remains obscure to the reader. The fact that alienation is involved gives the impression that the general will is expressed when particular citizens surrender their own wills, sacrifice their personal interests, and agree to give themselves entirely to the common cause. In fact, such a reading is not possible. Rousseau is not asking his citizens to abandon their love of self [amour de soi], their love of what he follows Pascal in calling le moi [the "I" or the self]. He is asking them to redirect this love and to love themselves as citizens. As he writes in Émile, the formation of a general will assumes that the institutions of the people concerned are able to "transport the I [le moi] into the common unity, with the result that each individual believes himself no longer one but a part of the unity and no longer feels except within the whole."[51] This transport of the self is clearly the key to the solution, since it involves precisely the movement by which an "I" [moi] comes to coincide with a "we," as Hegel would later put it in a famous formula.[52]

To transport the I into the common unity, yes, but from what is the representation of this "common unity" derived? Pure political individualism sees no reason to place it anywhere but within the universal human community. For the internationalist, it is by associating with other individuals that an individual becomes a citizen of a republic, which is—virtually, in any case—a universal community. Utopians who dream of making the empirical republic coincide with the universal republic persist within a conception of society as a collection of individuals. According to them, there is no need to locate the principle of individuation of the group within a *domain* (the national territory). It suffices that a general will has been expressed. But can a general will be formed out of a simple plurality of individuals? If that were the case, it would not be necessary to *individuate* the subject of the general will—i.e., there would be no need for an identity criterion to distinguish one "we" from another "we."

We can start from the fact that the social contract is drawn up in the first-person plural: "Each of us puts his person and all his power in

---

51. Jean-Jacques Rousseau, *Émile, or On Education*, trans. Allan Bloom (New York: Basic Books, 1979), 40.
52. G. W. F. Hegel, *The Phenomenology of Spirit*, trans. A. V. Miller (Oxford: Oxford University Press, 1977), § 177 (110).

common under the supreme direction of the general will; and we receive each member as an indivisible part of the whole."[53] Our question is, then, what does "we" mean in this statement, which is meant to found the political community? Is it to be understood as individuated—i.e., endowed with a "collective identity" of its own, in this case an identity of a political kind?

---

53. Jean-Jacques Rousseau, *The Social Contract*, in *Discourse on Political Economy and the Social Contract*, trans. Christopher Betts (Oxford: Oxford University Press, 1994), Book 1, Chapter 6 (55) [translation modified].

6

THE "WE" AS INSTITUTING POWER

The Individuation of a "We"

When a "we" is emitted by a human mouth, who is speaking? When a hand writes "we" on a piece of paper, who is involved? Who can use this form of self-expression? It is sometimes said that the "we" is the mark that the speaker is a "plural subject." This is not quite right. There is a plurality involved; however, as linguists often stress, the pronouns "we" or "us" are not plurals of "I" or "me." If one asks, "Who was in the concert hall?" and the response is "I and I and I," then that implies that the audience was but a single person (there was only I). As Edmond Ortigues remarks, the word "we" does not refer to a plurality of people (each of whom is saying "I"), but a "complex moral person."[1] The word "we" is used to posit an individual (in the logico-semantic sense of an identifiable entity). And there is therefore every reason to ask what it is that makes this complex "moral" person into a unit—i.e., to consider its mode of composition.

The pronoun "we" is not the plural of "I," because, in reality, the word "I" (in Latin, *ego*) *has no plural*. It cannot be used as an individuative term. It is therefore an error to speak of someone else as an *alter ego* and

---

1. See Edmond Ortigues, *Le discours et le symbole* (1962; Paris: Éditions Beauchesne, 2007), 172. Ortigues here harks back to Pufendorf's *persona moralis composita*.

imagine that one has thereby escaped the "solipsism" of the *ego*. Émile Benveniste explains this peculiarity that is constitutive of the pronouns "me" and "I" as follows: "The reason for this is that 'we' is not a quantified or multiplied 'I'; it is an 'I' expanded beyond the strict limits of the person, enlarged and at the same time amorphous."[2] In order to move from "I" to "we," I must add to my own person other people who are specified as being other than I, the speaker. The "we" must be *assembled* in its identity, and our entire problem is now this: how does one manage to assemble a *collective identity* out of oneself?

There would appear to be two ways of doing this. Linguists distinguish two semantic values of the pronoun "we" considered in its pragmatic use—i.e., in a situation of interlocution:

1. the "we" that has an *inclusive* sense (e.g., me, you, and you, and therefore *me* and *you* [plural] in contrast to *them*);
2. the "we" whose sense is *exclusive* (e.g., *me* and *them* in contrast to *you*).[3]

This difference depends on the fact that the word "we" is a term of address. By saying "we" (rather than "I"), the speaker takes a position relative to his interlocutor, allowing the latter to situate him. The terms "inclusive" and "exclusive" must be understood beginning from the speech act. The idea is not that there is one form that would be open to others and another that is closed to them, for both of these forms must shift someone other than the speaker to the side of the "I" in order to form, for the occasion, a "we." If the speaking subject addresses his interlocutor in the *inclusive* mode, it means that all of the individuals included in the "we" are present for the speech act. In this case, the people involved are these: *I* who am speaking and *you* to whom I am speaking. By contrast, if the speaking subject addresses his interlocutor in the *exclusive* mode, it means that the other members of the "we" are not present for the speech act, either because they are remaining silent

---

2. Émile Benveniste, "Relationships of Person in the Verb," in his *Problems in General Linguistics*, trans. Mary Elizabeth Meek (Coral Gables, FL: University of Miami Press, 1971), 203.
3. See Lucien Tesnière, *Éléments de syntaxe structurale*, 2nd ed. (1959; Paris: Klincksieck, 1988), 123-125. Tesnière notes that the French expression *nous autres* has an exclusive sense ("us and them, but not you"). He also points out that the similar phrase "Uns andere Laien" ("we laypeople") can be found in Goethe.

or because they are not physically present; in either case, they are *represented* by the speaker.

If "we" is an expanded "je," as Benveniste claims, the problem is one of determining its *contours*, or, to put it another way, of individuating it. This problem does not arise when the speaker says only "I," because the speaker who says "I" is necessarily speaking about herself even where she cannot identify herself any more precisely. There are, however, several ways that a speaker might delimit the contours of her "we." This is why uses of "we" can always be challenged, but in different ways depending on whether it is used in the inclusive or the exclusive mode. In the case of an inclusive "we," the interlocutors can immediately call the speaker's authority into question. Someone may stand up and say that he does not accept what the speaker has said in the name of all those present. He thereby demands to be excluded from the "we" that the speaker was trying to set up. Things happen somewhat differently when the speaker is using the exclusive "we." In that case, she is addressing people who are not required to identify with what she is saying to them. They cannot therefore challenge from within the use of an exclusive "we"; they can only do it from without (by objecting that the speaker is not in fact the spokesperson for the collective she claims to represent and therefore has no right to their "we").

In certain languages, the two values of our single pronoun are morphologically distinct. Otto Jesperson relates an anecdote that provides a good illustration of the semantic difference at issue.[4] The story features a British missionary who is addressing a group of Africans in their own language and wants to say to them "We are all of us sinners, and we all need conversion." Unfortunately, the pastor does not realize that the local language has both forms of "we" and that the "we" that he used is the exclusive one. What the audience heard, then, was this: "I and mine, to the exclusion of you whom I am addressing, are all of us sinners, and we all need conversion."

But can one not imagine a term of address that would be the synthesis of these two forms, aiming to include both the present interlocutors and all those who are not present, without any human person being placed outside of this community? Can one say "we" in the name of the human community as a whole? One can, of course, do this, but if the

---

4. Otto Jesperson, *The Philosophy of Grammar* (1924; New York: Routledge, 2007), 192.

pronoun remains one that marks the capacity in which the interlocutor is being spoken to, then the speaker will have to specify the status of those she is addressing. If she wants to speak to someone about all humans, she will have to come up with an interlocutor who is outside of this universal human community, as a Christian does in addressing her prayer to God in the form of a *Pater noster*. Otherwise, the speaker is the one setting herself outside of the human community by adopting a point of view from Sirius or Jupiter. Or—third possibility—if she wants to include herself among the totality of humans that she brings together in the "you" to whom she is speaking, she will have to posit an *absent third person* to represent the "them" or "him" before which she can posit the community that "we, human beings" constitute.

§§ Recall Rousseau's statement of the terms in which the founding contract of a society as a body politic is drawn up: "Each of us puts his person and all his power in common under the supreme direction of the general will; and we receive each member as an indivisible part of the whole."

Is this "we" used in Rousseau's formulation of the social contract *inclusive* or *exclusive*? At first glance, it seems inclusive, to be decided by those present. Rousseau gives the impression of lodging sovereignty within the actuality (*esse in actu*) of a meeting of all citizens in the form of an assembly or plebiscite. And, in fact, the political philosophy that features the notion of the general will—namely, the philosophy of republicanism—would appear to know only the inclusive "we." This suggests that the expression of a consensus must be the result of a negotiation among those present.

But how does it happen that all of these individuals, who are independent from one another, nevertheless manage simultaneously to form the "we" in the same terms? In other words, how is it that each one composes his "we" so as to form exactly the same "common unity" as that formed by every other person included by each of those assembled in his or her own complex moral individual? In the end and only as a result of a monumental coincidence, the same people would have to find themselves together in the composition of a unique "we." Moreover, the inclusive "we" of a social contract could bestow only a synchronic identity on the body politic, one that would be determined by the identity of the members participating in the founding act. Such a society would be literally contractual—i.e., it would be the association of those signing the contract and only those people. Such a society, born of what in private law is called a "contract of *societas*," would be dissolved as soon as one of its members withdrew or died. Yet the body politic for which Rousseau seeks a foundation is one that is meant to maintain its existence across the generations. When the legislator takes up the cause of the education of future generations, it is clear that the community's "we" has ceased to be an inclusive one: the act by which the city is founded turns out to be one that requires the participation of citizens that are currently absent and whom we cannot even name—our future descendants.

This, however, is not Rousseau's last word on the subject. One cannot remain with the image of a meeting of members that together would produce a general will by somehow coming to speak together *with a single voice*. As long as one abides by this view of the "we" as given in the present, the general will remains unintelligible, corresponding to nothing in our human experience. Things are different if we introduce the temporal dimension and the succession of generations. What makes possible the expression of a general will would then be that the elders look after the education of the young, concerning themselves with their entry into adult life and with inculcating good manners within them. Rousseau can then write that it is within such education that the real constitution of the city should be sought. He thus returns to Plato and Aristotle's concern with including within their treatises on political philosophy consideration of *paideia*.

The adherence of the citizenry to the institutions of their city is an identification overseen by Rousseau's legislator, a superhuman character able to carry out "the establishment of a people."[5] Having distinguished among three kinds of law that make up the legislative system (fundamental law, civil law, and criminal law), Rousseau goes on to say this:

> In addition to these three categories of law there is a fourth, which
> is the most important of all; it is not graven in marble or bronze,
> but in citizens' hearts; in it lies the true constitution of the state; its

---

5. Jean-Jacques Rousseau, *The Social Contract*, in *Discourse on Political Economy and The Social Contract*, trans. Christopher Betts (Oxford: Oxford University Press, 1994) Book, 2, Chapter 7 (76).

strength augments day by day; when other laws decay or become extinct it revives or replaces them, it maintains in the nation the spirit of its constitution, and imperceptibly changes the force of authority into the force of habit. I refer to moral standards, to custom, and above all to public opinion. . . . [6]

That Rousseau's thinking here is indeed the distant precursor of our identitarian idiom is clearly shown in the advice he gives to the Poles in his considerations on *The Government of Poland*. In it, he recommends allegiance to all of the customs that are likely to form a national character so that, according to him, the country will be unable to be annexed by one of its neighbors:

You cannot possibly keep them from swallowing you; see to it, at least, that they shall not be able to digest you. . . . See to it that every Pole is incapable of becoming a Russian, and I answer for it that Russia will never subjugate Poland.[7]

How is one to avoid being absorbed by one's larger neighbor? Rousseau advocates the cultivation of "national institutions," by which he means practices such as games, sports, festivals, dances, the commemoration of great historical deeds, the teaching of history, etc. Note that these are not "realms of memory," but rather "future realms" or, if you prefer, "realms in which a future can be imagined."

I repeat: *national institutions.* That is what gives form to the genius, the character, the tastes, and the customs of a people; what causes it to be itself rather than some other people; what arouses in it that ardent love of fatherland that is founded upon habits of mind impossible to uproot; what makes unbearably tedious for its citizens every moment spent away from home—even when they find themselves surrounded by delights that are denied them in their own country.[8]

---

6. Ibid, Book 2, Chapter 12 (89–90).
7. Jean-Jacques Rousseau, *The Government of Poland*, trans. Willmoore Kendall (Indianapolis: Hackett, 1985), 11.
8. Ibid.

Such social practices are what confer collective identity on a people. Through such practices, the people that engages in them *makes itself* into "itself rather than some other people."

§§§ In his initial presentation in Book 1 of *The Social Contract*, Rousseau borrows his conceptual framework from theorists of natural law. There he represents the normative establishment of society as a contract concluded among independent individuals (i.e., normative individuals). At that point, the unity of the body politic can only appear as a "moral person," an abstract juridical construct. One gets a sense of the distance covered when Rousseau comes to discussing what the legislator must anticipate with regard to the civic education of the citizenry. Once the anthropological dimension of time is added through the succession of generations, this unity becomes an authentic "collective unity" in the moral psychological sense. Here is the account that Rousseau himself gives of this psychology in a passage in which he describes the mental mutation that transforms a simple human plurality (a "multitude") into a city:

> As soon as the multitude is united thus in one body, it is impossible to injure one of its members without attacking the body, and still less to injure the body without its members being affected.[9]

It is clear that the moral psychology of a citizen according to Rousseau is the same as that described by Mauss. It is characterized by an extreme sensitivity to anything felt to be an aggression against the collective body. This is not about some *duty* to stand together, but rather an *experience* in which each citizen feels implicated by whatever happens to any member of the body (provided that that member has been attacked in his capacity as a member of the body). This is not about the citizen's dedication to the *res publica*, but his care for himself and his dignity after having "expanded" or "enlarged" his *I*—as Benveniste put it—to the dimensions of a "we."

§§§ Voltaire wants nothing to do with such a collective consciousness. He wrote the following in the margin of his copy of *The Social Contract*,

---

9. Rousseau, *The Social Contract*, Book 1, Chapter 7 (57).

next to the passage cited above: "This is pitiful. If someone gives Jean-Jacques a whipping, does he give a whipping to the Republic?"[10] Voltaire's gibe is a good illustration of the gap between individualist common sense and Rousseau's protosociological view. What does Voltaire object to? Is it the fact of collective consciousness manifested in what we would call "identitarian" reactions? More probably, Voltaire is deploring such reactions and calling into question what seems irrational to him: namely, that an entire people might feel offended simply because one of its members has been. After all, one cannot give the Republic a whipping. As it was wittily put in a line often attributed to Samuel Johnson, "Corporations have no soul to save and no bottom to kick."

Here one might respond to Voltaire by pointing out that his reasoning amounts to denying that a *part* might stand for the *whole*. By the same reasoning, as Hegel pointed out, an arsonist might reject all responsibility for the fire that destroyed the pine forest. "I did not set fire to the forest," he might say, "but rather dropped the butt of my still-glowing cigarette on a tiny portion of the ground of planet Earth." Similarly, the lout who jostles me or steps on my foot can always say that he did not injure my person as a whole but only a very small part of my body.[11]

Before it can be inclusive, the "we" of the general will must first be exclusive. By forming its general will, the social body is addressing the external world.

The Composition of a "We"

Rousseau, who is undeniably the philosopher of the general will, alerts us to the fact that the constitution of the state must be inscribed in the hearts of the people—in the form of *ways of doing things*, *customs*, and *opinion*—before being inscribed as law. One might say that Rousseau does not want to limit the notion of a constitution to its juridical sense of a collection of measures set out in a document called by that name. He persists in conceiving of it as a *politeia*. As Aristotle explained, a *politeia* is a way for the citizenry to be arranged with regard to one

10. Marginal note cited by Bertrand de Jouvenel in his edition of *Du contrat social* (Paris: Livre de Poche/Pluriel, 1978), 183 n 2.
11. G. W. F. Hegel, *Outlines of the Philosophy of Right*, trans. T. M. Knox, rev. and ed. Stephen Houlgate (Oxford: Oxford University Press, 2008), § 119 (118–119).

another—not just by constitutional laws, but also by the totality of their collective ways of doing things. Understood in this way, the constitution conceived of by Rousseau's "legislator" includes not only the "fundamental law" of the constitution, nor even the entire corpus of laws in the legislative sense. It is the name that he gives to the set of social institutions, including, for example, ways of raising children, forms of children's play, and ways of organizing collective pastimes.

One may well be concerned by the image that Rousseau gives of his "legislator." Is there not something totalitarian about the expansion of constitutional normativity to the entirety of what we today would call the "cultural identity" of a people? Rousseau believes that the political identity of a people—the "we" of the general will—assumes that the people look after their moral unity, i.e., the identity of their ways of doing things and their customs. His position is therefore far removed from those of contemporary theorists of democracy who, on the contrary, ask that we dissociate a society's political identity from its cultural practices. According to them, there is nothing preventing a society from being united in its democratic political identity while made up of multiple cultural traditions. Jürgen Habermas's "constitutional patriotism" is certainly not a patriotism of the *politeia* as understood in the broad sense of the ancients and Rousseau, since it bears only upon the "fundamental law."

Are we to conclude that Rousseau is a dangerous thinker, the precursor of nationalist or even totalitarian ideologues? Or should we view him as Durkheim does, as a brilliant precursor of a sociological view of human beings?[12]

These questions are not only difficult but both topical and controversial and not liable to be cleared up in a few sentences here. However, it is possible for us to ask how we should ask these questions from the perspective of a logic of the concept of identity and a semantics of the pronoun "we." I will do this in two phases. First I will touch on two contemporary political debates: the debate on the "right to difference" and the debate on the possibility of a multicultural democracy. Then I will stress the need to distinguish the "constituent power," which is the

---

12. See Émile Durkheim, "Rousseau's Social Contract" (1918), reprinted in his *Montesquieu and Rousseau: Forerunners of Sociology*, trans. Ralph Manheim (Ann Arbor, MI: University of Michigan Press, 1960), 65–138.

power to establish or remake the constitution, from the "instituting power," which produces and reproduces all of a society's institutions.

§§§ I begin with those discussions that have arisen from the irruption within the panoply of democratic demands of claims to a "right to difference." Does the democratic principle of the equality of all citizens not lead to the recognition of a right to be different from others, knowing that there is no single model of human perfection toward which all humans must aspire? For example, does not equality between men and women require that the image of the citizen be altered so as to be accepted equally by individuals of the female sex and of the male sex? Today, this demand is expressed in different idioms: sometimes in the classical vocabulary of human emancipation, sometimes in terms of a "recognition of the other in his otherness." It is on this latter point that our philosophical considerations may have some bearing.

I will begin with a remark by Louis Dumont concerning the notion of social recognition. Claims of a "right to difference" are demands for society's recognition, which is not the mere recording of a brute fact but the attribution of a *value*. Dumont reminds us that there are two ways for a society to accord a value to something. Social anthropology indeed distinguishes between two possible sorts of organization among people: *equistatutory* or *hierarchical*. There will then be two possible ways for those to whom a demand for recognition has been addressed to accord a value to someone and his customary ways of behavior: by holding him to be our equal or by assigning him a different rank to ours (either superior or inferior).

What, then, is the content of a demand for "recognition"?

If the demand is for equal treatment, the claim is for an *equistatutory* recognition. This means that the demand is for the end of a form of discrimination and a call for the establishment of rules against differentiation and distinction. This might arise for an individual whose way of life is different (it matters little here whether this is out of choice or out of necessity). She demands to be held to be the equal of others *despite the fact* that her way of life is different. In order to fulfill such a demand, the difference in question will have to be declared to be of no normative significance. The difference that sets someone apart must in some sense be canceled out or at least reduced to insignificance and judged to be of no value. As Dumont notes, such a demand gives rise to no problems of principle since it is egalitarian in character. It must therefore be assessed by the consideration of its particular content.

By contrast, if the aim of the demand for recognition is that a value be accorded to a difference, what is being asked for is a *hierarchical* recognition, since in order to satisfy the demand, a special status will have to be given to one category of the population in the name of this difference. In this case, "to recognize" does not have the sense of *observing* that someone behaves in a particular way; it is to attach a value and thus also a *rank* and a *status* to this particularity.

Dumont therefore concludes that a choice must be made between recognition of the other as a human being like oneself—i.e., a recognition that is egalitarian because it is equistatutory—and recognizing the other "as other" than oneself, a hierarchical recognition that assigns to him a value *other* than one's own. An intellectual contradiction—and the certain failure of any political program based on it—would follow from the demand to be both recognized as an equal and, at the same time, "as other." Dumont does not hesitate to write regarding the recognition of the Other in his alterity:

> I submit that such recognition can only be hierarchical. . . . To be explicit: *alter* will then be thought of as superior or inferior to Ego, with the important qualification of reversal. . . . That is to say that, if *alter* was taken as globally inferior, he would turn out as superior on secondary levels of consideration.
>
> What I maintain is that, if the advocates of difference claim for it both equality and recognition, they claim the impossible.[13]

Our earlier examination of the logic of the concept of identity confirms Dumont's conclusion here. As we saw then, the two adjectives "same" and "other" cannot be used as if, standing on their own, they referred to qualities of the object concerned. As "Geach's Rule" reminds us, the use of the adjectives "same" and "other" presupposes a context allowing us to understand what we are talking about. Outside of any context, we can only ask, "the same *what*?" or "another *what*?" Given this, what does recognition of the other's otherness commit us to? It

---

13. Louis Dumont, *Essays on Individualism: Modern Ideology in Anthropological Perspective* (Chicago: University of Chicago Press, 1986), 266.

might simply be a commitment to recognize in him another *human person* and therefore a peer—an equistatutory recognition of his alterity. By being a person other than me, the different individual is a person just as I am and thus the equal of all of us. Or—and this is the second possible interpretation—the demand in fact bears upon the differences in ways of life of some relative to others: here it is not a matter of seeing the difference as negligible but, on the contrary, according it an importance for this group and, above all, for the way in which this group represents itself. For example, a place will have to be officially reserved for it in the public space, in school textbooks, and in collective celebrations. Yes, but what sort of place? Major or minor? It is at this point that the question arises for society of the hierarchical ranking of these different ways of life, which is to say that we will find ourselves immersed in the contradictions of an "identity politics," since this hierarchy will be put in place in the name of the equality of all citizens.

The semantics of "we" leads us to this same conclusion from another angle. The "we" has two possible semantic values because there are two distinct ways of addressing people as "you." The speaker who upholds a "right to difference" claims this right for a group (and not, of course, just for himself). About whom is he speaking and to whom? His "we" is exclusive because it emphasizes the "alterity" of those in whose name he is speaking. He therefore excludes from the group on behalf of which he says "we" the entirety of those whose recognition he is demanding. True, but he is asking them for a civil right in the name of the equality of all citizens. He is therefore addressing his demand to his own fellow citizens and thereby includes his interlocutors in the "we" that he seeks to form around himself. One might well join Dumont in concluding that he does not know what he is demanding, because he does not know that he is demanding it of himself. Knowing neither what he is asking for nor of whom, he is certain not to obtain it.

§§§ Let us turn now to another public debate, one called to mind by the word "multiculturalism." The word "culture" unfortunately gives rise to multiple confusions, because many of those who use it appear to have forgotten that it was originally an anthropological term meant to encompass the ways of doing and thinking of groups other than one's own, ways that are transmitted from one generation to another. The word is therefore correctly used only if, first, it serves to posit a *global* difference among ways of doing things and, second, it refers to established ways of doing and thinking that a group regards as precious and worthy of being *transmitted*. Contained within the notion of culture or cultural belonging there is thus also the notion of a call from the elders to the young not to neglect the proper ways of doing and thinking. The problem of multiculturalism is therefore the result of multiple such appeals, received by a single individual, to be faithful to the spirit of his tradition. Provided they see such appeals as equally legitimate, how can all of those who find themselves in this position—i.e., all of us to varying degrees, if one thinks about it—respond to all of these demands for the transmission of various ways of life?

Several cultural traditions contend for the allegiance of a single individual. How can she define herself in such conditions? Here I will attempt to sketch out a general line of reasoning. Imagine that someone partakes in two collective histories, one of group A and the other of group B. This person will have two ways of defining her position within a historical storyline. Since each group is a historical community, our individual participates in two cultures, A and B. She can therefore formulate two *we*'s: the *we* of those who call themselves "the A" and the *we* of those who call themselves "the B." Our individual's problem is then one of *composing* for herself an identity of the type AB. She will have to be able to say not only that "I am an A" and "I am a B," but also that "I am an AB." She may also want to be able to say in the name of others like her that "We are ABs."

How can she? It would appear that she can do this in two ways, since the relation between the two groups can be, within the consciousness of this individual, either *equistatutory* or *hierarchical*.

Let us assume that the two groups to which she belongs are of equal rank in her mind. In that case, the AB-type identity will be composed through temporal juxtaposition. To be an AB will consist in behaving sometimes like an A and sometimes like a B, depending on what the circumstances require. As a result, such composition through simple *juxtaposition* can only result in a "plural identity"—i.e., a plurality of identities—that has as its awkward effect to require a *doubling* of the individual. Imagine, for example, that our individual has dual citizenship but that neither country allows for this possibility, requiring their citizens to have only a single nationality. Under such a hypothesis, she will have to fulfill her civic duties twice: do her military service twice, pass her school exams twice, pay her taxes twice, etc.

The composition of an identity through juxtaposition is therefore only viable if the doubling of the individual that it requires can be carried out at different times. Notice, however, that what is at issue here is not really the *plurality of adherences*, but rather the *mode of composition* of this plurality within a formula that is compatible with the individuation of the person concerned. The soothing phrase "plural identity" is equivocal, since it gives one to understand that there has been a successful reconciliation of a person's various allegiances with the fact of her individuation, but without supplying her with any means to avoid conflicts other than to divide up into different times the activities required by the various communities of which she sees herself as a loyal member. The conflicts are therefore avoided only at the price of a fracturing of her life into separate compartments.

The solution to our problem is clearly to allow the individual who is solicited from all sides in this way to define herself by an identity that is not also *several* identities and that will not require her to double herself or to pretend to lead multiple lives at once. We now move to the other possibility: a composition *AB* in which the two communities *A* and *B* are not on the same level, since one of them is included within the other as one of its components or subordinate parts. Suppose that group *A* is the *encompassing* group and *B* is the *encompassed* one. It is then natural that the encompassing group claims primacy over the encompassed one. We should recognize this principle of composition. It is none other than the superiority of the more universal good over a more particular good. This principle is what grounds republican universalism (in the French sense): *particular* interests must give way to the *common* interest, unless one admits to being corporative or feudal in outlook.

Rousseau theorizes this republican hierarchy when he discusses, in his *Discourse on Political Economy*, the "particular societies" that form within political society. Every society, whether encompassing or encompassed, is defined by a common interest and therefore possesses a general will. The citizen must then compare his individual will with two general wills—that of the smaller society *B* to which he belongs and that of the general society *A* to which he also belongs. He is thereby a participant in *two general wills*. How should he behave so as to reconcile these two general wills, knowing that the will of the smaller society is *general* relative to its members but becomes a *particular* will when put forward within the greater society? A simple appeal to dedicate himself to what is vaguely referred to as the "collective" will not work, for there are two possibilities for devotion, and they are sometimes incompatible. As Rousseau puts it, "a man can be a devout priest, or a courageous soldier, or a zealous lawyer, but a bad citizen."[14] By assigning degrees of generality to wills, Rousseau posits a principle of composition according to which the encompassed must yield to the encompassing.

The solution provided by republican universalism seems entirely rational on paper, but it can prove to be problematic in its application. This is so for two reasons.

First, there is often the possibility of an appeal to an even more encompassing general will. Over and above our national republic lies the republic of European nations, and beyond that the universal republic. A republicanism that claimed to achieve universalism within the confines of a nation's borders would present nothing more than the travesty of a *cosmopolitanism within a single country*.

Second, the hierarchical relation that is instituted by the primacy of the encompassing over the encompassed remains a linear one. A consequence is that general will *A* will *always* carry the day over general will *B*. Smaller societies will never warrant our concern. If *A* always takes precedence because it is encompassing, *B* will never be anything but second, which implies that it can never expect our attention. But that means that the overarching society takes no interest in the vitality of the small voluntary communities that nonetheless have their own role to play in the well-being and success of the encompassing society.

What, then, are we to think about this other possibility, the converse of the one Rousseau adduced—that a man could be a good citizen yet a bad priest, a bad soldier, and a bad lawyer? Surely that would be an odd idea of civic duty. Therefore, to allow the more general interest to take precedence over the more particular will not be sufficient to compose an identity that reconciles these different allegiances and the demands for loyalty and gratitude that flow from them.

We might seek a solution to these difficulties by looking to the semantics of the pronouns "we" and "you." When someone takes on the role of spokesperson for the encompassed group *B* and states that "We are the

---

14. Rousseau, *Discourse on Political Economy*, in *Discourse on Political Economy and The Social Contract*, 8.

AB," to whom is he speaking? The difficulty is that even if his "we" is supposed to establish the AB in the eyes of the rest of group A, he is using an inclusive "we," since he is himself an A and identifies himself as such. But if he does this, then his membership in group B must take a backseat, with the result that the spokesperson for the ABs finds himself professing a strict republicanism according to which A always comes before B. Let us nevertheless suppose that he wants to maintain his identity B in the face of a "you" made up of the other members of group A. In that case, the spokesperson of the AB confirms the worst fears of the stern guardians of linear universalism, showing himself to be a secessionist by excluding himself from the community of the A. And if he does secede, it can only mean that he puts his membership in group B *on the same level* as his membership in group A, which brings us back to the earlier case of a simple juxtaposition of A and B.

This is why the only solution to these difficulties lies in the hierarchical use of structural identification. By "structural identification," I mean one that proceeds by positing a *distinctive opposition* within a totality. In the case that concerns us, this solution will consist in the representative of the B setting up his "you" as all those As who are not Bs. The distinctive opposition will not then be between group B and group A, but between group B and the non-B group within the overarching group A (along the lines of the dichotomies between the North and the South, the Country and the City, Corsica and the Continent, the Left Bank and the Right Bank, etc.). Here we can make use of the theory of structural identification sketched out by Evans-Pritchard in his study of the Nuer.[15]

Evans-Pritchard explains the concept as follows. When one asks a Nuer about his affiliation, his responses seem in contradiction with one another. For example, he is asked if he feels bound to a given subgroup of his people. His answers seem to indicate that he does but also that he does not. Evans-Pritchard shows that the contradiction is only apparent. Indeed, it is all a matter of context. When questioned, where does the individual Nuer feel at home? That depends on where he is when asked. Evans-Pritchard compares our own way of defining the place where we feel at home:

---

15. E. E. Evans-Pritchard, *The Nuer: A Description of the Modes of Livelihood and Political Institutions of a Nilotic People* (Oxford: Clarendon Press, 1940).

If one meets an Englishman in Germany and asks him where his home is, he may reply that it is England. If one meets the same man in London and asks him the same question he will tell one that his home is in Oxfordshire, whereas if one meets him in that county he will tell one the name of the town or village in which he lives.[16]

As a general rule, the Nuer's responses conform to the principle of the "structural relativity" of social groups.[17] Reference to structural relativity means that one needs two reference points in order to identify a social group: an encompassing group to which it belongs (group *A* in our example) and a segmentation of this encompassing group into two subgroups by means of a distinctive opposition (our subgroups *B* and not-*B*).

It then falls to the individual *AB* to distinguish, on the one hand, the situations in which his "we" is addressed to other *A*s, thereby forming a collective identity of *A*s surrounding a speaker who includes himself in their number, and, on the other hand, those situations in which he is speaking to his interlocutors as a *B* addressing people who, in his eyes, are non-*B*. This solution to the problem raised for the individual by cultural diversity is a hierarchical one. It is the one put forward by Louis Dumont and taken up in turn by Mona Ozouf in her splendid autobiographical essay, *Composition française* [French Composition].[18]

There is then the following difference between the world of the Nuer and our own. Among the Nuer, the overall political society may be segmented. As Evans-Pritchard writes, "a man is a member of a political group of any kind by virtue of his non-membership of other groups of the same kind."[19] For us, political society presents itself as the political individual *par excellence* and, as such, as indivisible. This individual is the nation (in the modern—political—sense of the word). It requires of us a complete loyalty rather than a loyalty that depends on context. But the point that we have in common with the Nuer is that we must both posit a distinctive opposition between ourselves and a neighboring group (within an encompassing whole) in order to identify the community to

---

16. Ibid., 136.

17. Ibid., 135.

18. Mona Ozouf, *Composition française: Retour sur une enfance bretonne* (Paris: Gallimard, 2009), 246–247.

19. Evans-Pritchard, *The Nuer*, 136.

which we belong. In political terms, this structural necessity governing the group's representation of itself implies the primacy of *foreign* policy [*la politique extérieure*] over *internal* politics [*la politique intérieure*].

The Instituting Power

Can the constitution of the city that is written in texts (political identity) be dissociated from the constitution inscribed in the hearts of the citizenry (cultural identity)? In grounding the former on the latter, does Rousseau show himself to be a defender of the "closed society" against the modern project of an "open society"? The preceding analyses allow us to set aside this overly simplistic characterization of the problem of collective identity. There are not, on the one hand, the closed societies of the past and, on the other, the open societies of the present, for every human society, insofar as it offers a representation of itself, must provide itself with the possibility of a "we." It must therefore represent itself as being at one and the same time closed and open, defined in its own being by one or another principle of individuation while, at the same time, related to the external world by the precise distinctive opposition that it uses both to define itself and to address itself to other societies. To take an extreme example, for an entire period of its history, Japanese society sought to isolate itself from the rest of the world. However, this very closing off of Japanese society, far from detaching it from the external world, served to continue to relate it to that world.

Regardless of the strength of its democratic convictions, no society fails to distinguish between the status of *citizen* and that of *noncitizen*. This incontestable fact led Cornelius Castoriadis, in his seminars, to make a distinction that will provide me with my conclusion: the distinction between the "instituting power" and the "constituent power." Where is the rule stated that determines the conditions for membership in the body politic? In the constitution. Who established this rule and is able to modify it if need be? In a democracy, the sovereign people, in accordance with the procedures set down by that constitution. So it is that the rule determines who has the right to vote, and those who have the right to vote decide on the rule. There is thus a circular logic of constituent power.

We again find this circularity if we imagine ourselves present at the establishment of the rule setting up the functioning of political institutions. Imagine that a group of people has come together and says, "We are people X, and we decree the following constitutional rules . . ." Who are these people? With what authority are they speaking? What does their "we" represent? If they have been duly delegated by various elements of people X, then we are already at a later stage in the political history of this people, since it would have already provided itself with means to express its general will by giving particular people the authority necessary for the promulgation of constitutional rules. If, instead, these people are well and truly in the process of creating people X, then we are bearing witness to a philosophical miracle: a normative self-positing. By an act of pure *fiat*, a collective agent decides to create itself *ex nihilo* and to bestow upon itself authority over the lives of a great many people.

So it is that the entire exercise of the constituent power seems arbitrary in nature. In what does the circularity inhere? Is every kind of institution contradictory in nature, or is this merely a flaw in our way of talking about it? I believe that the flaw consists in treating political authorities and law in supernatural, rather than human, terms. What is needed is for us to *humanize* the inaugural scene.

To show this, let me refer to an anecdote recounted by H. L. A. Hart to illustrate the relationship between positive law and customs.[20] He tells the story (which he admits is "perhaps apocryphal") of a declaration made at the beginning of the school year by the headmaster of "a new English public school": from the beginning of the following term, he announces, it will be a tradition of the school that senior boys will wear a certain outfit. The difficulty, as Hart notes, is that one cannot *inaugurate* a tradition or a custom: there is a logical incompatibility between the very notion of a tradition and that of a choice or "deliberate enactment." The headmaster can hope that such a custom be established, he can set out a rule requiring a uniform, he can take strong measures to ensure that his rule is obeyed—all of which is a matter of will and depends on him and his administration. But the headmaster cannot create or establish a tradition through a legislative act. When historians refer to the "invention of a tradition," they do so in full awareness of the paradox. Someone who seeks to establish a tradition that he has just

---

20. H. L. A. Hart, *The Concept of Law*, 2nd ed. (1961; Oxford: Clarendon Press, 1994), 176.

invented will have to get others to believe that it has long existed and simply been forgotten or misunderstood in recent times.

This anecdote tells us something crucial concerning what can be called the *instituting power*, the power to establish ways of acting and doing things. As a matter of principle, it is impossible for the *entirety* of the instituting power to be lodged in the *particular person* of a Founder (whatever his authority may be). Every attempt to individualize such power—i.e., to make it the personal attribute of an individual—turns it into something magical or supernatural; for example, one ends up talking, as Max Weber did, of *charisma* in order to explain the extraordinary role of the Founder.

Yet that is not all. The headmaster of the school cannot inaugurate a tradition. And what he is unable to do by himself he is also unable to do with the rest of the school. Indeed, the collective formed by the students, the teachers, and the administrators also cannot make it the case that there will henceforth be a tradition. Even if they bring together all of their powers, they will still fail, since, one might say, these powers are confined to the present moment and cannot decide the future. In other words, it is not possible to lodge the entirety of the instituting power in a group of Founders or even in an entire generation of Founders.

Whence the question: if an individual agent, even one endowed with the sort of authority the headmaster possesses, cannot establish a tradition through a declarative act, and if a collective agent made up of the headmaster, the staff, and the students also cannot do it, then who can? How does the will establish a custom? Here we again take up the question of collective identity, the question of the "we" insofar as the "we" designates the author of established norms.

§§ How does one escape from the circle of self-positing? In order to escape it, we will have to *humanize* our entire description of the foundation by introducing into it the dimension of anthropological time. The rules that we decree can have some authority on generations to come— rather than just on us, now—only if we ourselves are not captive within the present. But to humanize our notion of authority or introduce anthropological time into it will come down to representing the group that seeks its own constitution as a historical series of generations. If the rules are to allow this group to constitute itself and to recognize itself in the "we" proffered by one of its members, these rules must be transmissible. This is why, behind the fact of a *constituent* power, the exercise of an *instituting* power must be recognized. Social life does not consist in applying rules that have already been decided by an assembly of citizens. We should instead take the inverse view. If it is possible to bring together an assembly of citizens in order to organize a collective deliberation on the policy to be implemented, then there must already be a social life, the social life of an *already-instituted* society. All of this is made possible by the exercise of a power that precedes every properly political exercise of public authority. Castoriadis sometimes calls it an "implicit power," sometimes an "infra-power." He writes:

> [F]or the fundamental "power" in a society, the prime power upon which all the others depend, what I have already called the infra-power, is the instituting power. And unless one is under the spell of the "constitutional delusion," this power is neither locatable nor formalizable, for it pertains to the instituting imaginary. Language, "family," customs, "ideas," a host of other things as well as their evolution are beyond the scope of legislation in their essential part. Moreover, to the degree that this power can be participated in, it is participated in by all. Everybody is, potentially, a coauthor of the evolution of language, of the family, of customs, and so on.[21]

Castoriadis removes what was troubling in the Rousseauist image of a superhuman legislator codifying in advance all of the actions of our lives, from the way we nurse infants or teach our children to dance to the smallest details of costumes and festivals. Rousseau writes: "Within the state, the legislator is a man extraordinary in every respect."[22] In reality, he is more of a mythological figure intended to fill the gap that separates the concept of a contractual society that is limited to its members, on the one hand, from the concept of a historical society with a diachronic identity that opens up an undefined future for its members, on the other. Those things that fall within the purview of the "instituting power"—for example, language and customs—are precisely what

---

21. Cornelius Castoriadis, "Power, Politics, Autonomy," in his *Philosophy, Politics, Autonomy*, ed. David Ames Curtis (New York: Oxford University Press, 1991), 168 [translation modified].
22. Rousseau, *The Social Contract*, Book 2, Chapter 7 (77).

falls outside of the domain of legislation. Legislation cannot create the very language in which legislation is produced, any more than it can create the customs whose support is essential if it is to be more than a dead letter.

Instead and in place of a mythical representation of the foundation of our community in some miraculous inaugural self-positing, it would be better to take as our paradigm the way in which each of us makes use of the instituting power through the reproduction and modification of the countless customs that make up a culture. Castoriadis's "implicit power" corresponds fairly closely to what the word "custom" [*coutume*] referred to in the works of authors such as Montaigne and Pascal. As it does in their works, the word designates a habit, a second nature, and, as a result, an expressive power of the individual.

Castoriadis refers to an "imaginary" (rather than to a "custom," or to an "ideology" as Dumont does) because he wants to stress the fact that participation in a historical tradition requires the exercise of the imagination, in the sense of the faculty of invention and conception. One cannot merely *receive* a tradition like a kind of bequest. In order to speak the same language as one's ancestors, one must reinstitute and re-create it, and that means that it cannot be transmitted without at the same time being altered, renewed, and transformed.

Envoi

We started with a question: what are we to think of the concept of collective identity that has today become part of public discourse? Some people speak about their identity as a way of communicating their deeply held convictions and claims regarding it. They say, for example, "This custom, this way of doing things, this principle are part of our identity; we cannot therefore accept the idea of losing them." Others will use the term in an interrogative mood as a way of expressing uneasiness: "Who are we?"

The philosopher's contribution to a discussion about collective identity can only consist in answering this question: is this concept of collective identity a legitimate one? In my view, there were two kinds of critiques directed at the use of this concept. A first-degree critique weakened the common belief in the authenticity of a given tradition or monument. But a more radical, second-degree critique called into question the theoretical legitimacy of the very concept of collective identity, claiming that any application of this concept to empirical reality is a mystification.

What is at issue, as we have seen, is the possibility of seeing a human group as the subject of its own history. Indeed, such a possibility assumes that two conditions have been met. First, one must be able to attribute a diachronic identity to the group so that its historical transformations can be traced. Second, one must be able to attribute self-consciousness to the group. In short, the group's own representation must in some way be constitutive of the group itself.

That issue ultimately came down to the question of the possibility of a historical "we." How can an individual speaker be in a position to legitimately utter a "we" that represents a historical community? It is true that such a "we" seems like a mere "construction" or "representation." The discerning jurists of the Middle Ages invented the idea of a "moral person" but saw it as a useful juridical fiction and not as a sociological concept. The *persona moralis* is an "entity" about which we may speak and, eventually, through a second fiction, one that we may endow with a voice. However, it is out of the question that it might ever really express itself. In order to have the concept of collective identity, one must accept that people can say things like "We are the Romans, who long ago defeated the Carthaginians." Are such people laboring under an illusion? Are they not taking the *persona ficta* of Rome, which is a pure construction surrounding a *nomen universitatis*, for a reality equivalent to a "mystical body"?

The objection is therefore that collective identity is of the realm of the imaginary. To this I respond by borrowing from Cornelius Castoriadis his distinction between two meanings of the imaginary. First, there is the imaginary in the sense of what does not exist here and now but that exists elsewhere or has existed at other times or could have existed at some time. In this case, "imaginary" means something like *unreal*, or even mystifying. This imaginary represents, in its absence, something that is not present where we are but is present elsewhere, or was in a former time, or could be. Then there is the imaginary in the sense of the *instituting* power. My response to the objection is then that collective identity does involve imagining or representing things, but the imaginary that it involves is an instituting imaginary and not an unreal imaginary.

The existence of two meanings of the word "imaginary" can be explained by returning to the Latin word *imago*. Recall that the Romans called *imagines* the effigies of the ancestors of noble families (those families that had a right to ancestors, *jus imaginum*) that were carried in a procession during funeral rites. It is easy to see what is unreal about such images. When the ancestor's *imago* is paraded during a ceremony, the ancestor himself is not being paraded, since he is no longer of this world. In his absence, one can carry only his image.

At the same time, the representative function of these *imagines* is not just to give an unreal presence to ancestors but also to give them a place within the reality of the ritual, a place that confers an authority on those who are participating in the ritual today. I say "the reality of the ritual" because we distinguish between a real ceremony and a mere imitation of one (for example, a dress rehearsal or a ceremony carried out in a fictional film).

For the Romans, these figures are indispensable as a way of marking the rank of one's family, carrying out funeral rites, and so on. They are thus a requirement for the performance of every kind of social act that requires a reference to dead ancestors. In this function, the images are given their meaning by an instituting imagination rather than a mere reproductive or imitative imagination. The fact that the figure meant to stand for the ancestor is (more or less) made in his image involves the side of the imagination that is productive of a false reality. But the fact that the figure allows a rite or a status to be established and thereby for an authority to be founded involves the instituting side of the imagination: for a rite is not an unreal reproduction of a natural way of behaving, and a status is not the fiction of a natural superiority. Ritual activities have no sort of natural meaning; they are a pure exercise of the instituting imagination.

So in answer to the objection that holds that collective identity is nothing but *a fiction devoid of reality*, I would reply with a *distinguo*. If the objection means that it is *devoid of a natural reality to be taken as a model for the faithful representation of the group's historical continuity*, then I will concede the point, for the claim is entirely correct. But if the objection means that it is *devoid of any reality of any kind*, I must reject it, for we are here discussing a historical society, one that is therefore defined by the transmission of institutions through time from one generation to a generation that follows and has been prepared for this role through *paideia*. Collective identity therefore has all of the reality necessary for the legitimacy of the concept, but a reality that is in conformity with its mode of existence, that of a founding by way of what Pascal called *un établissement humain*—a human institution.

§§ Benveniste writes that the "we" is not a multiplied "I"; it is an "I" expanded. It is incumbent on the speaker to determine its contours. The concept of identity, taken in the moral psychological sense, is precisely the concept of these contours that set limits to the expansion of the "I." To identify oneself in the literal sense is to state one's *surname*, *forenames*, and *occupation*. To identify oneself in the new figurative sense that has become established in the last half century is to provide a definition of oneself in the sense of delimiting the part that one thinks one plays in worldly affairs and the course of events.

Modern man is someone who "thinks as an individual" (Dumont) and who therefore wants to think of himself as an individual in the normative sense.[23] He means to posit for himself the conditions for his self-satisfaction—indeed, for his self-esteem. He wants to uphold his right as a particular individual to self-satisfaction (Hegel). For the thinkers of the Enlightenment, a "right of the subject" could only mean one thing: man has the *right* to liberate himself from every social dependency, and, moreover, he has the *duty* to do this. But to the great surprise of their contemporary heirs, the man of today, while still holding that the right of the subject is a right to emancipation, also interprets it as a right to define himself in his identity *as he conceives of it*, and this leads him to include within it social bonds that have nothing to do with any social contract. He uses the identitarian idiom to take a step toward a reconciliation with his own humanity.

The notion of identity in the moral sense allows such an individual to find herself outside of herself, authorizing her to label things other than herself as "me." Aristotle had already taken note of this when he deployed the distinction between potentiality and actuality to explain why artists treat their own works as parents do their children. The fact of being able to see oneself as the author of something allows one to maintain an

---

23. Louis Dumont, "World Renunciation in Indian Religions," Appendix B to *Homo Hierarchicus: The Caste System and Its Implications*, trans. Mark Sainsbury, Louis Dumont, and Basia Gulati (1966; Chicago: University of Chicago Press, 1980), 275.

expressive relation with that thing. The appreciation that the public shows for the thing is an evaluation of a work, and it bears upon the being-in-action of what was a potentiality of the artist. If one compliments my work, one is complimenting *me*, as if it were a part of me.

An individual searching for her own identity does not merely ask, "What are my works?" She also asks, "Of what history am I the work?"

The *Port-Royal Logic* severely criticized the reasoning according to which, merely by being a Roman, a Roman could take pride in the history of that people. This particular Roman, according to the Port-Royal logicians, hopes to glory in a victory in which he had no part. To follow these Jansenist logicians, the particular individual ought to refrain from *expanding* his "I" to the dimensions of a "we." Far from seeking to enlarge his "I" in this way, he ought to concentrate his efforts on *shrinking* it, first by renouncing treatment of his institutional identity [*identité d'établissement*] as his own and then by renouncing everything in his potential self-portrait that is the result of historical contingency.

However, the fact that a particular individual seeks to expand the contours of his "I" so as to include members of a community within his "we" in no way implies that he is claiming to have been victorious (or defeated) before he was even born. The passage from an "I" to a "we" is not necessarily a sign of inflation in the idea the individual has of himself. On the contrary, it may be a way for him to reestablish himself within his human condition and to put his feet firmly on the ground by laying claim to his individuation—in which he had no part—as an acknowledged condition for any self-satisfaction whatever. At that point, the word "identity" has as its function to effect a semantic reversal. The individual defines himself by stating what it is that, in his eyes, forms part of his identity. But what forms part of his identity is precisely what he is a part of. By representing his human bonds as components of his identity, he makes plain that his right to subjective satisfaction *as an individual* [*en tant que particulier*] authorizes him to include the fact of his contingent individuation within his definition of himself.

WORKS CITED

Anscombe, G. E. M. "The Principle of Individuation." In *The Collected Philosophical Papers of G. E. M. Anscombe*. Vol. 1, *From Parmenides to Wittgenstein,* 57–65. Oxford: Blackwell, 1981.

Aristotle. *Nicomachean Ethics*. Translated by Christopher Rowe. Edited by Christopher Rowe and Sarah Broadie. Oxford: Oxford University Press, 2002.

Arnauld, Antoine, and Pierre Nicole. *Logic or the Art of Thinking*. Translated and edited by Jill Vance Buroker. Cambridge: Cambridge University Press, 1996.

Aron, Raymond. *History and the Dialectic of Violence: An Analysis of Sartre's "Critique de la Raison Dialectique."* Translated by Barry Cooper. 1973. Oxford: Basil Blackwell, 1975.

Balibar, Etienne. *Citoyen Sujet et autres essais d'anthropologie philosophique*. Paris: Presses Universitaires de France, 2011.

Benveniste, Émile. "Relationships of Person in the Verb." In *Problems in General Linguistics,* translated by Mary Elizabeth Meek, 195–204. Coral Gables, FL: University of Miami Press, 1971.

Berger, Peter L., and Thomas Luckmann. *The Social Construction of Reality: A Treatise in the Sociology of Knowledge*. 1966. New York: Penguin Books, 1971.

Brubaker, Rogers, and Frederick Cooper. "Beyond 'Identity.'" *Theory and Society* 29 (2000): 1–47.

Butler, Joseph. "Of Personal Identity." 1736. In *Personal Identity,* 2nd ed., edited by John Perry, 99–105. Berkeley: University of California Press, 2008.

Castoriadis, Cornelius. "Power, Politics, Autonomy." In *Philosophy, Politics, Autonomy,* edited by David Ames Curtis, 143–174. New York: Oxford University Press, 1991.

Chauvier, Stéphane. *Qu'est-ce qu'une personne?* Paris: J. Vrin, 2003.

Chisholm, Roderick M. "The Loose and Popular and the Strict and Philosophical Senses of Identity." In *Perception and Personal Identity,* edited by Norman S. Care and Robert H. Grimm, 82–106. Cleveland: Press of Case Western Reserve University, 1969.

———. *Person and Object: A Metaphysical Study*. London: George Allen & Unwin, 1976.

Davidson, Donald. "The Individuation of Events." In *Essays on Actions and Events,* 163–180. New York: Oxford University Press, 1980.

Diogenes Laertius. *Lives of the Eminent Philosophers*. Vol. 1. Translated by Robert Drew Hicks. Cambridge, MA: Harvard University Press, 1925.

Dumont, Louis. *Essays on Individualism: Modern Ideology in Anthropological Perspective*. Chicago: University of Chicago Press, 1986.

———. *German Ideology: From France to Germany and Back*. Chicago: University of Chicago Press, 1994.

———. *Homo Hierarchicus: The Caste System and Its Implications*. 1966. Translated by Mark Sainsbury, Louis Dumont, and Basia Gulati. Chicago: University of Chicago Press, 1980.

Durkheim, Émile. "Rousseau's Social Contract." 1918. In *Montesquieu and Rousseau: Forerunners of Sociology,* translated by Ralph Manheim, 65–138. Ann Arbor, MI: University of Michigan Press, 1960.

Erikson, Erik H. *Childhood and Society*. 1950. 3rd ed. New York: Norton, 1986.

———. *Gandhi's Truth: On the Origins of Militant Nonviolence*. New York: Norton, 1969.

———. "Identity, Psychosocial." In *International Encyclopedia of the Social Sciences,* vol. 7, edited by David L. Sills, 61–63. New York: Macmillan, 1968.

———. *Identity: Youth and Crisis*. New York: Norton, 1968.

———. *Life History and the Historical Moment*. New York: Norton, 1975.

———. *Young Man Luther: A Study in Psychoanalysis and History*. 1958. New York: Norton, 1962.

Evans-Pritchard, E. E. *The Nuer: A Description of the Modes of Livelihood and Political Institutions of a Nilotic People*. Oxford: Clarendon Press, 1940.

Frege, Gottlob. *The Foundations of Arithmetic: A Logico-Mathematic Enquiry Into the Concept of Number*. 1950. 2nd rev. ed. Translated by J. L. Austin. New York: Harper Torchbooks, 1960.

Geach, Peter. *Mental Acts: Their Content and Their Objects*. London: Routledge and Kegan Paul, 1957.

———. "Ontological Relativity and Relative Identity." In *Logic and Ontology,* edited by Milton K. Munitz, 287–302. New York: New York University Press, 1973.

———. *Reference and Generality: An Examination of Some Medieval and Modern Theories*. 3rd ed. Ithaca: Cornell University Press, 1980.

Gleason. Philip. "American Identity and Americanization." In *Harvard Encyclopedia of American Ethnic Groups,* edited by Stephan Thernstrom, Ann Orlov, and Oscar Handlin, 31–58. Cambridge, MA: Harvard University Press, 1980.

———. "Identifying Identity: A Semantic History." *Journal of American History* 69 (1983): 910–931.

——. *Speaking of Diversity: Language and Ethnicity in Twentieth-Century America.* Baltimore: Johns Hopkins University Press, 1992.

Goffman, Erving. *Stigma: Notes on the Management of Spoiled Identity.* Englewood Cliffs, NJ: Prentice Hall, 1963.

Goyet, Francis. "Hamlet, étudiant du XVIe siècle." *Poétique* 113 (1998): 3–15.

——. *Le sublime du "lieu commun": L'invention rhétorique dans l'Antiquité et à la Renaissance.* Paris: Honoré Champion, 1993.

Hadot, Pierre. *Philosophy as a Way of Life: Spiritual Exercises From Socrates to Foucault.* Edited by Arnold Davidson. Translated by Michael Chase. Malden, MA: Blackwell, 1995.

Hart, H. L. A. *The Concept of Law.* 1961. 2nd ed. Oxford: Clarendon Press, 1994.

Hegel, G. W. F. *Aesthetics: Lectures on Fine Art.* Vol. 1. Translated by T. M. Knox. Oxford: Clarendon Press, 1975.

——. *Outlines of the Philosophy of Right.* Translated by T. M. Knox. Revised and edited by Stephen Houlgate. Oxford: Oxford University Press, 2008.

——. *The Phenomenology of Spirit.* Translated by A. V. Miller. Oxford: Oxford University Press, 1977.

Heidegger, Martin. *Being and Time: A Translation of "Sein und Zeit."* Translated by Joan Stambaugh. Albany: State University of New York Press, 1996.

Herberg, Will. *Protestant-Catholic-Jew: An Essay in Religious Sociology.* 1955. Chicago: University of Chicago Press, 1983.

Homer. *The Odyssey.* Translated by Allen Mandelbaum. New York: Bantam, 1991.

James, William. *The Principles of Psychology.* 1890. Cambridge, MA: Harvard University Press, 1983.

Jesperson, Otto. *The Philosophy of Grammar.* 1924. New York: Routledge, 2007.

Jouvenel, Bertrand de, ed. *Du contrat social.* By Jean-Jacques Rousseau. Paris: Livre de Poche/Pluriel, 1978.

Kantorowicz, Ernst. *The King's Two Bodies: A Study in Mediaeval Political Theology.* 1957. Princeton: Princeton University Press, 1981.

Kripke, Saul. *Naming and Necessity.* Cambridge, MA: Harvard University Press, 1980.

Lacan, Jacques. "The Neurotic's Individual Myth." 1953. Translated by Martha Noel Evans. *Psychoanalytic Quarterly* 48 (1979): 405–425.

Locke, John. *An Essay Concerning Human Understanding.* Edited by Peter H. Nidditch. Oxford: Oxford University Press, 1975.

Mauss, Marcel. "La nation." 1953–1954. In *Oeuvres.* Vol. 3, *Cohésion sociale et divisions de la sociologie,* edited by Victor Karady, 573–625. Paris: Les Éditions de Minuit, 1969.

Molière. *The Miser.* In *The Miser and Other Plays: A New Selection.* Translated by John Woods. Revised by David Coward. New York: Penguin, 2000.

Montefiore, Alan. *A Philosophical Retrospective: Facts, Values, and Jewish Identity.* New York: Columbia University Press, 2011.

Montesquieu. *The Spirit of the Laws.* Edited and translated by Anne M. Cohler, Basia C. Miller, and Harold S. Stone. Cambridge: Cambridge University Press, 1989.

Nicole, Pierre. Preamble to "Trois discours sur la condition des Grands," by Blaise Pascal. In *Pensées et opuscules,* edited by Léon Brunschvicg, 231–233. Paris: Classiques Hachette, 1990.

Noiriel, Gérard. *A quoi sert "l'identité nationale"?* Marseille: Agone, 2007.

Nora, Pierre. "Les avatars de l'identité française." *Le Débat* 159 (March-April 2010): 4–20.

O'Meara, Barry E. *Complément du Mémorial de Sainte-Hélène: Napoléon en exil.* 1822. Vol. 2. Paris: Garnier Frères, 1897.

Ortigues, Edmond. *Le discours et le symbole.* 1962. Paris: Éditions Beauchesne, 2007.

Ozouf, Mona. *Composition française: Retour sur une enfance bretonne.* Paris: Gallimard, 2009.

Pascal, Blaise. "Discourses on the Condition of the Great." Translated by O. W. Wight. In *Thoughts, Letters, Minor Works,* 382–388. New York: P. F. Collier & Son, 1910.

———. *Pensées and Other Writings.* Translated by Honor Levi. Edited by Anthony Levi. Oxford: Oxford University Press, 1995.

Plutarch. *Moralia.* Vol. 7 (523c–612b). Translated by Phillip H. de Lacy and Benedict Einarson. Cambridge, MA: Harvard University Press, 1959.

———. *Plutarch's Lives.* Vol. 1. Translated by Bernadotte Perrin. Cambridge, MA: Harvard University Press, 1914.

Polanyi, Karl. *The Great Transformation: The Political and Economic Origins of Our Time.* 1944. Boston: Beacon Press, 1957.

Popper, Karl. *The Poverty of Historicism.* 1957. New York: Routledge, 2002.

Prior, Arthur N. "Identifiable Individuals." In *Papers on Time and Tense,* 66–77. Oxford: Clarendon Press, 1968.

Proust, Marcel. *The Guermantes Way.* Vol. 3 of *In Search of Lost Time.* Translated by C. K. Scott Moncrieff and Terence Kilmartin. Revised by D. J. Enright. New York: The Modern Library, 1993.

Quine, Willard van Orman. *Ontological Relativity and Other Essays.* New York: Columbia University Press, 1969.

———. *Theories and Things.* Cambridge, MA: Harvard University Press, 1981.

Reid, Thomas. "Of Identity." 1785. In *Personal Identity,* 2nd ed., edited by John Perry, 107–112. Berkeley: University of California Press, 2008.

Rome: Le guide du routard. Paris: Hachette, 2008.

Rosset, Clément. *Loin de moi: Étude sur l'identité.* Paris: Les Editions de Minuit, 1999.

Rousseau, Jean-Jacques. *The Confessions.* Translated by J. M. Cohen. New York: Penguin, 1953.

———. *Discourse on Political Economy.* In *Discourse on Political Economy and The Social Contract,* translated by Christopher Betts, 1–41. Oxford: Oxford University Press, 1994.

——. *Émile, or On Education.* Translated by Allan Bloom. New York: Basic Books, 1979.

——. *The Government of Poland.* Translated by Willmoore Kendall. Indianapolis: Hackett, 1985.

——. *Rousseau, Judge of Jean-Jacques: Dialogues.* Edited by Roger D. Masters and Christopher Kelly. Translated by Judith R. Bush, Christopher Kelly, and Roger D. Masters. Hanover, NH: University Press of New England, 1990.

——. *The Social Contract.* In *Discourse on Political Economy and The Social Contract,* translated by Christopher Betts, 43-168. Oxford: Oxford University Press, 1994.

Sartre, Jean-Paul. *Being and Nothingness: An Essay on Phenomenological Ontology.* 1956. 2nd ed. Translated by Hazel E. Barnes. New York: Routledge, 2003.

Sedley, David. "The Stoic Criterion of Identity." *Phronesis* 27 (1982): 255-275.

Sen, Amartya. *Identity and Violence: The Illusion of Destiny.* New York: Norton, 2006.

Sorabji, Richard. *Self: Ancient and Modern Insights About Individuality, Life, and Death.* Chicago: University of Chicago Press, 2006.

Spitzer, Leo. "Milieu and Ambiance: An Essay in Historical Semantics." *Philosophy and Phenomenological Research* 3, no. 1 (Sept. 1942): 1-42; no. 2 (Dec. 1942): 169-218.

Taylor, Charles. "Action as Expression." In *Intention and Intentionality: Essays in Honour of G. E. M. Anscombe,* edited by Cora Diamond and Jenny Teichman, 73-89. Brighton: Harvester Press, 1979.

——. *Human Agency and Language: Philosophical Papers 1.* Cambridge: Cambridge University Press, 1985.

——. "Legitimation Crisis?" In *Philosophy and the Human Sciences: Philosophical Papers 2.* Cambridge: Cambridge University Press, 1985.

——. *A Secular Age.* Cambridge, MA: Harvard University Press, 2007.

Tesnière, Lucien. *Éléments de syntaxe structurale.* 1959. 2nd ed. Paris: Klincksieck, 1988.

Thatcher, Margaret. "Aids, Education, and the Year 2000! Interview with Douglas Keay." *Women's Own* (October 31, 1987): 8-10.

Thiesse, Anne-Marie. *La création des identités nationales: Europe XVIIIe-XXe siècle.* Paris: Les Editions du Seuil, 1999.

Thomas Aquinas. *Summa Theologiae.* Vol. 49 (3a. 7-15), *The Grace of Christ.* Edited and Translated by Liam G. Walsh, O. P. Cambridge: Cambridge University Press, 1974.

Thomas, Yan. *Les opérations du droit.* Paris: Gallimard/Seuil, 2011.

Tocqueville, Alexis de. *Democracy in America.* Edited and translated by Harvey C. Mansfield and Delba Winthrop. Chicago: University of Chicago Press, 2000.

Tugendhat, Ernst. *Self-Consciousness and Self-Determination.* Translated by Paul Stern. Cambridge, MA: MIT Press, 1986.

Voltaire. *The Ignorant Philosopher.* Girard, KS: Haldeman-Julius Company, n.d.

——. "Le philosophe ignorant." 1766. In *Mélanges,* edited by Jacques Van den Heuvel, 877–930. Paris: Gallimard/Pléiade, 1961.

——. "Traité de métaphysique." 1734–1738. In *Mélanges,* edited by Jacques Van den Heuvel, 157–202. Paris: Gallimard/Pléiade, 1961.

Wiggins, David. *Sameness and Substance Renewed.* Cambridge: Cambridge University Press, 2001.

Wittgenstein, Ludwig. *Philosophical Investigations.* 1953. Rev. 4th ed. Edited by P. M. S. Hacker and Joachim Schulte. Translated by G. E. M. Anscombe, P. M. S. Hacker, and Joachim Schulte. Oxford: Wiley-Blackwell, 2009.

——. *Tractatus Logico-Philosophicus.* 1922. Rev. ed. Translated by D. F. Pears and B. F. McGuinness. New York: Routledge, 1981.